19 MAY 2015

Vicki,

I really enjoyed meet... have heard great things about what you are doing in the DMUS area.

Hope you find this book useful.

Dick Thompson

Praise for *The Stress Effect*

"Good leaders make good decisions under stress, and the ability to do this depends on their emotional intelligence. Thompson masterfully walks the reader through this all-important connecting link, which represents one of the best predictors of successful leadership."

—Reuven Bar-On, the person who developed
the concept of EQ

"If your job involves leadership—or if you aspire to be a leader—read this book. Thompson tells you what you need to know about managing stress as a leader. You'll learn from research-backed examples, good and bad, what you need to do in the kinds of difficult situations that every leader faces."

—Steven J. Stein, coauthor, *The EQ Edge*, and CEO,
Multi-Health Systems

"*The Stress Effect* presents a compelling story of the impact stress has on decision making and why it matters for leaders. It is the only book of its kind to explain the relationship of decision making, cognitive intelligence, emotional intelligence, and stress as they relate to leadership. You will find the practical examples and stories engrossing and the description of research studies accessible and understandable."

—David Caruso, cofounder, EI Skills Group

"Thompson provides a valuable resource for connecting the dots between emotions, stress, and productivity. Read it now and practice his suggestions!"

—Marcia Hughes, author,
The Emotionally Intelligent Team

"As the CEO of a fast-growing company and as a fighter pilot, understanding how decisions are affected by stress is critical. In *The Stress Effect*, Thompson offers an introspective look at how stress, cognition, and emotions impact the effectiveness of rapid decision making. This book should be on the short list for CEOs and fighter pilots alike."

—Jeffrey Parker, CEO, ATAC

"Thompson has studied, consulted in, and led organizations in stressful environments that constantly demand effective decision making from leaders. I highly recommend this gem of a book to anyone who needs to know more about stress and stress resiliency in order to fulfill their various leadership roles."

—Brendan J. Croskery, retired chief superintendent, Calgary Board of Education, Canada

The
STRESS
EFFECT

Why Smart Leaders
Make Dumb Decisions
—And What to Do About It

HENRY L. THOMPSON, PH.D.

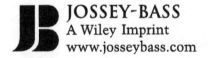

JOSSEY-BASS
A Wiley Imprint
www.josseybass.com

Published by Jossey-Bass
A Wiley Imprint
989 Market Street, San Francisco, CA 94103-1741—www.josseybass.com

Jossey-Bass books and products are available through most bookstores. To contact Jossey-Bass directly call our Customer Care Department within the U.S. at 800-956-7739, outside the U.S. at 317-572-3986, or fax 317-572-4002.

Jossey-Bass also publishes its books in a variety of electronic formats. Some content that appears in print may not be available in electronic books.

Library of Congress Cataloging-in-Publication Data

Thompson, Henry L.
   The stress effect : why smart leaders make dumb decisions—and what to do about it / Henry L. Thompson.—1st ed.
      p. cm.
   Includes bibliographical references and index.
   ISBN 978-0-470-58903-8 (cloth)
1. Decision making. 2. Leadership. 3. Stress (Psychology)   I. Title.
HD30.23.T468 2010
658.4'03–dc22

Printed in the United States of America
FIRST EDITION
HB Printing   10 9 8 7 6 5 4 3

Contents

Introduction: Good Leaders Make Good Decisions Under Stress   1

1   How Leaders Make Decisions   11
2   How Cognitive Intelligence Influences Decision Making   49
3   Emotional Intelligence and Decision Making   81
4   Stress and Decision Making   109
5   How Stress Leads to Poor Decision Making   137
6   Increasing Stress Management Capacity   167
7   Developing Cognitive Resilience   193
8   Building Stress Resilient Emotional Intelligence   221
9   The Seven Best Practices to Prevent Stress   243

Conclusion   283
Notes   287
Acknowledgments   311
About the Author   315
Index   316

To my wife, Grenae Thompson,
for her undying support over the years
and relentless effort to make this book become a reality

Introduction: Good Leaders Make Good Decisions Under Stress

Every great decision creates ripples—like a huge boulder dropped in a lake. The ripples merge, rebound off the banks in unforeseeable ways. The heavier the decision, the larger the waves, the more uncertain the consequences.

BENJAMIN DISRAELI

O n January 15, 2009, approximately ninety seconds after the start of "another day at the office," the work got unusually stressful—very, very stressful. This story has been told thousands of times, awards and accolades have been bestowed to the heroes (and some blame has been doled out to others), and the actions, decisions, and events that followed have been endlessly scrutinized. In the course of this book, I'm going to return to this story again and from many perspectives to help you gain an understanding of what happens when leaders make decisions under high stress—extreme stress in the case of US Airways Flight 1549.

What follows is an abridged version of the actual cockpit conversations between Captain Chesley Sullenberger and First Officer Jeffrey Skiles and between the departure control, Patrick Harten, and Captain Sullenberger, beginning just after takeoff. (Most conversations between departure control and other aircraft have been omitted.) As you look at the times, notice that something is being communicated almost every second:

15:26:37 Sullenberger: Uh, what a view of the Hudson today.[1]

15:26:42 Skiles: Yeah.

15:26:52 Skiles: Flaps up, please, After Takeoff Checklist.

15:26:54 Sullenberger: Flaps up.

15:27:07 Sullenberger: After Takeoff Checklist complete.

15:27:10 Sullenberger: Birds. [At 3,200 feet.]

15:27:11 Skiles: Whoa!

15:27:11: (Sound of thumps/thuds followed by shuddering sound.)

15:27:12 Skiles: Oh (expletive)!

15:27:13 Sullenberger: Oh yeah.

15:27:13 (Sound similar to decrease in engine noise/frequency begins.)

15:27:14 Skiles: Uh-oh.

15:27:15 Sullenberger: We got one rol—both of 'em rolling back.

15:27:18 (Rumbling sound begins and continues until approximately 15:28:08.)

15:27:18 Sullenberger: Ignition, start. [The plane is now dropping at eighteen feet per second and is approximately three minutes from impact.]

15:27:32 Sullenberger: Mayday! Mayday! Mayday! Uh this is uh Cactus fifteen thirty nine.[2] Hit birds. We've lost thrust in both engines. We're turning back towards LaGuardia. [Incorrect call sign.]

15:27:42 Departure control (Patrick Harten): Okay uh, you need to return to LaGuardia? Turn left heading of uh two two zero.

15:27:43 (Sound similar to electrical noise from engine igniters begins.)

15:28:02 Skiles: Airspeed optimum. Relight. Three hundred knots. We don't have that.

15:28:03 (Flight warning computer): (Sound of single chime.)

15:28:05 Sullenberger: We don't.

15:28:05 Departure control: Cactus fifteen twenty nine, if we can get it for you do you want to try to land runway one three?[3] [Incorrect call sign.]

15:28:05 Skiles: If three nineteen ...

15:28:10 Sullenberger: We're unable. We may end up in the Hudson. [By sixty seconds, he has consciously considered the Hudson and is moving in that direction.]

15:28:31 Departure control: Alright, Cactus fifteen forty nine it's gonna be left traffic for runway, three one. [Harten, who is talking to other aircraft and clearing a runway does not process that Flight 1549 cannot return to LaGuardia.]

15:28:35 Sullenberger: Unable.

15:28:36 (Traffic Collision Avoidance System): Traffic! Traffic!

15:28:36 Departure control: Okay, what do you need to land?

15:28:37 Skiles: (He wants us) to come in and land on one three ... for whatever.

15:28:45 (Predictive Windshear System): Go around! Windshear ahead!

15:28:45 Skiles: FAC (Flight Augmentation Computer) one off, then on.

15:28:46 Departure control: Cactus fifteen twenty nine runway four's available if you wanna make left traffic to runway four. [Harten is still trying to get him back to LaGuardia. Incorrect call sign.]

15:28:49 Sullenberger: I'm not sure we can make any runway. Uh what's over to our right? Anything in New Jersey? Maybe Teterboro?

15:28:55 Departure control: Okay yeah, off your right side is Teterboro Airport.

15:28:59 (Traffic Collision Avoidance System): Monitor vertical speed!

15:29:00 Skiles: No relight after thirty seconds, engine master one and two confirm ...

15:29:02 Departure control: You wanna try and go to Teterboro?

15:29:03 Sullenberger: Yes.

15:29:11 Sullenberger (over public address system): This is the Captain. Brace for impact!

15:29:21 Departure control: Cactus fifteen twenty nine turn right two eight zero, you can land runway one at Teterboro. [Incorrect call sign.]

15:29:21 Skiles: Is that all the power you got? . . . Wanna number one?

15:29:25 Sullenberger: We can't do it.

15:29:26 Sullenberger: Go ahead, try number one.

15:29:27 Departure control: 'Kay which runway would you like at Teterboro? [Harten did not process Sullenberger's, "We can't do it." He's still trying to send him to Teterboro.]

15:29:27 (Flight Warning Computer): (Sound of continuous repetitive chime for 9.6 seconds.)

15:29:28 Sullenberger: We're gonna be in the Hudson.

15:29:33 Departure control: I'm sorry say again Cactus? [Harten did not consciously perceive Sullenberger's, "We're gonna be in the Hudson." He's still trying to send him to another airport.]

15:29:53 Departure control: Cactus fifteen forty nine radar contact is lost. You also got Newark airport off your two o'clock in about seven miles.

15:29:55 (Enhanced Ground Proximity Warning System): Pull up! Pull up! Pull up! Pull up! Pull up! Pull up!

15:30:01 Skiles: Got flaps out.

15:30:03 Skiles: Two hundred fifty feet in the air.

15:30:04 (Ground Proximity Warning System): Too low! Terrain!

15:30:06 (Ground Proximity Warning System): Too low! Gear!

15:30:06 Skiles: Hundred and seventy knots.

15:30:09 Skiles: Got no power on either one? Try the other one.

15:30:09 (Radio from another plane): Two one zero uh forty seven eighteen. I think he said he's going in the Hudson.

15:30:15 (Enhanced Ground Proximity Warning System): Caution! Terrain!

15:30:16 Skiles: Hundred and fifty knots.

15:30:17 Skiles: Got flaps two, you want more?

15:30:19 Sullenberger: No let's stay at two.

15:30:21 Sullenberger: Got any ideas?

15:30:22 Departure control: Cactus fifteen twenty nine if you can uh . . . you got uh runway uh two nine available at Newark it'll be two o'clock and seven miles. [Harten still has not fully processed that Flight 1549 is going into the Hudson. He's still trying to send the plane to another airport. He is using the incorrect call sign.]

15:30:23 (Enhanced Ground Proximity Warning System): Caution! Terrain!

15:30:23 Skiles: Actually not.

15:30:24 (Enhanced Ground Proximity Warning System): Terrain! Terrain! Pull up! Pull up! ["Pull up!" repeats until the end of the recording.]

15:30:38 Sullenberger: We're gonna brace.

Seconds later US Airways Flight 1549 executed a perfect water landing in the Hudson River, and the next crisis began for the crew and passengers. They had survived the crash but now were sitting in a plane filling with thirty-four-degree water in a swiftly moving current. Yet as we all know, every person on Flight 1549 was rescued that day.

Having survived a helicopter crash, several parachute malfunctions, and other near-death experiences, I can say that nothing gets your attention like the finality of knowing how many seconds you have left before you die. The instant those Canada geese flew into the plane's engines, the lives of everyone on Flight 1549 were put on a three-minute timer that was rapidly ticking toward zero.

No one was more aware of the countdown timer than Captain Sullenberger. He was under extreme stress, yet he was able to make a series of complex decisions while executing precise control over a plane that was literally falling out of the sky, filtering through a vast amount of incoming data to find the critical pieces, carrying on conversations with departure control and First Officer Skiles, and maintaining a delicate balance of air speed, lift, nose attitude, and control as the plane hit the water. *The Stress Effect* focuses on how leaders like Captain Sullenberger make decisions under high levels of stress; some have successful outcomes, and others do not. The "miracle on the Hudson," as the day's events came to be known, was not just the result of good luck. It was the result of some very good decision making despite some very bad conditions.

Smart Leaders, Dumb Decisions:
How Does It Happen?

Why do seasoned leaders with proven track records sometimes suddenly begin making really bad decisions—or no decisions at all? Numerous highly publicized examples involving companies such as Enron, World-Com, Tyco, Fannie Mae, Freddie Mac, and AIG or events like Hurricane Katrina illustrate catastrophic leadership decisions. Moreover, though they don't make the headlines or result in anyone's going to jail, thousands of poor decisions are being made by leaders every minute of every day and in every field imaginable. CEOs were replaced at a record-high rate of 7.6 per business day in the United States in 2005.[4] Over 28 percent of those CEOs had been in place less than three years and 13 percent less than one year. By January 2009, CEO turnover reached a new record with an estimated 1,484 leaving their jobs in 2008.[5]

"CEOs are under intense pressure," says John Challenger of the outplacement consultant group Challenger, Gray & Christmas. "They have little room for error." And things aren't about to get any easier any time soon. As economic pressures at home combine with an ever-changing global economy, the demands on leaders will continue to mount, as will the stress levels in organizations. We're virtually guaranteeing an epidemic of leaders' making unsound decisions and resulting organizational failures if we overlook the relationship between stress and decision making—and if we don't take that relationship into account when we ourselves lead or choose others to do so.

Leadership isn't just about the right credentials: having worked at the best companies, getting promoted into bigger and bigger jobs, taking home larger paychecks each passing year. Leadership, pure and simple, is about being able to make good decisions during bad times.

Beyond the Résumé: Two Essential Qualities

As the founder and president of High Performing Systems, my job is to figure out what makes leaders tick. Over the years, we've worked with companies large and small, as well as organizations like the U.S. Army,

Mohawk Industries, Georgia Pacific, Delta Airlines, and Wipro. In addition to being well versed in leadership styles and their effectiveness, I have extensive experience observing and studying the impact of stress on people in decision-making positions. I served as an instructor for both the U.S. Army Rangers and Special Forces (Green Berets) and led these units, and other special operations units, in combat. During the early 1980s I was one of the U.S. Army's subject matter experts on stress in general and stress on the battlefield in particular. My work has led me to study and experience stress from an academic research perspective as well as through practical experience and field research. My experience and knowledge range from the battlefield to the boardroom.

My work, as well as that of others you'll read about in this book, points clearly to one explanation for why stressed leaders sometimes make very poor decisions: stress has an enormous impact on the brain's cognitive and emotional intelligences, two abilities required for making sound leadership decisions at all organizational levels.

Research on leadership, stress, cognitive intelligence, emotional intelligence, and decision making over the past thirty years indicates that when a leader's stress level is sufficiently elevated—whether on the front line of a manufacturing process, in the emergency room, in the boardroom, or on the battlefield—his or her ability to fully and effectively use the right blend of cognitive intelligence and emotional intelligence to make timely and effective decisions may be significantly impaired, sometimes leading to poor decisions: the bolt is affixed too tightly, the incorrect medicine is given, the merger is killed, the wrong order is given.

Decisions that leaders make can be grouped into two strategies: intuitive and rational. Intuitive decisions are made quickly, automatically, emotionally, and mostly unconsciously, and they tend to be of a routine or emergency nature. Leaders use this mostly unconscious strategy to make decisions on a regular basis every day. Rational decisions tend to be much more complex and more conscious, take longer, and use more structured processes than intuitive decision making. Leaders are also involved in these types of decisions to some extent each day. (In the case of the US Airways water landing, Captain Sullenberger led his crew through a deft and dizzying combination of intuitive and rational decision making, as we'll see later.)

In the ongoing war for talent, hiring, developing, and retaining talented leaders with high cognitive intelligence and emotional intelligence, the two essential leadership qualities we'll explore in depth in this book, are the major battles to be fought. The war will be won by selecting leaders who have the right skills and abilities to work at particular levels within the organization *and* who are able to control stress and make effective decisions, both intuitive and rational.

Why *The Stress Effect* Approach to Leadership Is New—and Necessary

As a leader, or as someone charged with identifying leaders in your organization, you've probably read extensively on the topic and have attended specialized workshops and seminars. You've heard over and over again the same information on "what makes a great leader." He or she is goal oriented, pays attention to detail but sees the big picture, works long hours, is well liked, and so on. Yet most of the traditional descriptions of leadership characteristics leave out a crucial ability—one that should probably be at the top of the list: good decision making under extreme stress. That is the focus of *The Stress Effect*. It's not simply about how leaders make decisions; it's about how leaders make decisions under high stress and how they can improve their abilities to do so.

There is substantial research to support all aspects of what is presented in this book, such as that of psychologist Richard Boyatzis and his team at Case Western Reserve University.[6] Boyatzis, along with his colleagues Melvin Smith and Nancy Blaize, have contributed to the foundation of a relationship between stress and leadership.[7]

This book explores how the stress effect affects a leader's cognitive intelligence, emotional intelligence, and decision making, as well as how building capacity in three key factors—stress management capacity, cognitive resilience, and stress resilient emotional intelligence—bolsters a leader's resistance to stress. In addition, you will learn how seven best practices—Awareness, Rest, Support, Exercise, Nutrition, Attitude, and Learning (ARSENAL)—build capacity in the three key factors and contribute to developing and maintaining a stress resilient system.

Although the key aspects of brain functioning will be addressed as they relate to decision making, this is not a book that spends a lot of time detailing the intricate workings of the brain and following signals along neuronal paths. This is also not a book primarily focused on the academic studies that have been conducted on decision making over the past hundred years, although a few of these studies will be mentioned to make specific points.

The stories and examples I've selected encompass a wide range of industries and leaders in decision-making positions, from frontline supervisors and squad leaders to CEOs and generals. Everything in this book is based on the real world and backed by science.

I am in favor of and support the practice of ethical decision making at all leadership levels; however, this topic will not be addressed in this book. A number of books have been published that cover ethics and decision making in-depth, and I will defer to their expertise.

Leaders who use the techniques and best practices described in this book to strengthen their resistance to stress will see the likelihood of their making bad decisions decrease. Even more important, the resulting increase in a leader's access to his or her cognitive and emotional abilities produces increased job performance, better health, more effective interpersonal relationships, and a lowering of stress.

The information provided in this book is, of course, not exhaustive; no book can be that thorough. In many cases, however, I have included small bites of information to pique your curiosity and inspire you to seek more in-depth information on a particular topic, to stimulate Lifelong Learning—the "L" in ARSENAL.

Now let's turn our attention to the topic at hand, using our full capacity, including cognitive and emotional intelligences, to make the best decisions possible when under stress.

I How Leaders Make Decisions

Most decisions are seat-of-the-pants judgments. You can create a rationale for anything. In the end, most decisions are based on intuition and faith.
NATHAN MYHRVOLD

Just a few weeks before the collapse of industry giant Enron in December 2001, CEO and founder Ken Lay told his twenty-eight thousand employees, "Our liquidity is fine. As a matter of fact, it's better than fine, it's strong." Yet at the same time he was urging employees not to panic, Lay, who had a Ph.D. in economics, sold 918,000 shares of his own Enron stock for $26 million.

Lay and other Enron executives blamed the company's collapse on Andrew Fastow, the chief financial officer, who pleaded guilty to falsifying Enron's balance sheet and conspiring with other employees to skim millions of dollars. "I think the primary reason for Enron's collapse was Andy Fastow and his little group of people and what they did," Lay said in an interview on *60 Minutes*. "But certainly I didn't know he was doing anything that was criminal."[1]

Following convictions of other Enron executives, Lay himself was convicted in May 2006 of conspiring to inflate stock prices and misleading investors and employees. Facing the prospect of spending life in prison, Lay maintained his innocence until his death two months later of coronary artery disease.

The collapse of investment banking legend Bear Stearns came on the watch of Jimmy Cayne, who had become CEO in 1993.[2] During the next fourteen years under his leadership, the company's stock skyrocketed from $16.61 to a high of $172.69 per share in January 2007. But a series of poor management decisions and the collapse of two hedge funds in 2007 plunged the Wall Street giant into a crisis unlike any other in its eighty-five-year history. In May 2008, Bear Stearns became a bargain basement steal for J. P. Morgan Chase at ten dollars a share.

Less than a year earlier, however, Cayne had reassured investors that the firm would rebound, saying confidently, "You can count on us." The former CEO would eventually admit that he was paralyzed with indecision during the firm's crisis: "It was not knowing what to do. It's not being able to make a definitive decision one way or the other, because I just couldn't tell you what was going to happen."

Here are some more famous last words from other CEOs of major corporations, spoken during the months prior to the crash of their respective companies in 2008. All of these comments indicate a serious lapse in decision-making capabilities:

> "Do we have some stuff on the books that's going to kill us? Of course not." — Richard Fuld, CEO, Lehman Brothers

> "We believe the probability that it [portfolio of credit default swaps] will sustain an economic loss is close to zero." — Martin Sullivan, CEO, AIG

> "The home-loans business had a challenging first half of the year, but ... we think we're back on track to get that unit back to profitability before the end of the year even in these challenging conditions." — Kerry Killinger, CEO, Washington Mutual[3]

It's hard not to grimace at those statements now because there is nothing humorous about the impact of a failed organization — particularly on the employees, clients, and others who depended on them for their livelihoods. Starting in 2007, major companies began to fall like dominos: first Enron, then WorldCom, followed by Tyco and a series of major failures in large U.S. corporations. The U.S. financial system began to implode, sending shock waves throughout the global economy. At the center of this crisis were leaders in major decision-making roles. As we know all too well by now, some of these men and women made the right calls, but far too many of them, unable to perform under increasingly higher levels of stress, made bad choices for their organizations.

At the same time, the U.S. presidential campaign was in full force. Throughout the campaign, the focus turned to which Democratic candidate could handle the "3:00 A.M. phone call."[4] In other words, voters wanted to know who could best make critical world-changing decisions. As the campaign narrowed to John McCain and Barack Obama, the question of which candidate had the knowledge, experience, and ability to make global decisions on issues such as Iraq, Afghanistan, Iran, and North Korea was foremost in the minds of American voters.

But as more financial institutions began to fail, the focus of the campaign shifted from the Iraq war to the economy, taking the momentum away from John McCain, whose strengths seemed to be foreign affairs and defense, and moving it to Barack Obama. As Fannie Mae, Freddie Mac, Bear Stearns, AIG, General Motors, and other major institutions fell apart, the focus of the campaign became which candidate would make better decisions about the economy.

If the financial crisis has taught people nothing else, it made one fact abundantly clear: we no longer live in a world where the leaders of the top companies in the United States make financial decisions that affect only America. The decisions that the CEO of General Motors or AIG makes reverberate around the world. The global financial system is woven together in an intricate web in which a slight movement by any major player will send ripples throughout the entire system. As Thomas Friedman says, the world may have become "flat."[5]

The Art of Choosing a Leader

How did we get to the point where CEOs are paid incredible salaries and bonuses regardless of the quality and effectiveness of their decisions and the performance of their companies? Have the world, and the organizations in the world, become too complex for humans to lead? Has leadership become too complex? Has the complexity of decision making in large corporations outstripped human decision-making capacity? I don't think so. But I do think that perhaps our worldview of leadership has become archaic. Many of us still buy into the antiquated notion that anyone can successfully lead a large corporation or be successful in a high-level government position.

This is America, after all, the land of opportunity. "You can be anything!" we tell our children. But is that really the truth? Can anyone be a *Fortune* 500 CEO? Can anyone be the head of a Hollywood studio? Can anyone lead a platoon, a ballet company, a high school, a town council? Of course not. But telling our children, "Well, you probably can't be *anything* . . . but you can be great at *something!*" doesn't exactly hit the right note. And especially in the professional world, holding to the idea that not everyone can make it to the top smacks of elitism or social hierarchies, making many people, including those in charge of identifying and managing leaders, uncomfortable.

As you will see in the chapters that follow, we actually have the knowledge to understand how the best leaders think. Yet we don't always call on it to select our decision makers and then hold them accountable. Instead we prefer to cling to the old notion that anyone who works hard can rise to the top and be successful. It's precisely because of our collective blind spot that organizations, and the leaders we put in charge of them, fail. Perhaps if we'd taken off those blinders and chosen our decision makers realistically, we could have prevented the economic meltdown and its global impact.

In addition, many may be unaware that we have the knowledge and ability to understand the complexities of leadership and decision making, that we can know what happened in organizations such as

Enron, Chrysler, Washington Mutual, and the U.S. government, and that we could have prevented the catastrophic failure of the global economy.

At the close of the first decade of the twenty-first century, the domain of leadership is reeling from the effects of questionable decisions made by supposedly smart leaders who had been placed in roles that exceeded their competence and ability levels. Lawrence Peter must be experiencing the paradoxical feelings of pride and concern: pride because he knows that his Peter principle—*In a hierarchy every employee tends to rise to his level of incompetence*—is being proven every day, and fear and concern for the country because the principle is correct.[6] The current approach to selecting leaders and not holding them accountable has created large bureaucracies populated by leaders incapable of making effective and efficient decisions or of responding to the dynamic, rapidly changing landscape of the global environment.

The leaders who uttered those famous last words a few pages back rose to the top of what were some of the largest and most powerful companies in the world. Our research at High Performing Systems indicates that CEOs of large corporations have an average IQ of 125.[7] Some CEOs we have assessed have IQs over 140. To put this in perspective, the average IQ of the general population is about 100. An IQ of 140 typically falls in the top 2 percent of IQ scores and makes those with this IQ eligible for membership in Mensa, the high-IQ society. We have not found any CEOs of multi-billion-dollar corporations with IQs less than 115. We have also found that many CEOs hold Ph.D.s. These are smart people, yet many appear to have created a culture of incompetent decision making, greed, and lack of accountability. This culture is not limited to the executive suite. It permeates deep into the hearts of their companies. "Dumb" decisions are being made by "smart" leaders at every level.

Some of these bad decisions can be attributed to inexperience, lack of knowledge, or poor judgment. Others can be attributed to a lack of understanding that organizations are systems, and as such, are perfectly designed to produce the results they are currently getting, even if those results are negative. However, bad decision making can also be the result of severe stress on the leader's cognitive and emotional functioning. As I pointed out in the Introduction, these two abilities—cognitive and emotional intelligences—are necessary for quality decision making.

Leaders must have the knowledge and ability to make decisions at the level of complexity required at their role level. In other words, we have to put the right person in the right job. When leaders with experience make decisions to put young, inexperienced, and unskilled leaders into positions of responsibility where they can cripple the financial foundation of the company (or stall its progress, frustrate employees, and alienate clients), they demonstrate a form of irresponsible decision making.

We begin to learn decision strategies in infancy and develop preferred approaches for making decisions. Decision strategies vary from unconscious, almost instant decisions to longer, more deliberate processes such as strategic planning. Each of these processes is discussed in detail in this book.

The ability to make complex decisions is driven by the leader's own decision-making ability, strategies, and timeliness. I explain the two major decision categories, rational and intuitive, in more detail and give examples to aid in recognizing to which category a given decision belongs and give examples of how to choose the appropriate strategy when dealing with that type of decision.

A discussion of decision making would not be complete without examining some of the more common and controversial factors, such as gender and age, that moderate the decision-making process. Each of these is discussed in turn in this book, too. Leaders are in a perpetual state of decision making throughout their waking hours, and some argue that decision making continues during sleep. Based on the results of some of the failed companies mentioned above (not to mention less famous but daily failures in countless other organizations), we seem to have some leaders who are sleepwalking.

Let's move forward and examine leadership, organizational complexity and decision making from the perspective of how leaders get work done and the impact of complexity on the decisions they make, the time span for making decisions, and the difficulty in making decisions at the various organizational levels.

Leadership: Redefining What It Takes

In their book *In Search of Excellence,* Tom Peters and Robert Waterman suggest that significant differences exist in how leaders think, how complex organizations are, and how decisions are made.[8] All three of these factors influence the success of organizations. These findings reinforce that the core essence of leadership is decision making. Leaders make decisions throughout the day, every day. A staff is required to orchestrate a top CEO's daily schedule. Each event on the schedule represents a decision or hundreds of decisions already made and preparation for hundreds more to be made. Everything a leader does or does not do is a decision with significant implications.

The approach to leadership in large organizations has been to create bureaucracies, which are incapable of operating efficiently, effectively, and with accountability. And the anointed leaders have lost sight of what leadership is about. The solution is not more bureaucracy or more people talking about leaders with vision, but rather a change in our leadership paradigm. There was a time when leaders served the organizations they led, not the other way around.

Not only have some leaders lost focus, but many do not understand that not everyone has the "right stuff," and getting the right stuff doesn't happen by attending management seminars or higher-level meetings or by being elected to a board of directors or a political office. As I mentioned at the beginning of this chapter, we seem to have a blind spot when it comes to identifying leaders, as we'd like to believe that "anyone" can do "anything" in our society.

When *Good to Great* author Jim Collins talks about getting the right people on the bus, the wrong people off the bus, and the people on the bus in the right seats, he doesn't mean this "just happens."[9] On the contrary, getting the right people on the bus is a deliberate and difficult task requiring the understanding that not everyone has the right stuff to be the CEO, a senator, or a general. Assessing a leader's ability to make timely and effective decisions at role levels above where he currently works is problematic and is made worse by the belief that decision making is no different at higher levels than it is at lower levels—"Just add some zeros to the size of the budget they control." I have actually heard this comment, or versions of it, numerous times in senior management meetings, where the solution to finding the right leader was simply to promote someone to the next level. That's not to say that promoting from within is a bad solution—often the right candidate is sitting down the hall from the position that needs to be filled—but there's more to it than just moving people up the organizational chain.

It is time to change our understanding of how leaders at each level of the organization think and make decisions, especially when under stress. Studying and understanding how leaders think and make decisions can help us get the right people on the bus and in the right seats. Researchers Shelley Kirkpatrick and Edwin Locke state, "It is unequivocally clear that leaders are not like other people. Leaders do not have to be great men or women by being intellectual geniuses or omniscient prophets to succeed, but they do need to have the 'right stuff' and this stuff is not equally present in all people."[10]

The difficulty lies in determining who has the "right stuff," especially under stress. One of the most critical components of the right stuff is having the right abilities, including the ability to make timely and effective decisions at the next role level in which the leader will be working. This seems to have remained invisible to many who are tasked with the responsibility of identifying leaders with the "right stuff." Consequently organizations are heavily burdened with leaders who constrain the organization's performance. "Having the most talented people in *each* of our businesses is the most important thing," Jack Welch says. "If we don't, we lose."[11] The talented people he refers to have the abilities required to be high performers—to make timely and effective decisions—at their role level.

For the past thirty years, I have worked with organizations to identify, select, and promote leaders at all organizational levels—from frontline supervisors to CEOs and board chairpersons. Early in this journey, I discovered that there are, in Six Sigma terminology, a few critical-to-quality components required to be able to predict the potential success of a leader, not just at the CEO level but at any organizational level.[12] Each level is characterized by a unique level of complexity that requires leaders with a particular set of knowledge, skills, abilities, and experience in order to make effective decisions. An old Wendy's commercial promoting higher-quality chicken claimed that to their fast food competitors, "Parts is parts"—a sentiment that does not hold true for leaders either. Leaders are not created with equal amounts of all abilities and cannot be randomly assigned or promoted, then be expected to make effective decisions automatically.

Organizational Complexity Levels: One Size Does Not Fit All

An organization's complexity varies depending on its type and size. For example, the complexity of a $5 million local uniform cleaning company tends to be significantly less than that of a billion-dollar international uniform manufacturing company. Within an organization, suborganizations (for example, manufacturing plants) may have varying degrees of complexity. Successfully managing a particular plant does not ensure success managing a more complex plant, even in the same organization. There is a dramatic difference in complexity at the CEO level in the local cleaning company and the international manufacturer, so a CEO who makes effective decisions for a $5 million company is not ensured of the same success at the billion-dollar international level. In fact, this experience running a smaller, less complex, company might contribute to not being successful in the more complex large one. To put it very simply, parts is *not* parts.

In 1984 I was working for the U.S. Army Center for Army Leadership. One of my duties, in addition to working on how to develop high performing leaders and battle staffs for the twenty-first century, was to evaluate new human technologies and processes that might be used to enhance leadership performance. While in this role, I met Elliott Jaques, one of the world's leading psychologists and a pioneer in human development theory, and explored his stratified systems theory of leadership, which proved to be a profoundly powerful approach to understanding leadership and leadership assessment. At its core, Jaques's theory posited that work within organizations could be divided into levels of complexity, which would then drive organizational structure and the cognitive ability required by leaders to be successful at these different levels. (Jaques had amassed a database of over 220,000 leaders from several countries.) He and his colleague, Gillian Stamp, had created an assessment process for determining a leader's cognitive ability to work at a particular level of complexity. Cognitive ability, which has an IQ or intelligence component, refers to how we bring information into our system, structure it, and create and make sense of our view of the world. Later in this chapter, I will explain this more thoroughly.

Later in 1984, I spent time with Stamp, went through her assessment process, and studied her ground-breaking techniques and methodology. She and Jaques had found a way to assess cognitive ability by having leaders look for patterns during card sorts and asking the leader being assessed to complete a series of sentence stems, for example, "The most important step in decision making is . . . ," as well as other questions. Their assessment identified a leader's current cognitive ability level that could be matched to organizational complexity and role levels and predicted growth of the leader's cognitive ability in the future.

I recommended that the Center for Army Leadership work with Jaques and Stamp to incorporate their theory and assessment method-ology into the U.S. military. Later that year, Jaques began to work with a colleague of mine, Owen Jacobs, the senior scientist for leadership at the U.S. Army Research Institute.[13] The cognitive ability assessment methodology implemented in the mid-1980s is still being used by the U.S. Army's senior service colleges as of this writing. (Over the years, I have refined the basic concepts into the Leadership Potential

Equation, which has proven to be a vital assessment tool for numerous organizations I have worked with.[14])

Organizations can be stratified into five levels of complexity, each with a set of defining characteristics: Production, Tactical, Organizational, Strategic, and Visionary. The following overview of the five complexity levels is in order from lowest to highest:

o o o

• *Production:* The focus at this level is on the fundamental work of the organization—producing a product or providing a service. Typically 70 to 80 percent of an organization's employees work at this level. Examples of work at the Production level are typing reports, driving a forklift, teaching fifth grade, carrying extra ammunition for a machine gun, writing a computer program, and taking a patient's vital signs.

• *Tactical:* The focus at this level is leading the production of a product, delivery of a service or creation of something new, and organizing work teams to accomplish the fundamental work of the organization. The level of complexity of the work is relatively low and tends to be easy to understand or learn, uses linear reasoning processes, and implements single solutions to solve problems with relatively good predictability of how well the solutions will work. Examples of work at the Tactical complexity level are creating daily, weekly, monthly, and quarterly production schedules; managing the quarterly sales plan; creating large pieces of a computer program; doing annual performance counseling; and managing a quarterly school improvement plan.

• *Organizational:* Work at this complexity level is more sophisticated and at a higher systemic level than at the Tactical level. The focus is on organizing, coordinating, and managing large pieces of the organization. Examples of work at the Organizational level are managing large projects, processing improvement projects stretching out over twelve to thirty-six months, completing and implementing large computer programs, organizational alignment, business unit integration, and school district (system) realignment.

• *Strategic:* Work at this complexity level represents a profound change in the level of complexity from the previous levels. Work at the Strategic level changes from concrete to abstract. The focus is on creating, developing, and implementing strategies and strategic goals that will move the organization toward its vision over thirty-six to sixty months. Work at the Strategic level of complexity includes creating and implementing strategic plans, large-scale organizational change, mergers and acquisitions, enterprisewide compensation systems, enterprisewide restructuring, product realignment, and military combat theater strategy changes.

• *Visionary:* The focus of this level is on connecting the organization with global resources that allow reaching the organization's vision. Visionary work is complex and unfolds across very long timescales. Work of this complexity relies on a combination of innaté growth of cognitive ability and experience that has resulted in the development of mental theories built over time through an extensive series of work experiences. Problems at this level have multiple solutions that branch into multiple solutions, all with multiple unintended consequences. There is no best solution, only temporary compromises and trade-offs that will evolve into new solutions through an unfolding, emergent process across time. Work at the Visionary level of complexity includes institution development, global resource acquisition, global combat theater alignment, global environmental policy, and long-range planning.

Role Level and Complexity: Matching the Leader to the Job

A leader's role level is determined by the organizational complexity level. For example, leaders working at the Tactical level are Tactical leaders and therefore must have the ability to lead work teams of Production-level employees. Examples of work at the Tactical level are supervising or managing an office or production shift, leading an infantry platoon, managing the human resources department, directing a ready-mix concrete region, and managing a school as a principal.

Leader role levels range from the most complex at the Visionary level (CEO, chairman) to the least complex at the Tactical level (frontline supervisor). The CEO role for the billion-dollar uniform manufacturer is much more complex than that of the $5 million local uniform cleaning company. The complexity of the roles of senior-level executives—vice presidents, directors, and managers—will also vary between the two companies, with the larger, more complex company having more complex leadership roles and more demanding decision-making requirements. When hiring or promoting leaders, an organization must be able to accurately match a leader's ability to the complexity of the role. Placing an under- or overqualified person in a leadership role will result in predictable negative outcomes for the leader, the leader's direct reports, and the organization.

Having worked for a highly successful company such as General Electric is not a valid indicator of a good leadership role fit with another organization. Companies often hire leaders using logic such as, "Well, this leader *must* be good if she worked for GE." Choosing someone to fill a leadership position based solely on the reputation of a previous employer can be a recipe for failure.

Learned ability, which includes job knowledge, skills, and experience, is a critical component of leadership and decision making. Selecting a former GE executive just because she was an employee of GE to run a hospital corporation or a publishing company does not make sense. Just because someone worked for an organization with an outstanding reputation doesn't necessarily mean that individual will become an outstanding leader who makes outstanding decisions, especially if she does not have the learned ability for that role level and industry. That is not to say that high performing leaders can't successfully switch organizations and assume higher role levels; however, it's not a given.

Ultimately the leader and the role level must be the right fit because the success of an organization is determined by a leader's ability to make the right decisions about the organization's resources, structure, and employees at a particular level of organizational complexity. The leader must have adequate resources to accomplish the job, including an appropriate organizational structure, a set of followers to perform the tasks, and certain leadership skills and abilities to make effective decisions. Leadership is a function of the leader's learned and innate abilities. High performance leadership results when the leader and the organizational role level are matched properly.

The skills component of leadership comprises three factors: technical skills, interpersonal skills, and leader skills. Technical skills are peculiar to the type of industry (for example, chemical, engineering, forest products) in which the organization operates. Interpersonal skills are those required to interact successfully with other people.

Matching the leader with the right skills and abilities to the right organizational role level and providing adequate resources and followers is critical for building high performing organizations that can compete as we move into the second decade of the twenty-first century.

Individual Leader Complexity: Find the Person Who Can Do the Work

Simply put, leader complexity refers to a leader's ability to handle the requirements of his or her job. Depending on the size and type of an organization, a leader's job is often enormously complex. Two factors determine ability to work at a particular level of complexity: learned and innate abilities.

Learned abilities consist of leadership skills, technical skills (peculiar to the type of industry), knowledge of the business, work experience, and the ability to make good decisions. These are those knowledge, skills, experiences, and judgment that the leader learns throughout the span of a career from formal education, job experience, coaching, individual studies, trial and error, and practice. Ideally a leader will grow and learn across his career and be able to progress to higher leadership positions.

In reality, all leaders have limitations to what they can learn and how far up the leadership ladder they can climb. Some of the limitations are imposed by the leader's innate abilities—those hardwired abilities or talents (for example, in music, math, or painting) that create individual differences across the population. A person can be born with an innate ability to become a great musician, an athlete, a scientist, or a CEO. All leaders have innate abilities and have discovered that some endeavors are easier than others. Innate ability as it pertains to leadership consists of four major factors: cognitive ability, emotional intelligence, motivation, and personality.

Cognitive Ability

Cognitive ability is how a leader processes, organizes, stores, and retrieves information, thus determining how she creates the world she lives in, makes sense of it, and acts on it. Cognitive ability is a key determinant of a leader's ability to be successful at different organizational role levels. Unlike learned skills, cognitive ability is not trainable; it is a hardwired ability that unfolds through a natural maturation process across one's life span. A leader's cognitive ability determines how she approaches problem solving, decision making, and interpersonal interactions. Let's look at the general characteristics of cognitive ability, going from high to low.

The higher a leader's cognitive ability level is, the lower the need for consistency in the information being processed. Consider the question, "Do cell phones cause brain cancer?" You can find as many studies that say it does as say it does not. At lower cognitive ability levels, most people would find the inconsistency in the research confusing. Their response would be: "There must be a right answer." The low cognitive ability leader may choose to ignore the data altogether or pick the data that support her position.

In contrast, the high cognitive ability leader understands that there is no single answer and tends to look at the implications of cell phone use in the organization or how to put in safeguards just in case the phones do cause cancer. She does not let the inconsistency prevent her from making a larger decision in which cell phones play a role.

Almost any topic contains some level of data inconsistency: what financial markets are going to do in the future, when the construction industry will rebound, which airlines will survive, and whether we need more F/A-22 Raptors (currently the world's most advanced fighter aircraft). The key is that high cognitive ability leaders rise above the level of inconsistency and make decisions.

Leaders with lower levels of cognitive ability are constrained by the information they receive. Information must be consistent for them to make sense of it. High cognitive ability leaders, by contrast, rely on themselves to provide missing information, look for more novel information, and search across more domains to find information. They show greater certainty in judging inconsistent information and are more focused on long-term strategies than low cognitive ability leaders are.

The leader with high cognitive ability uses multiple dimensions when processing information. This multidimensional approach creates a high probability that the leader will match some facet of herself with a facet of another person during interpersonal interactions. This leader is more inclined toward assimilation of information about herself than a leader with lower cognitive ability is. Thus, leaders with high cognitive ability show a propensity for receiving feedback. They seek out information about themselves, are open to feedback, and assimilate this information into knowledge about themselves. With this expanded knowledge and confidence, they can more easily find some aspect of others with which they can connect, and this connection allows them to gain more feedback and knowledge.

A leader with high cognitive ability perceives herself as being more complex than the average individual. In a decision-making situation, she might delay longer and submit a more complicated decision. Her interpersonal interactions tend to result in greater perceived similarities between herself and more senior people. She may perceive differences between herself and others more accurately than a leader with lower cognitive ability does. This complex internal structure results in a greater perception of the external environmental structure, which can manifest in intrapersonal conflict.

The high cognitive ability leader recognizes when she is communicating with others who are at a lower or higher cognitive ability. When talking to a lower cognitive ability leader, she recognizes that person's simpler language structure, linear thought process, and shorter-term focus and will understand that the lower cognitive ability leader might not get what she is saying. When she is talking to someone of equal or higher cognitive ability, she may find that the conversation moves faster and is more enjoyable and stimulating.

Low cognitive ability leaders tend to use fewer dimensions when processing stimuli, resulting in fewer and less complex information domains and a lower probability of matching some facet of themselves with that of another person. They tend to contrast themselves with others and are less open to feedback. In their interpersonal interactions, they tend to perceive themselves as being more similar to their peers and less similar to their superiors. They are predisposed to be more rigid and concrete in their thinking. The accuracy of their predictions about others is directly proportional to the amount of information they have about others. Their "concreteness" filters out more aspects of the external environmental structure, particularly when under stress.

Low cognitive ability leaders tend to have a relatively narrow set of interests and knowledge domains, although they may have in-depth knowledge in a few areas. Consequently they look for others who share one or more of their interests. Unlike the high cognitive ability leader, they do not have a broad range of areas of expertise they can use to connect with others.

The bottom line is that leaders with high cognitive ability are able to process greater amounts of information and operate more successfully in complex environments with a higher level of inconsistency and ambiguity than can leaders with low cognitive ability. As they rise to higher role levels in an organization, the problems they face become more complex and ambiguous. These leaders with high cognitive ability tend to perform well at upper organizational echelons.

Emotional Intelligence

Emotional intelligence focuses on the interpersonal and emotional aspects of innate ability.[15] It can be defined as a person's innate ability to perceive and manage his own emotions in a manner that results in successful interactions with the environment and, if others are present, to perceive and manage their emotions in a manner that results in successful interpersonal interactions.[16] Emotions and emotional intelligence play key roles in the decision-making process. (Emotional intelligence and its impact on decision making are more thoroughly explored in Chapter Three.)

As leaders advance in role level and responsibility, emotional intelligence becomes increasingly important in determining their likelihood of success. High emotional intelligence tends to be an enabler of other key leadership success factors.

Motivation

Motivation is a combination of work aspiration (the role level the leader aspires to reach), motivators (what drives the leader to be fully engaged at work), demotivators (what causes the leader to lose interest in work), and a drive for results (the leader's need to achieve). In general, motivation is highly associated with job performance and promotability. Research supports the idea that motivation has an innate core. Some aspects of motivation—for example, a desire to work in the health care field if one's parents were doctors or nurses—may be due to environmental influences. However, a drive for success and a need for achievement and power seem to be innate.[17]

Motivation can also be viewed as an energy or driving force that moves a leader to action. The leader wants the project to succeed, so she puts in extra hours to ensure its success. She wants to be promoted, so she attends school at night and on weekends to complete an M.B.A. It appears that Jimmy Cayne, the former CEO of Bear Stearns, reached a point in his career where he was more motivated to play bridge than to lead his company.[18] When a leader's dominant motivation shifts—temporarily or permanently—it changes her focus and behavior.

Personality

A leader's personality tends to be hardwired so that most of his core preferences for interacting with people, gathering information, decision making, and general orientation to life change little over the course of his life. These preferences influence how he perceives stimuli—or doesn't perceive them. Personality influences how he interacts with others, makes decisions, and leads in general.

Although personality has a significant influence on how a leader leads and makes decisions, we will not spend much time on the topic in this book. Numerous other books are dedicated specifically to leadership and personality, such as Roger Pearman's *Hardwired Leadership*, which would make excellent supplemental reading.[19]

Decision Complexity: Find the Leader Who Can Make the Right Decisions

The fundamental core of leadership is decision making. Everything a leader does or does not do is the result of decisions. Every day leaders are called on to make decisions, routine and nonroutine.

Routine decisions are made frequently and have standard responses based on experience: the more times a leader has made a particular decision, the easier it becomes to recognize the problem and make the appropriate decision again. A manufacturing supervisor, for example, occasionally has an employee who does not show up for work. The supervisor most likely has solved this problem many times before and knows what decisions have to be made to find someone to work the absent employee's shift. Many problems of this nature that occur throughout the day are easily solved based on experience. Such routine problems require standard decisions. Examples are shown in Table 1.1.

Nonroutine decisions arise out of never- or rarely seen situations. (For perhaps the most searing example, think of all the nonroutine

TABLE 1.1 Routine Decisions by Role

Leader	Routine Decisions
Manufacturing supervisor	Attendance report Overtime report Absenteeism
Commercial pilot	Plane inspection Takeoff checklist Landing checklist
School administrator (principal)	Safety checks Curriculum design Parent meetings
Brigade commander	Task force organization Troop deployment Security
CEO	Weekly financial review Weekly production review Quarterly financial report

decisions that had to be made on September 11, 2001.) In most cases, there is no standard or best solution. Decisions of this nature tend to be extremely complex and ambiguous and will be difficult for the leader to make effectively. Most basic leadership training classes include instruction on how to solve problems and make decisions, including nonroutine ones, using a standard problem-solving and decision-making model. The typical model consists of the seven steps shown in Figure 1.1.

Note that problem solving is just a series of decisions. It is also important to remember that if you make the right decision but make it at the wrong time or in the wrong way, the net result is a bad or ineffective decision. Timing is critical.

Similar models are taught in business schools, Six Sigma black belt training, process improvement classes, and other courses where leaders are required to solve problems and make decisions. This process is typically thought of as a logical, rational problem-solving and decision-making process. Examples of nonroutine decisions are shown in Table 1.2.

FIGURE 1.1 The Seven-Step Problem-Solving Model

In the past thirty years, I have trained thousands of leaders to make nonroutine, difficult decisions using the seven-step process above. I taught these leaders that it is imperative to fully understand the problem to be solved, gather all the relevant facts and data, reevaluate the problem to ensure that what was initially believed to be the problem is actually the problem and not a symptom of the problem, generate multiple solutions, use various analytical techniques to compare and evaluate potential solutions, select and implement the best solution, and evaluate how well the solution works.

The decision-making strategy for solving nonroutine problems requires this logical sequence. Over the years, however, I have found that most leaders tend not to follow these steps in making most decisions. When I observe them make quick decisions, in particular, it appears as

TABLE 1.2 Nonroutine Decisions by Role

Leader	Nonroutine Decisions
Manufacturing supervisor	Technology implementation New product line
Commercial pilot	Both engines shut down Passenger heart attack Smoke in cockpit
School administrator (principal)	School shooting Redistricting Major budget cut
Brigade commander	Successful enemy cyberattack Major strategy change Combat deployment extension
CEO	Acquiring a new company Replacing the CFO Nonprofitable quarter

if some other process is being used. A phrase often used in organizations is "Ready! Fire! Aim!"—referring to leaders making decisions without appearing to have all the facts available. (Many times this process seems to work, and we will explore this later in this chapter.)

The opposite of a rapid-fire decision-making style is called "analysis paralysis." This is when the leader gets bogged down in gathering and analyzing data to the degree that decisions are made very slowly or not made at all.

I often use the Emotional Quotient Inventory (EQ-i) to measure a leader's emotional intelligence.[20] Its Problem Solving scale assesses the degree to which a leader uses a logical decision-making process, such as the seven-step model in Figure 1.1. In fact, it is not uncommon for leaders who have demonstrated the ability to make tough decisions and solve difficult problems to score low on this particular EQ-i scale. And when they receive low scores, they tend to push back and say something to the effect that "I make difficult decisions throughout the day, every day. My job is about making decisions. I don't know how you can say that I'm not a good problem solver." In fact, when I look at their actual ability to solve problems and make decisions, too often I see a disconnect between their score on the Problem Solving scale and their actual ability. I believe the reason for this disconnect is that this scale is assessing the leader on how well he or she follows traditional problem-solving steps. Many leaders use this formal process for solving problems and making decisions only in certain circumstances (primarily nonroutine), which might cause them to get a lower than desired score on the scale.

Decision Strategies: Pick the One That Works

Leaders use two basic decision strategies to make decisions: rational and intuitive. Each uses different decision-making processes, and each has its own utility and blind spots. Each is also a trade-off between analysis and speed, conscious and unconscious processes, and comparative solutions and one solution at a time.

Rational Strategies
The rational decision-making strategy tends to be a logical, sequential, analytical, conscious, well-thought-out process that takes time and typically involves others. It generates and compares multiple solutions, then chooses the best solution for implementation. It follows a logical, sequential process designed to ensure that the decision maker considers all data, generates appropriate alternatives, and then evaluates alternatives before a solution is chosen and implemented. The problem-solving steps presented earlier are some of the basic tools of the rational strategy.[21]

Strategic planning is an example of rational decision making that is appropriate for the situation and works well. Planning of this nature tends to be relatively complex, mostly nonroutine, and carried out across an extended period of time. It is not uncommon for strategic planning to take several months to complete. It is also not uncommon to see trained decision makers using a similar process when purchasing a car, refrigerator, cell phone, or other item when there are several options from which to choose.

Rational decisions tend to be much more complex, more conscious, and of longer duration than intuitive strategies; use more methodical data collection and analysis; and may involve a longer-term impact on the organization.

Intuitive Strategies

In his book *Blink!* Malcolm Gladwell proposes that most decisions are made in the "blink of an eye"—that within two seconds we have made a decision.[22] We appear to have been "thinking without thinking." And according to Gladwell, these "blink" decisions are not only critical for survival situations, but are also how we make most complicated decisions.

Intuitive decisions are made very quickly, automatically, emotionally, and mostly unconsciously, and this is the type of decision usually made in routine or emergency situations. Leaders apply unconscious processes to make intuitive decisions throughout the day. There are two prominent intuitive decision-making models: the observe-orient-decide-act loop and recognition-primed decisions.

Observe-Orient-Decide-Act Loop

Colonel John R. Boyd, a retired U.S. Air Force fighter pilot, designed a way to "out-decision" his opponents by using an intuitive process to make faster decisions. He developed a reputation for being able to start air-to-air combat with his plane in a position of disadvantage and within forty seconds or less to be on the tail of his opponent. Legend has it that Boyd never failed to defeat an opponent within forty seconds, earning him the nickname "40 Second Boyd." Boyd called his decision-making process the observe-orient-decide-act loop (OODA). OODA was created as a model of how humans make Tactical decisions and as a way to teach fighter pilots how to make decisions faster than their opponents—to operate inside their opponent's OODA loop.[23]

The loop aspect of the model indicates that the process is repeated over and over as the situation constantly changes. You must change faster than your opponent changes, always keeping him confused and off balance. Harry Hillaker, one of Boyd's colleagues, once summed it up in an interview: "The key is to obscure your intentions and make them unpredictable to your opponent while you simultaneously clarify his intentions. That is, operate at a faster tempo to generate rapidly changing conditions that inhibit your opponent from adapting or reacting to those changes and that suppress or destroy his awareness. Thus, a hodgepodge of confusion and disorder occur to cause him to over- or under-react to conditions or activities that appear to be uncertain, ambiguous, or incomprehensible."[24]

The OODA loop appears simple on the surface, but it has many layers, mathematical equations, and decades of work, making it a deep and rich model. Over the years, the application of Boyd's model has been extended into numerous fields, from other branches of the military to business where leaders have to make relatively quick decisions.

Recognition–Primed Decision Model

The recognition-primed decision model (RPD), one of the best known and most studied rapid decision-making models, was developed by Gary Klein and explained in his book *Sources of Power*.[25] Klein is a psychologist who studies decision making by "living in the field" and observing leaders making decisions in real time. He has lived on aircraft carriers and in firefighter camps and has participated in military exercises and in many other environments that require rapid decision making. His research team has been called in to study some of the most infamous fast decisions, such as the shooting down of an Iranian Air Bus in 1988 by the *USS Vincennes*.

On the heels of the Iran-Iraq war, the *USS Vincennes*, a U.S. Navy–guided missile cruiser commanded by Captain Will Rogers, mistakenly shot down an Iranian civilian airliner on July 3, 1988, over the Strait of Hormuz, killing all 290 passengers (including sixty-six children) and crew aboard, sparking an intense international controversy. The U.S. Government claimed that Air Flight 655 was mistakenly identified as an attacking F-14 Tomcat fighter by the *Vincennes* crew, who had been warned of a possible attack.

Yet it was determined that the *Vincennes* was inside Iranian territorial waters at the time of the attack and the airliner was within Iranian airspace. The United States and Iran reached a settlement over the incident in 1996, with the United States agreeing to pay $61.8 million as compensation for the Iranians killed. Poor decision making and lack of training have been cited as contributors to the deadly attack.

Klein's work focuses on intuitive decision making, where leaders use their experience to quickly evaluate the situation and make fast decisions. A fireground commander looks at a house or building that is on fire and immediately begins shouting orders as to how to fight the fire or to get away from the building because it is about to collapse. Often the commander does not realize he was making decisions. He just thought that what needed to be done was obvious.

Klein's research indicates that in fast-moving, dynamic environments like firefighting, police work, and military combat where decisions have to be made in under sixty seconds, an intuitive-type decision-making process is used almost exclusively. He has found that even in situations favoring rational decision making, about 80 percent are made using the intuitive style. This type of decision making seems to be in conflict with the rational decision-making strategy taught in most business schools.

As Klein continued to collect data and study how decisions are made under time constraints, he developed the RPD model. Unlike the rational decision-making model taught in leadership courses and business schools, leaders rarely seem to follow a formal seven-step decision-making process, especially when under time constraints. Most decision making does not tend to be an exercise of generating and comparing alternative courses of action until the best one is chosen. What leaders actually do is to go with the first solution they come up with that they think might work. The solution is evaluated on its own merit. Leaders often do not generate or compare alternatives. This finding is in stark contrast to what is normally taught about how leaders should and do make decisions.

The RPD model sizes up the problem by recognizing cues that are tied to prior experience. These cues identify decisions that have worked before in similar situations and thus are primed to come forth as solutions. When a primed solution materializes, it is evaluated by using mental simulation. The leader imagines how the solution will be implemented and to what degree it will work. (Table 1.3 shows the steps and actions.)

The objective of the RPD model is to find a solution rapidly that will work. Generating and evaluating a long list of problems in a fast-moving problem space is inefficient and might lead to failure. After US Airways Flight 1549 hit the flock of birds as it was ascending, the plane had approximately three minutes until impact with the water. Captain Sullenberger had to make numerous decisions and take certain actions for everyone to survive. He made the decision to attempt to land on the Hudson River within seconds. There was no time to have a brainstorming session, generate thirty or forty possibilities, eliminate redundancies, consolidate similar ideas, expand on them, evaluate each idea in a weighted decision matrix, choose the optimal solution, plan its implementation, communicate it to others, and execute the plan. Captain Sullenberger appears to have used a decision-making process

TABLE 1.3 Klein's Recognition-Primed Decision Model Steps and Actions

Recognition-Primed Decision Steps	Actions
Assess the situation.	Judge it familiar.
Evaluate a course of action.	Imagine how it will be carried out.
Select an option.	Look for the first workable option.
Develop a solution set.	The set is usually very small.
Generate and evaluate options.	Generate and evaluate options one at a time.
Adjust the option.	Spot weaknesses, and find ways to avoid them.
Take action.	Be poised to act, not paralyzed.

similar to Klein's to choose a workable solution rather than work toward a perfect (maximized) solution.

Herbert Simon spent his career studying decision making and won the Nobel Memorial Prize in Economics in 1978 for his work. Simon, a psychologist and economist, made many advances in the field of decision making, but two of his contributions, satisficing and bounded reality, are particularly relevant to the RPD model.[26] The technique of satisficing allows a solution to be chosen that is not perfect but is sufficient to provide a satisfactory solution to the problem. The RPD model chooses the first solution that might work (a satisficing approach). Simon discovered that in most cases, trying to choose a solution using a maximizing (optimal or perfect) approach tends to be unrealistic and inefficient because the leader is making decisions in an environment where all the information about the problem and possible solutions are unknown. The leader is operating in a bounded reality, which makes the satisficing solution the most efficient, especially under time pressure. Most leaders use the satisficing technique even though they might not be aware they are using it.

Mental simulation is an important component of both Klein's RPD model and Simon's satisficing technique. During mental simulation, the leader imagines the implementation of the chosen solution and plays out the solution in her mind. If the solution does not appear to work, then it is either modified or discarded and another solution is selected; the simulation process starts again. For example, you have a flight out of the Atlanta airport tomorrow at 10:00 A.M. You need to decide when to leave your house for the airport. There are three basic parts to your mental simulation: (1) depart from your house, (2) travel, and (3) arrive at the gate. You know that you like to be at the gate an hour prior to flight time. That means you need to be at the gate at 9:00 A.M. The travel will take two hours. The latest you can depart from your house is 7:00 A.M. When you run this simulation, it appears to give you a workable solution.

As you might imagine, mental simulations require the use of mental resources. Klein found that most leaders are limited to a maximum of three moving parts (depart from your house, travel, arrive at the gate) and six steps (load the car, get in the car, drive to the airport, park, go through security, travel to the gate) during mental simulations. Going beyond three parts and six steps overtaxes most leaders' cognitive resources, especially under time pressure. It is possible for leaders to use a chunking process of combining several steps so as not to exceed the three-parts, six-steps rule. Reducing the mental resources required for the simulation may allow for larger simulations. In the airport example, drive to the airport, park, go through security, and travel to the gate were chunked into one part: travel.

Boost Your Working Memory with Chunking

George Miller coined the phrase "the magical number seven, plus or minus two" in relation to how many pieces of information the human mind can hold in working memory at one time. Quickly read the sequence of numbers that follows, then look away and try keeping them in your working memory; and, without looking, say the numbers in sequence: 3409112001.

This ten-digit sequence exceeds most people's seven-digit working memory capacity—unless you notice something familiar about the digits. For example, 09 could be the 9th month, 11 could be the 11th day, and 2001 could be the year. Miller called this *chunking*. Now you remember 3, 4, 09, 11, 2001—five chunks of information instead of ten. Some people might chunk 09112001 together, reducing the total pieces of information to three chunks. If 34 is your age, you might have only two chunks to remember, 34 and 09112001.

Source: Miller, G. (1956). The magical number seven, plus or minus two: Some limits on our capacity for processing information. *Psychological Review, 63,* 81–97.

Even with chunking, some simulations are too complex to do mentally, especially when you have many other actions competing for your mental resources. We will see later how stress can significantly reduce the amount of information you can hold in memory. Captain Sullenberger had to "just focus on flying the plane" and not allow himself to be overwhelmed by the competing demands for his mental resources—especially fear.

A significant portion of decision making takes place in the unconscious, where it appears that there are fewer limitations on the number of pieces of information you can manage. The downside to solving problems in the unconscious is that you are not aware of how you arrived at the solution. You have to trust your instinct to use intuitive decisions. As we will see later, there are times to make intuitive decisions and times to make rational decisions.

The U.S. Marine Corps implemented a version of Colonel Boyd's OODA loop decision-making process into its doctrine in 1989. The intent was to enable leaders to make decisions faster and better than the enemy could. This decision-making philosophy was consistent with Sun Tsu's belief that "speed is the essence of war" and Napoleon's belief that intuitive decision making was a "gift of nature" and critical for success in war.[27]

General Charles C. Krulak, the thirty-first commandant of the U.S. Marine Corps, coined the term "strategic corporal" and described the role it will play in the "three block war." A three block war is described by the Marine Corps as a conflict in which Marines may be confronted by the entire spectrum of tactical warfare within hours, all taking place in an urban area the size of three city blocks. A Marine corporal leading a fire team of four Marines will have to react almost instantly to visual cues in the environment and deploy his team against the enemy while taking into consideration hostile, neutral, and friendly forces in this limited space. Military leaders must be able to make intuitive decisions. To assist Marines in making effective intuitive decisions, General Krulak began implementing a version of Klein's RPD model into the Marine Corps for his strategic corporals in the late 1990s. It has also been evaluated for use by the U.S. Army.

In the chapters to come, we'll examine the latest neuroscience research on different decision-making strategies that leaders use. If you understand the whys and hows of decision making, particularly when people engage in it under stressful conditions, you'll be better able to recognize what makes an effective, decisive leader.

Using the Perception-Appraisal-Motivation-Action Model: What Was Sullenberger Thinking?

It makes sense to wrap up this discussion of decision making with one more look at US Airways Flight 1549, an event that called for a sweeping number of decisions that fell into just about every category, from routine to nonroutine. Let's look at one final model that can serve as a comprehensive model for both rational and intuitive strategies.

The Perception-Appraisal-Motivation-Action model (PAMA) provides a way of looking at and discussing the very complex information processing that takes place in the brain during decision making.[28] PAMA is admittedly an oversimplification of what is really happening, and the steps in its process do overlap somewhat: but this model provides a means of visualizing and talking about how decisions are made from a macro perspective. Each component in the process, shown in Figure 1.2, is described next using examples from US Airways Flight 1549.

Stimulus (External/Internal): "Birds"

The PAMA model is activated when a Stimulus is detected. The Stimulus can originate from outside the leader, such as seeing the Hudson River, or from inside, such as having a thought about a situation.

FIGURE 1.2 Perception-Appraisal-Motivation-Action Model

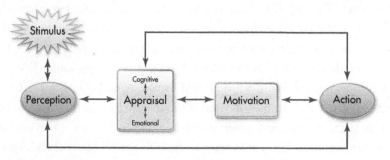

Source: Thompson, H. (2005). Exploring the interface of the type and emotional intelligence landscapes. *Bulletin of Psychological Type, 29*(3), 14–19.

At 15:26:37, or 3:26:37 P.M. Eastern Time, Captain Sullenberger enters a PAMA cycle by expressing his reaction to the aerial view of the Hudson River (the Perception of a Stimulus, an Appraisal of the Perception, a Motivation to express his Appraisal followed by the Action of making a comment) by saying, "Uh, what a view of the Hudson today." First Officer Skiles acknowledges the comment with, "Yeah," and continues with the After Takeoff Checklist: "Flaps up please, After Takeoff Checklist." Sullenberger responds at 15:26:54 with, "Flaps up" and thirteen seconds later at 15:27:07 with, "After Takeoff Checklist complete."

Sullenberger has several PAMA cycles running concurrently, and these cycles are transitioning in and out of consciousness. He and Skiles are going back and forth between the view of the Hudson River and the After Takeoff Checklist.

Think about the PAMAs involved when a person is driving to work. Driving is a relatively complex task. Simultaneous PAMAs are engaged for driving, navigation, rush-hour traffic, tuning the radio, a conversation with your passenger, a cell phone call from your spouse, checking your hair in the mirror, the presentation you have to give to your boss when you get to work, wondering why your boss is such a jerk, and, speaking of jerks, what about the one who just cut you off and now you will have to wait through the traffic light again, which means you'll be late to brief the boss jerk and so on. Your PAMAs move in and out of consciousness. The majority of a leader's PAMAs are running on autopilot in his unconscious.

At 15:27:10, Captain Sullenberger, three seconds after stating that the After Takeoff Checklist is complete, consciously perceives the Stimulus (the birds) and says, "Birds." This was *one second* before the plane made contact with the flock of Canada geese (15:27:11). As the birds made contact with the plane, First Officer Skiles said, "Whoa." The impact of the birds can be heard on the voice cockpit recorder as loud thumps and thuds, followed immediately by a shuttering sound. At 15:27:12, one second after contact, Skiles expresses an expletive, and the captain follows at 15:27:13 with, "Oh yeah!" Like Schrödinger's cat, the box has been opened, and all PAMAs collapse into consciousness as the birds strike the plane's engines.[29]

Perception (Conscious/Unconscious): "Oh [Expletive]"

The Perception of the Stimulus may be conscious or unconscious. For example, most stimuli are perceived unconsciously. In fact, the whole process from the origination of the Stimulus through Perception, Appraisal, Motivation, and Action can take place in the unconscious. There are always numerous PAMA cycles in process in the unconscious, and most never make it into consciousness. At 15:27:11 the bird strike PAMA is dominating the captain's and first officer's consciousness.

Flight 1549's impact with the birds generated numerous Stimuli that set hundreds of conscious PAMAs in motion for the 150 passengers, 3 flight attendants, and 2 pilots. At least one passenger sees fire coming from one of the engines and sends a "final" text message to his wife. Another sees some of the birds go by as gray streaks. Almost everyone hears the thuds of the birds and notices the sudden engine silence and the "tennis shoe-in-the-dryer sound" coming from one of the engines. They also feel a sudden forward deceleration, and their weight in the seats goes from heavy, the result of the g-force produced from the plane's upward acceleration, to lightness, due to the plane's suddenly beginning to descend at approximately eighteen feet per second. These and the Stimuli coming from the reaction of the other passengers initiate many PAMAs in each person.

In many normal situations, the PAMA process may become conscious only at the Motivation phase and the leader then realizes that he wants to take an Action. For the passengers on Flight 1549, many PAMAs have begun competing for space in each passenger's consciousness, but there is room for only seven pieces of information in consciousness, plus or minus two. For most people in situations like Flight 1549, fear-generated PAMAs tend to dominate consciousness.

Appraisal: "We May End Up in the Hudson"

The Appraisal phase takes place immediately on Perception of the Stimulus. The Appraisal is designed to make sense of the Stimulus and then create an appropriate Motivation followed by an appropriate Action. Keep in mind that the whole process from Stimulus to Action may take place in seconds or less, making it seem as if there were no Appraisal or Motivation phases.

Captain Sullenberger sees the birds (Stimulus 1) and completes a PAMA cycle in less than one second and knows he cannot avoid the birds. One second after he sees the birds, he hears their contact with the plane (Stimulus 2), which updates his PAMA cycle. He feels the deceleration and hears the change in the engine sounds. His Appraisal of the Perception Motivates him to begin the Action of assessing the damage. He hears the first officer say, "Uh-oh," and sees both engines' revolutions per minute rolling back (Stimulus 3). Sullenberger is now in his third update of the PAMA cycle and tells the first officer, "We got one rol—both of 'em rolling back." It has been five seconds from sighting the birds to confirming that the engines are shutting down. Sullenberger has run at least three updates to the bird PAMA cycles during this five-second period and has now initiated several more—some conscious, some unconscious. Two separate components play major roles during Appraisal: cognition and emotions.

Cognitive

The cognitive component of Appraisal provides the logical reasoning and intellectual processing of information received from the Perception of the Stimulus. This component moves relatively slowly (approximately 100 milliseconds) and deliberately to process and make sense of information coming into the system from various parts of the brain. It tries to control the Appraisal process by thinking about and understanding the meaning of the data. The cognitive component also attempts to maintain control of the emotional component.

The cognitive component identified the objects as being too close to avoid and calculated that the "birds" (information received from the emotional component) would hit the plane. It will later identify the birds as Canada geese. When the Stimulus evolves to the birds' hitting the plane, the PAMA cycle is updated, with the cognitive component now reacting to the bird strikes and processing the strike data. This process is overwritten with the new set of data: engines becoming quiet and changes in horizontal and vertical acceleration. The cognitive portion of the Appraisal says, "This is not good."

Emotional

The emotional component of the Appraisal process moves extremely quickly to process and interpret data, create a Motivation, and initiate an Action. There is a strong predisposition toward survival. Data are interpreted in a fuzzy manner. That is, incomplete data are interpreted by the best pattern available.

The emotional component recognized the pattern of the objects as belonging to the general category of "birds" and instantly (approximately 25 milliseconds) fed "birds" into the Appraisal process and triggered the verbal response (Action) of "Birds" from Captain Sullenberger. The captain's and first officer's brains are now experiencing a chemical bath. Hormones, such as adrenaline, are gushing throughout their brains and bodies, increasing heart and breathing rate (along with many other changes that are discussed in Chapter Four) in preparation to engage in some type of new and heightened Action. Fear is instantly present. Captain Sullenberger later stated in an interview, "I felt the adrenaline shoot straight through my heart." At this point the emotional component is trying to dominate the process. Captain Sullenberger also stated, "I knew I had to block out everything except flying the plane."[30] It was crucial that fear not be allowed to dominate his Actions.

The emotional component is designed to produce automatic responses in the event of potential danger. These responses are based on instinct, learning, and prior experience. This was Captain Sullenberger's first experience with losing both engines close to the ground. Fortunately for the other 154 people onboard this flight, it was not his first time bringing a plane down without power. He had once been a glider pilot, had practiced no-power landings in a simulator a few years earlier, had a lot of experience with this type of plane, was seated where he had the best view of the landmarks critical for making decisions about viable options for landing, and he had a very cool head. (Although I'm singling out Captain Sullenberger here, the passengers were extremely fortunate to have such a strong five-person flight crew. All were heroes that day.)

Motivation: "We've Lost Thrust on Both Engines"

Motivation provides the energy required to initiate an Action. When Sullenberger heard the impact of multiple large birds, felt the g-force changes, and heard the sounds of the engines change, he was Motivated to look for damages, problems, and solutions. Eight seconds after the bird strike (15:27:18), he was attempting to restart the engines. Fourteen seconds later (15:27:32), he knew the plane was going down and sent the distress call: "Mayday! Mayday! Mayday! Uh this is uh Cactus fifteen thirty nine [should have been 'fifteen forty nine']. Hit birds. We've lost thrust in both engines. We're turning back towards LaGuardia."

At this point the updated data have been Perceived and Appraised, and the captain is Motivated to get the plane back safely on the ground. Instinct (from the emotional component) told him to go back to where he just left from, and that's what he told the control tower he was going to do. His air speed and altitude were dropping fast. He had to angle the nose of the plane down a bit to increase his air speed so the plane would not stop flying and fall out of the sky. Increasing his angle of descent increased his air speed and flying ability of the plane, but this also increased his rate of descent. At 15:28:03, the plane's flight warning computer is beginning to sound an alarm.

Unconsciously Captain Sullenberger has completed the PAMA cycle and knows that he cannot make it back to LaGuardia or any other airfield. There are only two choices: crash into a populated area, killing everyone on board and possibly many people on the ground, or try to land on the Hudson River. The National Transportation Safety Board flight tracking system reveals that Flight 1549 is already moving toward the Hudson River. At 15:28:05, departure control gives Sullenberger directions for an emergency landing at LaGuardia, to which he replies, "We're unable. We may end up in the Hudson." It has been only sixty seconds since the bird strike, and the captain has now voiced what will be his final decision about where to land: the Hudson River.

Action: "We're Gonna Brace"

Motivation generates Action. The Action component is the behavioral output of the system. The traffic collision avoidance system begins shouting, "Traffic, Traffic," into Sullenberger's headset, along with the predictive windshear system's warnings of, "Go around! Windshear ahead!" But the captain wanted to check one more option and asked, "I'm not sure we can make any runway. Uh, what's over to our right? Anything in New Jersey? Maybe Teterboro?" He is told that Teterboro is off to his right. The traffic collision avoidance system shouts, "Monitor vertical speed!" He tells departure control that he wants to try it—but he already knows he can't do it.

At 15:29:11 he tells the passengers over the public address system, "This is the Captain. Brace for impact!" The flight attendants begin shouting instructions in unison. At 15:29:25 he tells departure control, "We can't do it." At 15:29:28, he says, "We're gonna be in the Hudson." He is now finalizing the Action to put Flight 1549 in the Hudson River's thirty-four-degree, swiftly moving water. Captain Sullenberger is totally focused on air speed, descent rate, keeping the nose angled upward, and executing a perfect water landing. He blocks out the multitude of alarms going off, asks First Officer Skiles if he has any ideas, braces, and then makes the storybook landing—and starts a new PAMA cycle for getting everyone out of the plane and to safety.

**Over and Over Again: The Recursive
Nature of PAMA**

You can see from the Flight 1549 example that the PAMA system is dynamic. The Stimulus is constantly changing, requiring the system to be continuously updating itself. This means that every component gets information from and provides information to every other component. Each component is continually being updated based on information and Actions generated.

Table 1.4 gives a brief comparison of the PAMA model with the two other decision strategies discussed in this chapter, and it shows the many similarities in the models. It seems clear that leaders use a

TABLE 1.4 PAMA, OODA Loop, and RPD: A Comparison

PAMA	OODA Loop	RPD
Perception	Observe	Recognize
Appraisal Cognitive Emotional	Orient	Select
Motivation	Decide	Simulate
Action	Act	Act

rapid decision-making process, especially when they are under time pressure. The PAMA model allows us to explore how the decision process works and potential pitfalls and the impact of other moderating factors such as stress.

The Takeaway on Leadership and Decision Making

In this chapter, we've looked at examples of "smart" corporate leaders in some of the largest U.S. companies who made decisions that could easily be categorized as dumb, illustrating that even proven leaders can make bad decisions under certain circumstances. That is not to say these leaders were not intelligent; rather, they lacked the right combinations of organizational complexity, role level, and individual leader complexity, and they took a wrong turn that eventually led their organizations to failure. On top of that, they lacked the right balance of cognitive and emotional intelligences that would have allowed them to make better decisions, particularly in stressful situations.

We know that effective decision making is at the core of leadership and that different types of decision environments and strategies influence leader success. Research has shown that as leaders' stress increases, two key factors determine the success of their decisions: cognitive and emotional intelligences, both of which we're about to look at more closely. We'll start with an in-depth examination of cognitive intelligence in general and the neuroscience of intelligence in particular.

2 How Cognitive Intelligence Influences Decision Making

I do not feel obliged to believe that the same God who has endowed us with sense, reason, and intellect has intended us to forgo their use.
GALILEO GALILEI

P lato, Socrates, Aristotle, Newton, and Einstein: these are names that come to mind when we think of cognitive intelligence, which broadly stated is the ability to learn and retrieve knowledge. The intellectual prowess of these great thinkers has been well documented. Sir Isaac Newton, for example, took a year off in 1665 when Cambridge University was closed because of the Great Plague.[1] He returned to his family home in Woolsthorpe, a safe distance away from Cambridge. It was during this break, sometimes called the Newtonian Revolution, that Newton created "the method of flowing fluents" (integral calculus), "the calculation of fluxions" (differential calculus), "the theory of colors," "the universal theory of gravity," and "the laws of motion." These were some of his greatest contributions to science—and he was only twenty-four years old.

Albert Einstein performed a similar feat during his own "miraculous year" in 1905 by writing six of his science-changing papers on: quantum theory; Brownian motion; special relativity; a follow-up to special relativity, with $E = mc^2$; determining molecular sizes; and a second paper on Brownian motion.

All of these people were intellectual geniuses with substantial amounts of cognitive intelligence. (I use *cognitive intelligence, intelligence,* and *IQ* interchangeably. *Cognitive ability* is used as a higher-level construct that has IQ as a subcomponent. See Chapter One.) They were also true leaders in their fields. Although these thinkers lived and worked in another time, their examples raise a contemporary question: How does cognitive intelligence affect a leader's decision-making ability? Let's bring this question to life by looking behind the scenes of one of our national pastimes: football. (And after you read this story, you will never use the phrase *dumb jock* again!)

Every February the best college football players in the world are invited to attend what is essentially a job interview: the National Football League (NFL) Scouting Combine in Indianapolis, Indiana, where executives, coaches, and scouts from all thirty-two NFL teams are present to evaluate the potential professional players prior to the NFL draft, when the teams select new players. The NFL Combine is an intense job interview. Performance during those four days has a significant effect on which players will be selected and when and how much money they will be offered.

The physical interview consists of six events: the forty-yard dash, bench press, vertical jump, broad jump, three-cone drill, and shuttle run. The NFL coaches believe these events are key physical performance indicators of how well the potential players will perform in their respective roles on the gridiron. American football is, to say the least, a very physical sport, so it makes sense that a job interview would include a standard measure of physical performance.

Years ago I was invited to dinner at a client CEO's home. We had become friends as we had worked together on his company. His son, an outstanding high school quarterback, was on the floor in the middle of the den with notebooks, worksheets, and other materials scattered around, and his father asked him to move his work to another room. "But, Dad," he responded, "I have to memorize all these offensive plays, how they work against all of the standard defenses, how to modify them based on the backs and ends present for a particular snap, where we are on the field and the time remaining. There must be 180 combinations!"

Leading a football team as a quarterback, even at the high school level, can be cognitively demanding. The cognitive demand goes up exponentially when the ball is snapped, knowing you have only seconds to make decisions—and you can sense several huge linemen and defensive ends closing on your position at a high velocity. As long as you have the ball—and a couple of seconds after—you are fair game to experience how it might feel to be hit by a Mack truck. At the college level, the players are bigger and much faster. At the professional level, there is a quantum leap in speed, leaving the quarterback with even less time to make the best decision and with a greater chance of injury.

The NFL scouts and coaches watch the prospective players play, watch videos of their previous games, and conduct numerous assessment techniques before each Combine. However, they also use a somewhat controversial objective measure that is not physical. The players take an IQ test called the Wonderlic Personnel Test.[2] The NFL teams believe that there is a relationship among IQ, how close a player is to the ball, and performance. The quarterback touches the ball more often than anyone else except the center, who snaps the ball to the quarterback. Therefore, the coaches prefer a quarterback who scores high on the Wonderlic.

Ben Fry, who received his doctorate from the Massachusetts Institute of Technology and runs a design and software consultancy specializing in designing visual data, has created the graphic shown in Figure 2.1 showing an offensive and defensive team, with circles representing the player positions. Each circle is sized based on the average Wonderlic score for that position, with the larger sizes representing higher scores. Notice how the larger circles surround the ball, which is located under the center (C) on the graphic.

It appears those helmets are protecting some brains with very high levels of cognitive intelligence. Clearly, whether you are leading a team of scientists, corporate executives, football players, ballet dancers, production-level workers, or just about any other group in need of an effective decision maker, cognitive intelligence plays a significant role in your ability to make smart and timely decisions.

FIGURE 2.1 ·Position by Wonderlic Score

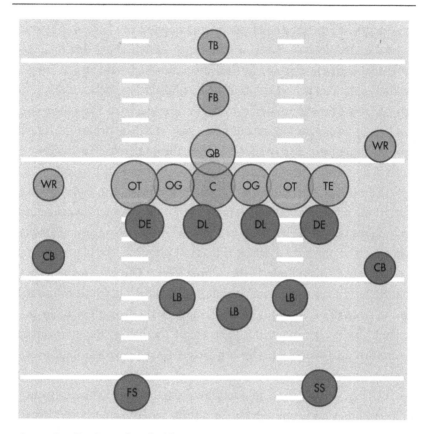

© 2008 Ben Fry. Reproduced with permission.

Cognitive Intelligence: What Every Leader Needs

Extensive research on leadership has firmly established the importance of cognitive intelligence in determining leader performance. In 1998, psychologists Frank Schmidt and John Hunter published their classic paper on a review of eighty-five years of leadership research, showing that general mental ability (cognitive intelligence) was one of the strongest predictors of leadership success.[3] Furthermore, they concluded that cognitive intelligence should be the primary personnel selection measure for hiring decisions, using the other eighteen measures they evaluated as supplements. They found this to be especially true for leaders in more complex jobs, such as jobs at higher role levels. In other words, as role levels increase, so should cognitive intelligence.

This chapter lays the foundation for understanding cognitive intelligence and its relation to how leaders make decisions. Understanding the relationship of cognitive intelligence, leadership, and decision making requires developing an intimacy with how these three concepts work independently, as well as how they interact to produce decision-making effectiveness. Cognitive intelligence will be examined from the perspective of how it is defined, its subcomponents, and methods for measuring it. Understanding cognitive intelligence requires exploring some of the latest neuroscience research as it relates to decision making.

Leadership can be especially difficult and challenging at a higher role level where cognitive intelligence significantly influences decision-making effectiveness. However, high cognitive intelligence is the price of admission to a higher leadership role level and the satisfaction such work can bring.

What Is Cognitive Intelligence?

There is a long-running debate in psychology about how best to define *cognitive intelligence.* In general, it refers to a person's ability to rapidly process, learn, and retrieve knowledge and procedures and to use learned knowledge and procedures along with abstract reasoning to solve complex problems. However, as we shall see, having cognitive intelligence and applying it are two different things.

In 1997, a group of fifty-two experts on cognitive intelligence, led by Linda Gottfredson, defined cognitive intelligence as

> *a very general mental capability that, among other things, involves the ability to reason, plan, solve problems, think abstractly, comprehend complex ideas, learn quickly and learn from experience. It is not merely book learning, a narrow academic skill, or test-taking smarts. Rather, it reflects a broader and deeper capability for comprehending our surroundings—"catching on," "making sense of things," or "figuring out" what to do.*[4]

That definition is an excellent starting point for thinking about leadership and decision making, especially the last point about "figuring out" a process. Cognitive intelligence doesn't begin and end with having some "smarts." An individual must know what to do with his or her cognitive intelligence. Consider the following story of a college student.

As a freshman, a young man named Robert Sternberg received a C in Introduction to Psychology. His professor told him, "There is a famous Sternberg in psychology, and it looks like there won't be another one." Sternberg decided to leave psychology and major in math. After failing the introductory course for math majors, he went back to psychology, deciding that a C in psychology was better than an F in math.

Thirty-five years later, Dr. Robert Sternberg became president of the prestigious American Psychological Association and is internationally known for his research (involving complex mathematics) on the psychology of intelligence. He had the cognitive intelligence to do outstanding intellectual work but needed to put more effort into applying his abilities.

Substantial evidence shows that cognitive intelligence varies across individuals. Not all of us have the cognitive intelligence of a Newton or Einstein. About 3 percent of the world population scores above 130 on IQ tests, which is considered the gifted range. This does not mean that people have more or less value than others because of differences in cognitive ability. It does mean that this ability, like other human characteristics, such as height, weight, running speed, and musical ability, is not evenly spread across the population. Certain jobs, such as leading an organization, require a certain level of cognitive intelligence to be successful.

Cognitive intelligence has an impact on the quality of decisions leaders make. As noted in Chapter One, the average IQ of CEOs of large corporations is around 125. This is more than enough cognitive intelligence to successfully run a multibillion-dollar corporation, if correctly applied along with other requirements to operate successfully at that role level.

Cognitive Intelligence as a Science

Cognitive intelligence under the label of IQ was first described as a "general factor" in 1904 by Charles Spearman.[5] Spearman, a British psychologist, studied student scores on different subjects and found a relationship between how well students performed across different subjects. If students performed well in one subject, they tended to perform well in others, and vice versa. He proposed that people have a general mental ability that enables them to perform at a certain level across subjects. Spearman's theory of general intelligence set off an argument that has lasted since he formulated it.

Three decades after Spearman's work, Louis Thurstone suggested that seven "primary mental abilities" make up the "general factor" of intelligence.[6] What became known as the g-factor accounts for approximately 50 percent of the variance in IQ tests.

In 1963, Raymond Cattell categorized cognitive intelligence into two general factor abilities, *fluid intelligence* (G*f*) and *crystallized intelligence* (G*c*).[7] Fluid intelligence refers to the ability to solve novel problems and draw inferences in the absence of information, involving learning and pattern recognition. When leaders solve problems they have never faced before, they are required to use fluid intelligence. Crystallized intelligence refers to the ability to use knowledge, skills, and experience—that is, people's ability to retrieve and apply what they have learned. It is more stable but depends on fluid intelligence to some degree for learning. When leaders face routine problems, they are able to draw on crystallized intelligence to make decisions about how to solve these problems.

John Horn, a student of Cattell, extended Cattell's model (G*f*-G*c*) to include nine broad abilities:

- Fluid reasoning
- Crystallized intelligence
- Visual processing
- Auditory processing

- Processing speed
- Short-term memory
- Long-term retrieval
- Quantitative knowledge
- Correct decision speed

This version of the model became known as the Cattell-Horn theory.

John Carroll concluded that the Cattell-Horn theory was the best available psychometric theory of intelligence. In his seminal work, *Human Cognitive Abilities*, Carroll reanalyzed over 460 intelligence studies to create a summary and an integrated model (see Figure 2.2).[8] Carroll called his model the "three Stratum model of human cognitive ability." His Stratum III, general intelligence, or g-factor, has eight broad abilities (Stratum II) which are broken down into over sixty-nine narrow abilities (Stratum I). The Stratum II abilities are:

- Fluid intelligence
- Crystallized intelligence
- General memory and learning
- Processing speed
- Broad cognitive speediness
- Broad retrieval ability
- Broad auditory perception
- Broad visual perception

Notice that Stratum II contains Cattell's and Horn's crystallized and fluid intelligences. In 2000, Cattell's and Horn's model was integrated with Carroll's to form the Cattell-Horn-Carroll theory, which remains the most complete hierarchical model of cognitive intelligence to date.[9]

Measuring Cognitive Intelligence

Along with the study of cognitive intelligence came the development of tests to measure it. One of the most debated concepts of cognitive intelligence is its measurement. Dozens of tests have been developed over the

FIGURE 2.2 John B. Carroll's Hierarchical
Representation of Mental Ability

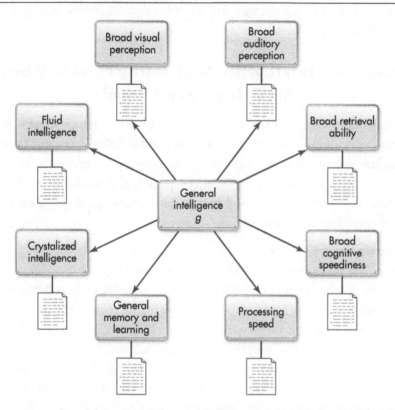

Source: Adapted from Carroll, J. B. (1993). *Human cognitive abilities: A survey of factor analytic studies.* Cambridge: Cambridge University Press. Copyright © 1993 by the American Psychological Association. Reproduced with permission. The use of this information does not imply endorsement by APA.

years, but the two most prominent full-scale tests today are the Stanford-Binet and the Wechsler Adult Intelligence Scale–III. They are typically used by psychologists for IQ assessment. These tests require specialized training to administer, interpret, and provide feedback and may take two or more hours to administer. The Wonderlic Personnel Test (WPT) mentioned at the beginning of this chapter takes twelve minutes to complete and is highly correlated with the Wechsler Adult Intelligence Scale–III.[10] The WPT works very well for a quick g-factor measure.

Consideration should be given to collecting this type of information on leader candidates who are preparing to move up to a higher role level. Research supports a strong correlation between cognitive intelligence and leadership effectiveness.

Cognitive Intelligence Moderating Factors: When All Things Aren't Equal

Moderators are common factors that influence a leader's cognitive intelligence and, consequently, ability to make effective decisions. These include environment, age, gender, physical conditioning, nutrition, and sleep. Extensive research has been conducted, and continues, on how these factors affect leaders' ability to make decisions across their career. Let's look briefly at some of these moderators.

Environment

It is not uncommon to read about the impact of the environment on the development of cognitive intelligence during early childhood.[11] Several studies have implied that cognitive intelligence can be enhanced or slowed based on the environment in which a child is raised. Craig Ramey and Frances Campbell of the Abecedarian Project wanted to determine whether children having IQs less than 70, allegedly caused by inadequate, nonstimulating environments, could raise their IQs if they were placed in high-quality preschool programs.[12]

The project looked at 107 low-income, high-risk families with children at risk of poor achievement. The children entered the program when they were four months of age and continued until kindergarten age. They were randomly assigned to either a control group or an intervention group. The intervention group attended an all-day, fifty-week program. All children participated in IQ assessments at the ages of twelve, eighteen, twenty-four, forty-two, forty-eight, and fifty-two months.

At eighteen months, the intervention group had IQs ten to eighteen points higher than the control group. At the five-year evaluation, the intervention group was still higher than the control group, but the range had closed to within eight points. By age eight, the difference was only three points. Even with the enriched environment, the intervention group maintained an average IQ of 100, the national average. The most prominent finding in the study was that the most powerful predictor of a child's IQ was not which group the child was assigned to but his or her mother's IQ.

Studies like the Abecedarian Project have become more political than scientific. Too often, only the results that support a particular group's objectives are reported. There does not appear to be any substantial body of research to suggest that IQ can be significantly changed by placing children in enriched programs or by watching videos such as the Baby Einstein series or similar videos. There is no doubt that the environment plays a role in cognitive intelligence development, but perhaps much less than most people, particularly parents, want to believe.[13]

One environmental advantage that a leadership role provides is constant cognitive stimulation that helps keep the brain functioning and decision-making skills sharp. High-level positions offer opportunities to interact, problem solve, and learn new skills. Such jobs may also bring certain levels of stress, but under the right conditions, stress can work as a positive environmental stimulant.

Age

In discussions of IQ in general and leadership and IQ in particular, age becomes important. After all, there are many well-known and truly senior high-level decision makers in both the public and private sectors. Rupert Murdoch is closing in on eighty, Robert Morgenthau headed up New York City's district attorney's office until he was ninety, and Senator Robert Byrd has been in the U.S. Congress since 1959. But does IQ change as people age, and if so, when and how much? If IQ changes, what impact does a leader's age have on his ability to make effective decisions?

Developmental psychologists such as Jean Piaget, Lev Vygotsky, and Jerome Kagan have shown how humans progress through various stages of learning and decision-making strategies from infancy through adulthood.[14] Some aspects of human development are relatively predictable. Most five year olds, for example, lack the ability to learn how to solve differential equations—and some will never learn how at any age. The maturation of the brain plays a major role in how humans learn, when they learn, and how they make decisions. On June 1, 1932, all 87,498 students in the Scotland school system who were born in 1921 took the Scottish Mental Survey 1932. The test covered vocabulary, sentences, numbers, shapes, codes, instructions, and other mental tasks.[15] These students, all between 10.5 and 11.5 years old, became part of the largest and longest longitudinal research project ever conducted on mental ability. On June 1, 1998, sixty-six years later to the day, 73 members of the original group took the same test under the same conditions as in 1932.[16] Some of the findings were:

- Most people scored better at age seventy-seven than they had at age eleven.
- The people who did well on the first test tended to do well the second time.
- Those who did not do well on the first test tended not to do well the second time.
- A few people made a significant improvement, and a few showed significant losses.
- Overall, there was substantial stability in rank order across time.

From this study, we see that IQ continues to develop after the age of eleven. Most cognitive intelligence researchers agree that various components of IQ mature along different time scales, but the overall g-factor matures for most people by the early twenties. General findings for the broad abilities of g-factor show that for most people:

- Inductive reasoning, spatial orientation, perceptual speed, and verbal memory show a steady decline from around the age of twenty-five to at least eighty.

- Verbal and numerical ability peak around middle age and then remain relatively stable.
- Abstract reasoning and processing speed decline steadily beginning in the late twenties.
- Crystallized intelligence remains relatively stable from midlife to old age.
- Fluid intelligence begins declining around the late twenties.

K. Warner Schaie's study of adult intellectual development of five thousand people across a period of thirty-five years with regular testing supports the findings of the Scottish Mental Survey 1932 cited previously. The ability to solve problems and make effective decisions changes as the leader ages, and the various IQ scales have different growth and decline rates. For example, Figure 2.3 shows a comparison of verbal ability, numeric ability, perceptual speed, and inductive reasoning across six major testing periods spanning thirty-five years. For most

FIGURE 2.3 Intellectual Ability Scales Change with Age

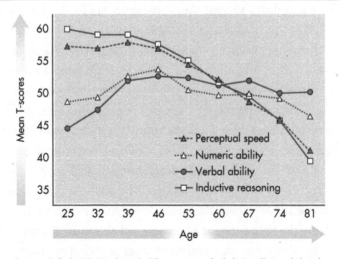

Source: Schaie, K. W. (1994). The course of adult intellectual development. *American Psychologist, 49,* 304–313. Copyright © 1994 by the American Psychological Association. Reproduced with permission. The use of this information does not imply endorsement by APA.

leaders, verbal and numeric ability peaked in the early thirties and then remained relatively stable until age eighty-one. Inductive reasoning and perceptual speed peaked by age twenty-five and then showed a steady decline until age eighty-one.

The Seattle Longitudinal Study by K. Warner Schaie found seven specific factors that seem to help preserve cognitive intelligence as people age:[17]

- The absence of cardiovascular and other chronic diseases
- A favorable environment, above-average education, occupational pursuits involving high complexity and low routine, above-average income, and the maintenance of intact families
- A complex and intellectually stimulating environment
- A flexible personality style at midlife
- Being married to a spouse with high cognitive intelligence
- Maintenance of high levels of perceptual processing speed
- Being satisfied with life's accomplishments

Schaie's findings suggest that there are ways for leaders to sustain levels of cognitive intelligence that will allow them to continue to lead well past the current retirement age. An article in *USA Today* on leaders over seventy years old pointed out, "While CEOs almost never get the job at 72, there are those who are effective at that age and beyond. Warren Buffett (BRKA) [turned] 78 the day after [John] McCain [turned] 72." It also mentions the ages, at the time the article was written (2008), of the following leaders: Walter Zable, CEO of electronics manufacturer Cubic, ninety-three; Marriott International CEO, Bill Marriott, seventy-six; News Corp. CEO, Rupert Murdoch, seventy-seven; Kirk Kerkorian, CEO of Tracinda, ninety-one; financier Carl Icahn, who "waded into the fight between Microsoft and Yahoo at 72"; and T. Boone Pickens, breaking into the alternative energy industry at age eighty.[18] The last chapter of this book is devoted to cutting-edge techniques for maintaining mental acuity and decision-making sharpness.

Memory

Memory is one of the most researched and discussed aspects of cognitive intelligence. Without memory, we exist only in the present. Clive Wearing, one of the most studied and famous "memory-related" subjects, is a good example to illustrate this point.[19] Clive, a former British musicologist, conductor, and keyboardist, has suffered from anterograde amnesia since 1985: he is unable to form new memories and consequently lives in a thirty-second world. If his wife asks him about something she said more than thirty seconds prior, he does not remember it. If she is out of sight for more than thirty seconds, he reacts as if she has just arrived and is excited to see her.

Clive does, however, retain his procedural memory from before the amnesia began. He can play the piano just as well as before but has no idea how he does it. For decades he spent his days writing down what he was doing as he did it—his angry outbursts and uncontrollable temper. For the past decade, however, he has controlled his temper and appears to be much happier, although still confused. Clive illustrates the point that without memory, we live only in the present.

When discussing the brain, we typically refer to memory from at least two perspectives: memory that is stored and can be retrieved and working memory. Stored memories give us the ability to learn and replicate procedures, such as playing the piano and recalling memories from our lives or episodic memories. Memory gives us a life. Without it, we, like goldfish, just exist.

Working memory is the conscious thinking space where we entertain thoughts, ideas, and knowledge about what is going on around us. We use it to make sense of the world and to solve problems. This is the "seven-plus-or-minus-two" work space. It is dynamic, with information constantly flowing into and out of it. We control it with the prefrontal cortex (PFC) and can retain pieces of information long enough to make connections and solve problems. Working memory is directly and significantly related to cognitive intelligence.

As the brain ages, working memory slows and becomes less effective, as does short-term memory. We begin to have "senior moments" and can't remember where we put the car keys or the glasses that are on top of our heads or, even worse, on our faces. Changes in memory speed, working memory space, and short-term retrieval can affect leaders as they age.

This reduced working memory can become problematic for leaders who are trying to manipulate numerous data streams as they make decisions—or remember decisions that were made that morning.

Gender

Lawrence Summers was forced to resign as president of Harvard University in 2005 after he created an international uproar by suggesting that women's underrepresentation in the top levels of academia was due to a "different availability of aptitude at the high end."[20]

Stereotypes around gender have been perpetuated over the centuries, including the notion that women are less mathematically inclined than men. Although there are some structural differences between men's and women's brains, research does not bear out that women are mathematically inferior to men. There is also a stereotype of women being better able to multitask than men, but the evidence is still mixed. There are physiological brain differences by gender, such as women tend to have a wider corpus callosum than men and varying amounts of hormones (estrogen is higher in women and testosterone higher in men). The genders are different in some ways, and this knowledge can be used to build our capabilities.

Elkhonon Goldberg, a clinical professor of neurology at the New York University School of Medicine, found that on the Cognitive Bias Test, which he developed, men were more context dependent (influenced more by the background or surrounding environment) and women more context independent (less influenced by the background or surrounding environment) when responding.[21] Other differences have been found that will be discussed later.

Psychologist Janet Hyde, at the University of Wisconsin at Madison, has found no difference between girls and boys on standardized math tests in the United States. When Hyde and her colleagues analyzed studies from around the world using the World Economic Forum's Gender Gap Index, they found that gaps existed when a country, such as India, had poor gender equality. Countries with gender equality did not show a math gender gap. Although one gender might not have an advantage over the other, there are some differences.[22]

Physical Conditioning

Waneen Spirduso and her colleagues have conducted extensive research that suggests exercise is significantly related to cognitive functioning and decision making. Exercise, done appropriately, influences a leader's ability to maintain a high level of cognitive functioning well into old age.[23] Even starting an exercise program late in life has a positive effect on performance and fighting off dementia and, possibly, Alzheimer's disease.

An extensive body of research supports the idea that physical conditioning can play a major role in delaying the onset of cognitive decline when stressed, as well as maintaining one's ability later in life. (This will be discussed more in Chapter Nine.)

Nutrition

Although the brain accounts for only approximately 2 percent of the body's total weight, it consumes approximately 20 percent of the energy generated by the body.[24] Looking at this from a different perspective, the average body consumes enough energy at rest to light up a 100-watt bulb. The brain, at rest, consumes enough energy to light up a 20-watt bulb! This energy comes from the food we eat. Children who do not begin the school day with an appropriate breakfast show significantly lower levels of learning than children who have a good breakfast. Food has many functions; providing the energy to power the energy-hungry PFC while it makes decisions is one of them.

It is important to eat the right kinds of "brain food" to nourish the brain, including healthy carbohydrates for energy, as well as omega-3s and other nutrients for proper growth and functioning. Unfortunately, based on the behavior I've observed over the years among many high-level leaders, most have diets that do not properly feed their brains (but do contribute to their waistlines). It's possible, however, to alter this modifier for the better. Consider your cognitive intelligence the next time you're ordering off the menu at a business dinner, or just eating out.

Sleep

One of the most overlooked and underrated moderators of cognitive intelligence and decision making is sleep: getting enough sleep and the right kind of sleep are critical. The brain rejuvenates itself during sleep, and this is the time when most learning and memory consolidation takes place. A tired brain does not make decisions well. For example, "historically, battles are won or lost at the small-unit level, due to the interaction—or lack of it—between individuals in squads and platoons," said Colonel Gregory Belenky, a psychiatrist who has studied sleep for the Army since 1984. "If you're sleep deprived, you're not going to make good decisions," he said.[25] During combat operations, poor decisions as a result of sleep loss are passed down to sleepy soldiers, who make additional bad decisions as they implement their orders.

A business leader who flies from Atlanta, Georgia, to Cologne, Germany, may lose as much as 15 percent of his cognitive ability during the flight and take one or two days to recover it. To try and counter this loss, many large companies buy first-class tickets for their leaders to allow them to sleep during the trip.

Although research on what actually happens during sleep is evolving, it is clear that a certain amount of sleep is necessary for all leaders. Some leaders may perform well on as little as six hours a night, while others may need eight or more. Each leader has a sleep requirement for effectiveness. When a leader is awake for twenty-four hours, his dopamine levels increase. Dopamine is a neurotransmitter that is associated with the pleasure system of the brain and is released in anticipation of pleasurable actions, resulting in the influence of motivation and learning. Most likely, this is the brain's attempt to ward off a drop in cognitive performance. The amount of dopamine produced may indicate not only how much sleep a particular leader needs but his sensitivity to sleep loss.

Are We Getting Smarter?

It would be difficult to talk about human intelligence, especially IQ, without mentioning the Flynn effect. The Flynn effect is based on the work of James R. Flynn, emeritus professor of political studies at the University of Otago in Dunedin, New Zealand. Flynn has documented rising IQ scores in countries around the world. A little-known fact by most nonpsychologists is that tests, such as IQ tests, must be renormalized periodically so that the standard deviation and average score remain the same across time.[26]

Flynn and IQ test publishers found that across time, people were gradually scoring higher on IQ tests—the average score was increasing beyond 100 by approximately three points per decade. Consequently, test publishers were (and still are) periodically renormalizing scores to bring the average back to 100.

Although children today have higher scores than children who took the tests fifty years ago, researchers are not sure that today's children actually have higher IQs. They might be better educated, exposed to more information and technology at a younger age, or better test takers than their grandparents. Whatever the reason, we might find that Generation Y and subsequent generations have more cognitive intelligence to apply to decision making.

Source: Flynn, J. R. (1984). The mean IQ of Americans: Massive gains 1932–1978. *Psychological Bulletin, 95*(1), 29–51. Flynn, J. R. (1987). Massive IQ gains in 14 nations: What IQ tests really measure. *Psychological Bulletin, 101*, 171–191.

Cognitive Intelligence Across Leadership Role Levels

We know that job complexity increases as people move from the bottom levels of an organization toward the top. Higher role levels within organizations also have a corresponding requirement for increased complexity. Consequently, the leaders filling these role levels must have the requisite amount of cognitive intelligence to make effective decisions in more complex environments.

Research conducted by High Performing Systems has found wide variation in IQ at the Tactical role level, ranging from 85 to 140.[27] At higher role levels, the range of IQ becomes smaller, with the lower end dropping off faster. For example, it is rare to find an Organizational role–level leader with an IQ of less than 105. At the Visionary role level (CEO), the lower end of the range is 115. The complexity of work and difficulty of decisions increase steadily as the role level increases, requiring leaders with higher cognitive intelligence. For example, complexity increases as you move from Production (data entry, report writing, running a tread splicing machine), to Tactical (supervising a production shift, being a school administrator), to Organizational (department director, plant manager), to Strategic (brigade commander, business unit president, superintendent of a 75,000 student school system), to Visionary (three- or four-star general, CEO of a multibillion-dollar global corporation) organizational levels.

Bernard Bass, a renowned leadership researcher and scientist, found that in eighteen of twenty-three studies that looked at the relationship between leader and team member cognitive intelligence, the leaders had higher cognitive intelligence than their team members.[28] He also found evidence that when a leader's cognitive intelligence was too much greater than that of team members, the disparity often had a detrimental effect on team performance.

Cognitive intelligence can be a double-edged sword. A leader with high cognitive intelligence can process information rapidly, solve complex problems quickly, and make effective decisions. He might also be perceived by his team as arrogant, condescending, and impatient. The leader knows he can do the work better and faster than his team members and may forget sometimes that they don't have his ability. Howard Gardner, a researcher and educator best known for his theory of multiple intelligences, found this same fragile effect for leaders who had very high cognitive intelligence.[29]

Cognitive Intelligence and the Brain: Where the Action Is

We have examined decision-making processes, strategies, and the role of cognitive intelligence, but where are decisions actually made? (The answer is not "in my car on the way to my office.") On a macrolevel, decisions are made in the brain. Confining intelligence to a specific area in the brain, however, becomes more problematic. Before trying to identify the specific brain structures responsible for cognitive intelligence, let's examine the lump of gray matter between our ears that was once thought to be a radiator for cooling the blood.

The human brain is typically described not only as the most complex organ in the human body, but as the most complex device known to exist. Weighing in at around three pounds, with over 100 billion cells and more connections in a cubic centimeter of brain tissue than there are stars in the Milky Way galaxy (estimated to have between 200 and 400 billion stars), the human brain gives us awareness and the ability to function.

To fully understand the impact of the brain on decision making, we should examine the structure of the brain itself and its various components and their roles (Figure 2.4).

The human brain can be described in various ways. Neurologists usually talk about the brain's components: the cerebrum, cerebellum, and brain stem. The cerebrum is divided into a right and left hemisphere, each composed of frontal (higher cognitive functions), temporal (smell, visual, and auditory memory), parietal (visuospatial, verbal/written understanding, sensation), and occipital (visual recognition, shapes, and colors) lobes. The outer layer of the cerebrum is the cerebral cortex, which provides us with consciousness and thought.

The cerebellum, located near the base of the head, is responsible for automatic responses, complex movements, balance, and coordination. Damage here may interfere with the ability to walk, talk, eat, or perform other complex motor tasks.

The brain stem connects the brain to the spinal cord. It is composed of three components: the midbrain, pons, and medulla oblongata. Our

FIGURE 2.4 Cross-Section of the Human Brain

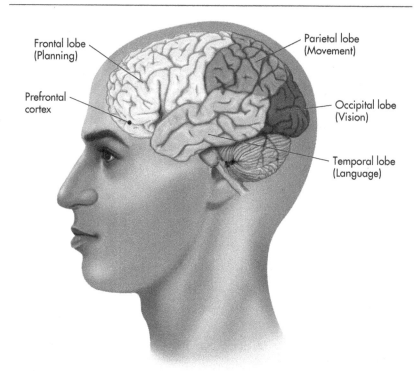

Frontal lobe
(Planning)

Prefrontal
cortex

Parietal lobe
(Movement)

Occipital lobe
(Vision)

Temporal lobe
(Language)

survival instincts and responses reside in the brain stem. These include breathing, digestion, heart rate, blood pressure, arousal, and attention. This region is sometimes referred to as the reptilian brain.

Although neuroscientists have learned a tremendous amount about how the brain operates, brain science is still in its infancy of knowledge.

How the Brain Communicates

Brain cells called *neurons* convert sensory stimuli into electrical signals that travel along the axon part of the cell and connect to other neurons (Figure 2.5). When the electrical signal reaches the junction, or *synapse,* between neurons, it causes the release of chemical messengers called *neurotransmitters.* Otto Loewi, later awarded the Nobel Prize in Physiology or Medicine, discovered the first neurotransmitter, acetylcholine, in 1926, and he demonstrated that it was responsible for transmitting a

FIGURE 2.5 Neuron Cell of the Human Brain

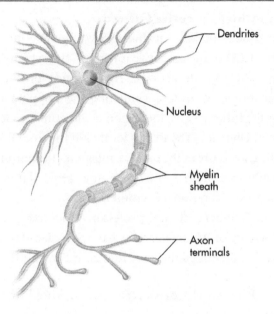

signal from the vagus nerve to the heart to slow cardiac rate. Since then, more than a hundred neurotransmitters have been discovered.

How the Brain Ages

As the brain ages, physical changes begin to occur; for example, the brain tends to shrink. This is partly due to the "death" of neurons. Other factors, such as hormone therapy, excessive alcohol, and lack of exercise, have been reported to influence changes in the brain's size during the aging process as well.

A study conducted by Helen Christensen, director for mental health research at Australian National University, found reductions in the brain's size for people over age sixty, but no related change in cognitive functioning. Her project, initiated in 1999, looked at magnetic resonance imaging scans of over 446 people in their sixties in Australia.[30]

Physical exercise may reduce brain shrinkage in older people.[31] On the positive side, particularly for older leaders, there is also evidence that as the brain ages, the two hemispheres can become more integrated, which results in increased cognitive ability.[32]

The Brain's Chief Executive Officer

Many brain regions make contributions to cognitive intelligence, but the PFC is the CEO of the executive functions, those high-level abilities that control and regulate actions. They include planning, thinking abstractly, adapting, controlling (initiating and stopping actions), and anticipating the future. Thus, the region is sometimes called the center of cognitive intelligence. The PFC is located in the frontal lobes, and as the controlling structure of the brain, it integrates the output from other structures within the brain. It interprets a vast array of information and is capable of powerful rational decision making.

Elkhonon Goldberg, clinical professor of neurology at New York University School of Medicine, who has spent decades studying the frontal lobes, has identified the basic functions (Table 2.1) of the PFC in

TABLE 2.1 Prefrontal Cortex Decision-Making Functions and Dysfunctions

Prefrontal Cortex Functions		
Mental representation of alternatives	Innovation	Creates models of things that don't exist
Imagination	Intentionality	Manipulates models
Freedom	Higher consciousness	Goal formation
Aerial view	Judgment	Self-consciousness
Brain's CEO	Empathy	Metacognition
Coordinating other areas	"Soul"	Organizes behavior in time
Flexibility	Foresight	Terminates activities
Decisiveness	Planning	"Personality"
Novelty	Forward looking	
	Projecting into the future	

Prefrontal Cortex Dysfunctions		
Short attention span	Chronic lateness	Difficulty learning from experience
Distractibility	Poor organization	Short-term memory problems
Lack of perseverance	Procrastination	Social anxiety
Impulse control problems	Lack of emotions	Lying
Hyperactivity	Poor judgment	Misperceptions

relation to decision making. This list provides a sense of the magnitude of what the PFC contributes to decision making, especially with the rational strategy.[33]

According to Goldberg, some historians have suggested that Napoleon's defeat at Waterloo might have been partially the result of his suffering from greatly inflamed hemorrhoids. Perhaps Napoleon's hemorrhoids did not negatively influence his leadership, but research, including Goldberg's, suggests that anything causing a distraction to the PFC leads to less than effective decision making. There is no way to know for sure if Napoleon's hemorrhoids helped pave the road to Waterloo, but leaders should be cautious about making major decisions when they are experiencing a lot of pain.[34]

Goldberg has also found that an underdeveloped PFC leads to risk taking, distraction, and poor-quality decisions. In many cases, the PFC is not fully developed until the late twenties or early thirties. This may account for some of the poor and more risky decisions teenagers and young adults make. When we consider very young leaders in high role levels who have been ineffective, we often attribute their poor decision making to inexperience. That may be true, but it may also be due to a still-developing PFC.

Cognitive Intelligence and Decision Making: Deciding How to Decide

At 2:47 on the afternoon of December 28, 1978, United Flight 173 left Denver, Colorado, en route to Portland International Airport, Portland, Oregon, with 181 passengers and 8 crew members on board.[35] The planned arrival time was 5:13 P.M. The flight from Denver to Portland was uneventful.

At 5:05 P.M. Flight 173 notified Portland Approach that it was at ten thousand feet and reducing airspeed. Portland responded to maintain heading for visual approach to runway 28. Flight 173 acknowledged the approach instructions and stated, "We have the field in sight."

As Flight 173 descended through eight thousand feet, the captain lowered the landing gear. He noticed loud thumping sounds and a "yaw to the right." Only the nose gear green light was on indicating that the nose gear had descended and locked in place. The crew was concerned that the other two landing gears were not down or had not locked in place, which would result in a crash landing. At 5:12 P.M. they requested permission to stay at five thousand feet and work on the problem.

At 6:13 P.M., one hour and one minute after the request to stay at five thousand feet and work on the problem, the captain instructed the first officer of Flight 173 to send a "Mayday" and notify Portland Approach that "the engines are flaming out. We are going down."

That was the last transmission before Flight 173 crashed into a wooded section of a populated area of suburban Portland at 6:15 P.M. Eight passengers, the flight engineer, and a flight attendant were killed. Twenty-one passengers and two crew members were seriously injured. The National Transportation Safety Board attributed the cause of the accident to a failure of the crew, led by the captain, to properly monitor and respond to the fuel state. The captain and crew became so distracted by preparing for a possible crash landing if the landing gears were not down and locked (which they actually were) that they circled for over an hour, ran out of fuel, and crashed six miles short of the airport.

The captain and crew engaged in extensive rational decision making and planning. It obviously takes a lot of cognitive intelligence to learn how to fly a plane and read the myriad instruments involved, as well as other tasks involved with flying a commercial aircraft. Not having enough cognitive intelligence to respond appropriately was not the issue. The crew, and especially the captain, became so distracted by the perceived emergency that they overloaded their collective PFCs to the point that they lost their priorities. They failed to keep the four most critical factors at the forefront of their actions: distance to the runway, time to reach the runway, fuel level, and direction. Every decision has one or more critical factors that drive the decision-making process and may actually change the problem being addressed by the decision. The more time the leader takes to make and implement a decision, the more the situation and which decision needs to be made first change. The result in this case was catastrophic. Sometimes a leader can get so caught up in the process of rational decision making that he runs out of time to make the key decision.

Cognitive Intelligence and Rational Decision Making

Rational decision making is about applying a logical, analytical decision-making process to choose the best decision under the circumstances. This process typically takes the form of the seven-step model presented in Chapter One and involves making comparisons of the alternatives that have been generated.

The PFC, the primary brain region involved in this decision-making strategy, needs plenty of energy and minimal distractions to function properly. In addition, the PFC has a finite amount of random access memory to use in decision making. If the PFC is overloaded with information, it cannot be used to focus on the future.

Processing Power

Everything else being equal, a leader with an IQ of 120 has significantly more information processing power and speed, retrieval ability, and working memory than a leader with an IQ of 100. The additional cognitive power inherent in a 120 IQ facilitates each step in the problem-solving and decision-making process. The high IQ leader gathers more information, generates and evaluates more potential solutions, and selects a best solution faster than a low IQ leader does. The additional cognitive power of the high IQ leader may allow for the entire problem-solving and decision-making process to take place mentally, appearing to the observer and the leader that an intuitive strategy was used. High IQ may give a leader the ability to perform more complex mental simulations involving more of the RPD model's moving parts and steps. Einstein was known for sitting in his favorite chair and "thinking" (performing mental simulations) for hours at a time, sometimes all day as he worked through his "thought experiments."

Problems come in differing levels of complexity, ranging from the routine to the nonroutine. The complexity of the problem can negate the value of high cognitive intelligence or exacerbate it. For example, a leader with an average IQ who has experience and expertise with a piece of equipment or a particular problem might make the right decision more easily than a leader with a much higher IQ who has no related experience. Leader performance was defined in Chapter One as a function of the leader's innate (one factor being cognitive intelligence) and learned (one factor being experience) abilities. Just being smart is not enough. Reading books and manuals about flying a plane does not make me a pilot, for example. I also need many hours of supervised experience.

As the problems become more complex or nonroutine, cognitive intelligence becomes a much more valuable factor in making the best decision. This is one reason leaders' cognitive intelligence tends to increase as the role level increases. As the organizational level increases, there is a corresponding increase in the complexity of work and decision-making requirements. As complexity increases it distracts or overloads the PFC, causing the accessible cognitive intelligence to be decreased, and tends to result in leaders' making less effective decisions. The captain and crew of Flight 173 experienced a collective drop in cognitive intelligence at a time they needed every IQ point they could muster to solve a relatively complex and nonroutine problem.

Cognitive Intelligence and Intuitive Decision Making

By definition, intuitive decision making occurs mostly in the unconscious, can be extremely fast, and tends to focus on an immediate situation. It is not uncommon for leaders to say that the decision "just came to me." Albert Einstein worked "rationally" to resolve the problem of the constancy of the speed of light, regardless of whether the source was moving toward or away from the observer, for a year before the solution "just came to him" during a conversation with his best friend as they walked to work. Einstein's intuitive solution to a nonroutine, extremely complex problem was aided by his high cognitive intelligence.[36]

Cognitive intelligence seems to contribute most to intuitive decision making in the areas of working memory, pattern recognition, information processing speed, and information retrieval, especially in nonroutine situations. Solutions to routine problems can be learned with experience, making intuitive decisions automatic. Driving a car, riding a bicycle, eating, and leading a daily team meeting involve a lot of decision making that becomes invisible and automatic. High cognitive intelligence is not required and in many cases may get in the way. Overthinking decisions can lead to "analysis paralysis." United Flight 173 is a good example of what can happen as a result of overthinking. Most decisions have a time constraint. A great decision (all the planning and preparation for how best to handle a crash landing on the runway) may be ineffective (the plane did not make it to the runway) because it (decision to fly to the runway) was implemented too late.

I have observed hundreds of teams negotiating what the military used to call "leader reaction courses" and what the corporate training world commonly refers to as "ropes courses" or "ropes initiatives." These reaction initiatives typically present a team with a novel obstacle to negotiate or task to perform within a short time limit and with limited resources and specific constraints.

One example is an exercise called the "wild woosey." A steel cable is fastened around three trees to form an open "V." At the closed end and the starting point, the two sides are approximately twelve inches apart, and the open ends are approximately ten feet apart. This apparatus is about three feet off the ground. The object is for two people to mount the "woosey" at the closed end and move together to the open end without falling off. They cannot use anything but their hands to hold on to each other. The cable is very shaky (woosey) and gets more so as it widens. The typical unsuccessful solution is to hold on to each other's hands, pulling on each other, as the pair moves toward the end. Eventually one person will pull the other off the cable. Some teams, however, are able to figure out the correct solution and implement it.

During one executive teambuilding session, a senior executive team included the president's executive assistant as part of the team. When I started the timer on this exercise, almost immediately she said, "All we have to do is ... " I thought, "Oh no! She has ruined the exercise by recognizing the solution so quickly." Then I realized that no one was listening to her. The executives (all men) were using a rational strategy to solve the problem. The assistant tried to tell them her intuitive solution twice more before time expired. The team was unsuccessful. There are many factors involved in what happened to this team, but one is that the assistant's intuitive solution was much faster and more accurate than the rational strategy of the executives. (It wasn't until the third exercise, and they had heard and seen her try to provide input, that the executives began to listen to the assistant's input. She did not always have the best solution, but they did begin to listen and include her as part of the team.)

The assistant did not have the same level of cognitive intelligence as the executives, but she was very good at solving practical problems like the woosey. I find that in general, employees at lower role levels tend to be better than the more cerebral senior leaders at solving practical problems. Each level of complexity requires a particular set of knowledge, skills, experience, and abilities to make effective decisions.

The impact of cognitive intelligence on decision-making strategies is strongly influenced by the complexity of the problem and the amount of time available to generate a solution. When the problem is low in complexity, the intuitive strategy works well. If the problem is high in complexity, the rational strategy might be better.

There are many intuitive decisions around each step in the problem-solving process: identifying the problem, determining what information to gather, deciding how to gather the information, the sources to use, the time line, and others. It is not uncommon for the rational decision-making strategy to consist of sets of intuitive decisions.

The Takeaway on the Link Between Cognitive Intelligence and Decision Making

The effectiveness of decisions that leaders make is significantly influenced by cognitive intelligence. A leader's ability to process information quickly, make associations among data, draw conclusions, and make effective decisions determines his or her success. The more complex the decision is, the more crucial the role of cognitive intelligence in that decision.

Cognitive intelligence provides the logical, analytical, and controlling process for decision making. In the real world, decisions have an emotional component, and emotions have a "mind of their own." Emotions and emotional intelligence combine with cognitive intelligence to lead the effective decision-making process. Chapter Three explores the dramatic impact that emotions have on effective decision making.

3 Emotional Intelligence and Decision Making

Anyone can become angry—that is easy. But to be angry with the right person, to the right degree, at the right time, for the right purpose, and in the right way—that is not easy.

ARISTOTLE, *THE NICOMACHEAN ETHICS*

In the early hours of Sunday morning, August 28, 2005, Hurricane Katrina tore along the Gulf coast, destroying lives, homes, businesses, and dreams in her wake. The fifth deadliest storm on record, Katrina left over eighteen hundred people dead, seven hundred still missing, countless numbers of physical and emotional injuries, and damage estimates near $100 billion.

Being totally caught off guard by Katrina, along with the unpredictability and intensity of her destructive forces, put local, state, and national leaders in the hot seat, sending stress levels soaring all around. This only added to the unbelievable amount of stress that victims of Hurricane Katrina were already under.

The general inexperience with this type of situation, confusion, name calling, and finger pointing by leaders in charge provided plenty of fodder for the media and slowed efforts to alleviate human suffering. Into this pressure cooker walked Lieutenant General Russ Honoré, the "John Wayne dude" who came to "get some stuff done" (as New Orleans mayor Ray Nagin put it). Shortly after arriving in New Orleans, Honoré said, "The more we saw of what the storm had done the more capacity we knew we had to build quickly."[1]

Lieutenant General Honoré, commander of Joint Task Force Katrina, was responsible for all active duty military personnel on the ground sent to save lives, facilitate evacuations of at-risk civilians, and help restore civil control. He brought to the already volatile leadership mix a reputation for being straight talking, outspoken, and results oriented, with years of experience and, more important, a heart for the people of the Gulf coast region, especially the poor, who were the majority of Katrina's victims. (Honoré is also a proud Louisiana native, of Creole descent.)

After surveying the region, he started to make things happen, meeting with leaders, getting information, and making decisions to accomplish the priority mission of saving lives. Next he turned his attention to evacuating the victims, continuing to work closely with local and national leaders. He would later write in his book, "We were in a constant problem-solving environment in which decisions had to be made quickly in order to save lives and keep things moving forward."[2]

As the human condition in the Gulf region began to improve, the issue of pets came to Honoré's attention in the form of an increasing number of calls to his office at Fort Gillem in Atlanta. He was aware that during Katrina, people had put themselves at risk to avoid abandoning their pets. In response, he decided that his troops would rescue any dogs and cats found abandoned. Although this was not part of his mission, he recognized the importance of the bond between people and their pets.

I first met Lieutenant General Honoré when he was beginning his military career in 1973. I was the commander of Bravo Company, 1st Battalion, 23rd Infantry, 2nd Infantry Division, and Honoré, then a lieutenant, was the executive officer of the battalion support company commanded by Captain Fred Hepler. There was no doubt in the minds of any of the company commanders, or our battalion commander, Lieutenant Colonel Howard Clark, that Russ Honoré was destined to reach the military rank of general. He exhibited the cognitive and emotional intelligence, motivation, and drive to excel that one would expect of someone destined to be great. As our paths crossed over the years, I watched him continue to grow and develop as he rose through the military ranks.

Emotional Intelligence and Decision Making

Honoré has a commanding presence that goes beyond his size. You know as soon as he starts talking that he is a decision maker and will move things forward rapidly. He is excellent at using the intuitive decision-making strategy: he sees a problem, makes a decision, and things happen. I have known him for over thirty years, and he has always been this way.

Under the surface, there is another side to this "John Wayne dude": a deep concern for people, particularly those who do not have an advocate in the system who can help or protect them. He demonstrated this with the victims of Hurricane Katrina. People realize quickly that he identifies with them, will stand up for and listen to them, and then "do the right thing."

Honoré is a leader with emotional intelligence. People like him and want to be around him. He influences others, manages their emotions, and takes care of people—and their pets, if necessary. Like the rest of us, he does not always exhibit perfect emotionally intelligent behavior. Sometimes his impulse control is less than ideal, and he might speak a little too quickly and a little too candidly, though always for the right reasons. But emotionally intelligent leaders have many techniques that they use to adapt to their situation. In high stress environments, these leaders might have difficulty accessing their cognitive intelligence and their emotional intelligence, as well. This chapter describes what happens to emotional intelligence when a leader's stress level increases.

All human decisions have some emotional component. That's the way the brain is wired, as you're about to see. The more a leader understands the emotional component of decision making, the more effective her decisions can become.

Great leaders like Lieutenant General Honoré know how to use their emotions, as well as the emotions of those they lead, to make the best decisions to accomplish their mission. His handling of the crisis created by Katrina exemplifies what leadership is about. He was able to operate from the highest political level down to the individual personal level of those caught in the disaster. His focus was first on doing the right things and then on doing things right.

Let's turn to the role of emotional intelligence in decision making, the neuroscience underlying emotional intelligence, and how it varies in importance across different types of decisions.

Emotions Happen: A Closer Look at Why We Feel the Way We Feel

Emotions are neural impulses that happen inside the brain and trigger a motivation to reach a goal. Emotions are goal oriented. Whenever you experience an emotion, there is an end goal that the emotion is trying to move you toward. Emotions have their beginning in the unconscious, and most of them stay there. When an emotion becomes conscious, we have a "feeling." For example, when the emotion of fear becomes conscious, I feel scared. Emotions can be viewed as providing situation reports about what is happening in the body—"Why am I shaking?" I feel scared.

Emotions have survival value. David Caruso and Peter Salovey, researchers and educators, provide the following linkages between emotions and survival.[3] Fear, from a survival standpoint, is, "Let's get out of here." Sadness is, "Help me." Disgust is, "Don't eat that." Anger is about fighting. When you get angry, the anger raises your energy level to overcome an obstacle in your path.

As an example, use the PAMA model introduced in Chapter One to see what happens to Mark, when his manager breaks this news to him: "Mark, you can't go on this trip because you don't have enough experience." This comment is a Stimulus Mark hears ("Perceives" in the PAMA model) and then Appraises as being a negative comment about his competence. Mark really wanted to go on the trip, but now his opportunity is being blocked because his manager does not think he has enough experience to go. During the Appraisal process, the emotion of anger arises because Mark's path to his goal (going on the trip) has been blocked. The emotion of anger raises his energy level and Motivates him to take Action in an attempt to overcome the obstacle in his path. If the energy associated with anger becomes too great, Mark may take an action that is inappropriate and make the situation worse.

Sometimes anger is accompanied by another emotion, such as sadness. Sadness has a dampening effect on energy level and helps deenergize anger. We rarely experience a single emotion. Emotions tend to occur in combination with other emotions, sometimes forming a *blend* that is more complex than the individual emotions making up the blend.

When Emotions Blend
Emotions follow rules. Perhaps the most visual model of this is Robert Plutchik's structural model of emotions that shows how the eight basic emotions (joy, trust, fear, surprise, sadness, disgust, anger, and anticipation) can be arrayed similar to Sir Isaac Newton's color wheel.[4] The words describing emotions can be arranged in terms of *intensity*, *similarity*, and *bipolarity* (oppositeness). Intensity refers to words that describe the same emotion in terms of strength, for example, *annoyance*, *anger*, and *rage*. Annoyance, for example, can escalate to anger, and anger can escalate to rage, a much more intense emotion than annoyance.

Some emotions are more similar than others. Fear and fright, for example, are more similar than fear and joy. This allows emotions to be arranged in the model according to their similarity.

A third characteristic in Plutchik's model is emotional bipolarity— opposites. Most people think of emotions in terms of opposites: love and hate, happiness and sadness. Oppositeness, when combined with intensity and similarity, allowed Plutchik to create the cone-shaped geometric model in Figure 3.1. The vertical dimension represents intensity. Cross-sectional pieces represent similarity, and opposite points on the circle represent opposites. Each "slice" of the model represents a basic emotion.

Plutchik's model provides a visual for understanding how various emotions can intensify and combine to form more complex emotions. Table 3.1 shows Plutchik's eight primary emotional dyads formed by combining two adjacent emotions. Anticipation and joy can blend to

FIGURE 3.1 Plutchik's Multidimensional Model of the Emotions

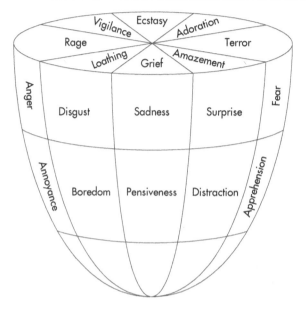

Source: Plutchik, R. (2002). *Emotions and life: Perspectives from psychology, biology and evolution* (p. 104). Washington, DC: American Psychological Association. Copyright © 2002 by the American Psychological Association. Reproduced with permission. The use of APA information does not imply endorsement by APA.

form optimism. Joy and trust blend to form love. In real life, most emotions are experienced as blends.

Table 3.1 is just the beginning. By varying the intensity level of the emotions that are mixed, hundreds of emotional dyads and their opposites can be produced. By varying intensity and the number of emotions mixed, thousands of advanced emotions can be generated.

Plutchik's model provides insight into how emotions transition in intensity, how they form blends, and how to use this information when making decisions. Emotionally intelligent leaders are aware of their emotions, the impact those emotions have on decisions, and how to use more favorable emotions when necessary.

TABLE 3.1 Plutchik's Emotional Dyads

Emotional Dyads	Blend of	Opposite Dyads
Optimism	Anticipation and joy	Disapproval
Love	Joy and trust	Remorse
Submission	Trust and fear	Contempt
Awe	Fear and surprise	Aggressiveness
Disapproval	Surprise and sadness	Optimism
Remorse	Sadness and disgust	Love
Contempt	Disgust and anger	Submission
Aggressiveness	Anger and anticipation	Awe

Knowledge of how emotions combine and the self-awareness to know which emotions you experienced earlier, as well as those you are experiencing in the present, provide valuable information for making effective decisions. Leaders who use emotional information in their decision-making process have a better chance of making the best decisions.

How Emotions Develop

Because human emotions develop sequentially and according to critical time periods starting in infancy, there is evidence that they are, at least to some degree, innate. It seems we are born prewired for emotional development.

Primary emotions emerge during the first six months of life. By three months, most infants have developed interest, joy, happiness, sadness, and disgust. You can watch the expressions of these emotions on their faces. Somewhere around four to six months of age, anger and surprise emerge. At seven to eight months, fear can be easily observed.

The *self-conscious* emotions develop between eighteen and twenty-four months and include embarrassment, empathy, and envy. Self-conscious emotions require the emergence of a new cognitive ability, objective self-awareness (or self-referential behavior). These emotions are much more complex than the primary emotions and are linked to the increasing development of complexity in the brain. The child must have developed self-awareness. Most two year olds can pass the "mirror test": they can recognize themselves in a mirror and therefore know they have a separate identity from other people.

The third set of emotions, *self-conscious evaluative* emotions, appears between thirty and thirty-six months and includes pride, shame, and guilt. Self-conscious evaluative emotions require the emergence of a second cognitive ability: the ability to compare personal behavior to a social standard.

Emotions, Motivations, and the PAMA Actions continue to evolve rapidly during infancy and slow as we get older. The plasticity of the younger brain and its neural connections allows the formation of new Motivations and Actions, or changes to earlier ones. As time goes by, however, changing established Actions may take more effort than a person is willing or capable of producing. For example, an adult with a long-held phobia may find it almost impossible to change her phobia-triggered emotions and the resulting Actions.

Facing Our Emotions (Literally): Why Our Bodies Won't Let Us Hide What Our Brains Are Feeling

Paul Ekman is one of the world's leading experts on reading microexpressions given off by the face, body, hands, and voice. He has analyzed numerous high-profile cases such as Yankee infielder Alex Rodriguez, who denied using performance-enhancing drugs in 2007 but later changed his story and admitted using them. Ekman studied a 2007 interview of Rodriguez by newscaster Katie Couric, which to him revealed consistent expressions of lying, for example, "gestural slips" (a slight raise of one shoulder), "unilateral contempt" (tightening and raising of the corner of the lip), and "microfear" (horizontal stretching of the lips). Although Ekman has said that you can never be totally sure whether a person is lying, his analysis of Rodriguez showed a high probability of deception. Two years later Ekman's analysis was confirmed when Rodriguez admitted the drug use.[5]

Ekman, a professor emeritus of psychology at the University of California at San Francisco, has spent more than forty years cataloging over ten thousand facial expressions produced by the forty-three muscles in the face. He is one of the world's leading authorities on emotional expressions, particularly facial expressions. His knowledge and expertise have been used by the FBI, the CIA, the Department of Defense, and, more recently, the TV series *Lie to Me* (he is the show's scientific advisor).

One of Ekman's discoveries is that the expression of emotions is normally very fast and that several emotions may be expressed in rapid succession. Watching the expression of emotions is not like looking at a static picture where you can take your time and study it. Most emotional expressions last less than half a second.

Obviously, in the real world, facial expressions are not as easy to read as those presented in crime shows like *Lie to Me* and are not as definitive. Ekman is convinced, however, that facial, body, and voice expressions communicate a person's internal emotional state and that these expressions can be used to determine whether a person is lying. Ekman's focus is on the person and the emotions she is expressing.

"The face is like a switch on a railroad track," says psychologist Alan Fridlund. "It affects the trajectory of the social interaction the way the switch would affect the path of the train."[6] Fridlund's work focuses on the effect of the facial expressions on the person who observes them. He sees facial expressions as tools used to influence social interactions that tend to occur at pivotal points in conversation such as greetings, for example.

Dutch psychologist Nico Frijda agrees with Fridlund that expressions are a means of influencing people and agrees with Ekman that they also represent the emotions a person is experiencing. All this research suggests that the face, body, and voice are outlets for the expression of emotions.[7]

One of the first and best books on emotion, *The Expression of the Emotions in Man and Animals,* was published in 1872 by Charles

FIGURE 3.2 An Angry Dog

Darwin. This book was the most comprehensive written account of the expression of emotions of that time and is still valid today.[8] Darwin specifically looked at how animals and people displayed emotions. He presents drawings of animals, such as dogs and cats, when they're happy or about to attack and describes their emotions and how they are displayed. He then relates the same emotions to people (Figure 3.2). He also found that emotions are expressed in a similar manner across cultures.

Emotional Intelligence: Awareness and Management

When researchers began studying cognitive intelligence, they discovered emotional aspects to the data. These aspects were not their focus, so they identified and labeled them and then set them aside. For example, in the 1920s, Edward Thorndike identified "social intelligence" and "emotional factors"; David Wechsler in the 1940s identified "non-intellective aspects of general intelligence"; R. W. Leeper identified "emotional thought" in 1948; B. Leuner published the term "emotional intelligence" in 1966; Howard Gardner identified "intra-psychic" and "personal intelligence" in 1983 as two of his eight multiple intelligences; Reuven Bar-On identified and coined the term "emotional quotient" in 1985; and in 1990, Peter Salovey and Jack Mayer expanded and refined the term "emotional intelligence" in their seminal paper.[9]

Emotional intelligence has always been present—and identified— but not valued as an "intelligence." In 1995, Daniel Goleman brought emotional intelligence into the world's consciousness with the publication of his best-selling book *Emotional Intelligence: Why It Can Matter More Than IQ.*[10] His book quickly spawned a proliferation of articles, books, workshops, training materials, assessments, and conferences on emotional intelligence. A cottage industry sprang up almost overnight.

The term *emotional intelligence* is used to describe a noncognitive type of intelligence. I define it as "a person's innate ability to perceive and manage his/her own emotions in a manner that results in successful interactions with the environment, and if others are present, to also perceive and manage their emotions in a manner that results in successful interpersonal interactions."[11] Note that this definition does not require interaction with another person. Emotional intelligence involves managing and controlling the awareness and Appraising of emotions and the resulting Motivation and Action in a manner that produces successful outcomes, whether in the presence or absence of others.

When other people are present and interpersonal interactions occur, the emotional intelligence process of managing outcomes becomes more complex. Now you have to manage the perceiving and appraising not only of your own dynamic emotional intelligence system, but the dynamic emotional intelligence systems of others in the interaction. Leaders make decisions every day in these complex interactions.

A simple model of emotional intelligence is shown in Table 3.2. According to this model, emotional intelligence consists of four basic processes: self-awareness (being aware of my emotions), self-management (managing my emotions), other awareness (being aware

TABLE 3.2 General Emotional Intelligence Model

	Self	Others
Awareness	Self-awareness	Other awareness
Management	Self-management	Relationship management

of others' emotions), and relationship management (managing the relationship). At the core level, emotional intelligence is about emotional awareness and management.

Consider the PAMA model once again. Managing the Perception of one's emotions and the emotions of others, if present (awareness), provides the foundation for being able to manage Appraisals and Actions. *Emotional intelligence begins by being aware of emotions and then managing and controlling them.* It manages a recursive cognitive and emotional Appraisal and the blending of emotions, Motivation, and Actions (see Figure 1.1). Intelligent responses to situations require appropriate management of the emotional system in a manner that produces the highest probability of successful interactions with the environment and others who are present.

Think of this process as a cycle that loops around and around. The entire process of awareness of the dynamic emotions in one's self and others and the dynamic Actions in myself and others is recursive, with each component continually feeding back into the system, making it a self-adjusting process that requires continuous, appropriate managing and controlling to produce "intelligent" results. Emotional intelligence is not a set of four or more separate linear processes that just happen to result in intelligent emotional management. It is about managing a dynamic process to produce successful outcomes. In other words, I am constantly reacting to you as you react to me, and vice versa.

Think about what happens when you are in rush hour traffic. You are constantly adjusting your speed based on the traffic around you. The car in front of you speeds up, then abruptly slows or stops. You have to decelerate quickly so you don't hit it, but not so quickly that the car behind you rear-ends you. You're doing all of this while watching the lanes of traffic on each side of you for cars that want to cut in front of you. This give and take of constantly adjusting to the other cars is similar to emotional intelligence: you have to constantly adjust to the people around you.

Emotional Intelligence and the Brain: Finding the Source

The brain's architecture is such that it provides emotional intelligence through the integration and synthesis of numerous brain regions, processes, and decision making at the cellular level, similar to cognitive intelligence. Let's look at the brain as a center of emotional intelligence.

The Emotional System

It is not uncommon for discussions of the brain and the emotional system to focus on Paul MacLean's triune brain.[12] According to MacLean, we actually have three brains, each representing a stage of evolutionary development. All three brains are interconnected, but each has responsibility for special functions. The oldest, most primitive brain is the reptilian brain (also called the primitive brain, basal brain, R-complex, or archipallium), which includes the brain stem and cerebellum. The reptilian brain is responsible for controlling the muscles, balance, breathing, and heartbeat. It tends to be rigid in its operation, repeating the same behaviors over and over and not learning from mistakes. This brain dominates the behavior of reptiles, hence the name *reptilian.*

MacLean coined the term *limbic system* for the middle part of the brain that evolved after the reptilian brain.[13] The limbic system is the second oldest part of the brain and includes the hypothalamus, hippocampus, and amygdalae. It is responsible for controlling long-term memory and retrieval, learning, attaching emotional markers to information, linking emotions to behavior, mediating emotions and feelings, bonding, and primal drives such as hunger and sex.

MacLean calls the most recently evolved part of the brain the *neocortex* (also called the cerebral cortex or neopallium). The neocortex makes up approximately five-sixths of the human brain. It contains the prefrontal cortex (the CEO of the brain), thus controlling thinking, logic, planning, and also language, voluntary movement, and the processing of sensory information.

Our focus will be more specifically on certain brain regions that have been shown to relate to emotional intelligence (see Figure 3.3).

The prefrontal cortex (PFC) has been discussed previously as "the CEO" of the brain and a significant contributor to cognitive intelligence; it also has a major role in controlling the emotional responses of the amygdala. Neuropsychologist Elkhonon Goldberg explains: "It has become increasingly clear that emotions are complex, multilayered processes under the combined control of subcortical structures, particularly the amygdala, and of the neocortex, particularly the prefrontal cortex."[14]

Anything that interferes with the functioning and focus of the PFC reduces our ability to make effective decisions. Distractions, stress,

FIGURE 3.3 Location of Emotional Intelligence
Centers in the Human Brain

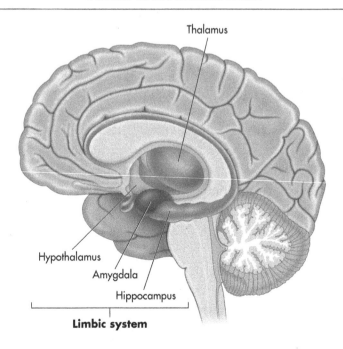

fatigue, or brain damage, to name a few, can reduce the functioning of the PFC.

Antoine Bechara, Antonio Damasio, and Reuven Bar-On have conducted extensive research to identify the brain circuitry that controls emotional intelligence. The specific neural emotional intelligence substructures they have identified are the amygdala, insular and somatosensory cortex, orbitofrontal/ventromedial prefrontal cortex, and anterior cingulate cortex. The roles of each of these emotional centers and their roles in decision making are shown in Table 3.3.

Obviously many areas of the brain are involved in emotional decision making, but Table 3.3 represents key brain regions that functional magnetic resonance imaging (fMRI) data have shown to be directly related to emotional intelligence. Damage, permanent or temporary, to any of these areas may result in a significant change in a leader's emotional intelligence and decision-making effectiveness.

Measuring Emotional Intelligence

As with cognitive intelligence, many approaches and different assessments can be employed to measure emotional intelligence, though most measures use one or more of three basic assessment methods: self-report, test, or multi-rater feedback. These methods assess emotional intelligence as ability or as skill sets. Emotional intelligence assessment instruments tend to be categorized as based on either an ability model or a mixed model.

John Mayer, Peter Salovey, and their colleague David Caruso designed the Mayer-Salovey-Caruso Emotional Intelligence Test (MSCEIT) to measure emotional intelligence ability.[15] The MSCEIT provides a MSCEIT total score, two area scores (Experiential and Strategic), four branch scores (Perceiving, Using, Understanding, and Managing), and eight task scores (Faces, Pictures, Sensation, Facilitation, Blends, Change, Emotional Management, and Social Management). The basic premise is that to be emotionally intelligent, a person must have the ability to perceive, use, understand, and manage emotions to make emotionally intelligent decisions.

TABLE 3.3 Functions of Emotional Intelligence Brain Centers

Brain Region	Function
Prefrontal cortex	The PFC is the CEO of the brain and controls the executive functions including cognitive and emotional processes. Information from all components of the brain is transmitted to and consolidated in the PFC. Consequently, anything that interferes with the functioning of the PFC degrades decision-making effectiveness.
Amygdala	The amygdala is like a survival radar continually scanning for anything that can be matched to a dangerous pattern, then responds immediately. When information created by the amygdala becomes conscious, it gives rise to emotional self-awareness and leads to feelings and the expression of emotions and feelings. The amygdala is the neurological foundation of emotional intelligence.
Insular and somatosensory cortex	These areas map emotions and convert them to feelings. Emotional self-awareness is enhanced through this process. These areas appear to be the neurological basis for empathy and adhering to social conventions.
Orbitofrontal/ ventromedial prefrontal cortex	This area governs the expression of feelings, social interaction, behavior, assertiveness, and interpersonal problem solving and decision making.
Anterior cingulate cortex	This area appears to be the nexus of where feelings emerge into consciousness. Emotional regulation, nondestructive expression of feelings, and adherence to social conventions are regulated by this area. This appears to be the seat of the "intelligence" component of emotional intelligence.

Source: This table is created from the findings of Bechara, A., Damasio, A., & Bar-On, R. (2007). The anatomy of emotional intelligence and implications for educating people to be emotionally intelligent. In R. Bar-On, J. G. Maree, & M. J. Elias (Eds.), *Educating people to be emotionally intelligent.* Westport, CT: Praeger.

The MSCEIT uses a variety of methods, such as faces, pictures, and emotional scenarios, to measure emotional intelligence abilities. A knowledge-based test, it relies heavily on a leader's emotional vocabulary, understanding of the "rules" that emotions follow, recognition of emotions in faces and pictures, and knowing how to use emotions to facilitate intra- and interpersonal interactions. MSCEIT scores tend to represent emotional intelligence potential, not necessarily application.

The MSCEIT falls into the ability model classification because it identifies and measures actual abilities associated with emotionally intelligent behavior using the test method. Respondents' scores reflect their ability to select the "right" answers.

The Emotional Quotient Inventory (EQ-i) is categorized as a mixed model because it measures a broad set of emotional intelligence skills ranging from empathy to problem solving. Developed by Reuven Bar-On, a clinical psychologist and researcher who coined the term "emotional quotient," the EQ-i uses a self-report method and provides scores for total emotional intelligence, five composite scales (Intrapersonal, Interpersonal, Stress Management, Adaptability, and General Mood), and fifteen subscales (Self-regard, Emotional Self-awareness, Assertiveness, Independence, Self-actualization, Empathy, Social Responsibility, Interpersonal Relationship, Stress Tolerance, Impulse Control, Reality Testing, Flexibility, Problem Solving, Optimism and Happiness).[16]

This self-report instrument "asks" the leader to tell how she would or does respond in various situations. These situations give a measure of her emotional intelligence across the various scales on the instrument. As a means to increase the reliability and validity of the EQ-i, "validity scales" are built into the assessment to indicate whether the leader is trying to make herself look good or bad and whether she is being inconsistent in answering the questions.

The EQ-i assessment also has a multi-rater version that allows the leader's boss, peers, direct reports, and others to provide their observations of her performance on these emotional intelligence scales. Others' perceptions of a leader can be a powerful source of additional feedback, important information the leader needs to increase awareness.

True emotional intelligence might be situationally dependent. That is, emotional intelligence might not be the total score produced by an emotional intelligence instrument, but rather a particular blend of emotional intelligence components. Moreover, this blend may vary by situation (for example, job, role level, company). This idea will be discussed more in the next section.

Emotional Intelligence and Leadership: What It Takes to Be a High Performer

In 2008, Leonard Abess, the owner and CEO of City National Bank based in Miami, sold his controlling stake in his company and gave $60 million to his 399 current employees and 72 former employees as a gift. Why would he do this? Abess said in an interview:

> *I tell young CEOs, that before you cut anybody's compensation, before you fire anybody for economic reasons, you deal with yourself. Your perks go, your bonus goes, your salary goes. I am very surprised when I see huge amounts of money that go to the people at the top [even] as there are massive layoffs, especially when they accept government money.*
>
> *We provided, I think, an atmosphere of caring. We were always there. I know my employees. I know their names. I know their spouse's names, their parents, their children. We have multiple generations there, multiple members of families, people who have met at work and married. And then their children have come to work there. So we always tried to have a family atmosphere. We attend each other's events—birthdays, weddings and funerals. In hardship, we try to take care of each other. I think we had an atmosphere that, for people, was comfortable and they felt welcome in, so they stayed.[17]*

Abess's comments reflect a high level of emotional intelligence and a leader who believes in leading by example. Unlike the leaders of the failed financial institutions described at the beginning of this book, who took extremely large salaries and bonuses while running their companies into the ground, Abess has the right philosophy. Leaders, whether of companies or teams, are responsible to make them successful; those who are unable to do so should be the first to accept responsibility—and cuts in compensation.

What does emotional intelligence have to do with leadership? Research indicates a relationship between emotional intelligence and leadership performance. I've looked at supervisors, managers, senior-level leaders, and CEOs in numerous types of organizations and compared their scores on emotional intelligence with their actual performance in the organization. Almost without exception, high performers have emotional intelligence components that set them apart from low performers. The higher the role level, the more pronounced the difference; hence, the more important emotional intelligence is. Leaders like Leonard Abess and Lieutenant General Honoré are mission focused and driven to make their organizations the best they can be, and they understand that this is accomplished by taking care of their people. There is a compassionate, people-focused side to high performance leadership.

The Ontario Principals Council Leadership study found that school principals with the highest leadership ratings scored higher on emotional intelligence, especially on the EQ-i subscales of Emotional Self-awareness, Independence, Interpersonal Relationship, Stress Tolerance, Impulse Control, Flexibility, and Problem Solving, than lower rated principals.[18] In a similar study with public education principals, I found that, in general, higher emotional intelligence, based on the EQ-i as well as the MSCEIT, predicted higher leadership performance.[19] A caveat to this finding is that it's typically not the total emotional intelligence score that predicts performance, but a specific combination of subscales that may be somewhat unique for a particular role level in a particular company. As role levels change and job descriptions change, so does the particular set of emotional intelligence components required for success. Think about the differences between a data entry specialist in a bank who spends his entire work day interacting with a computer terminal compared to a bank teller who is with one customer after another all day. Emotionally intelligent behavior tends to be situational.

Steven Stein, founder and CEO of Multi-Health Systems, the publisher of the EQ-i and MSCEIT, studied the leadership performance of seventy-six CEOs. He found that CEOs had higher EQ-i scores on Independence (105), Assertiveness (109), Optimism (112), Self-regard (107), and Self-actualization (108) than the average person (100). This suggests that a leader high on these five subscales of the EQ-i might make a good CEO. A regression analysis, however, revealed that Empathy, Self-regard, and Assertiveness were the key subscales that predicted the CEOs in the study group with the best financial performance.[20]

Reuven Bar-On analyzed twenty-six studies that looked at emotional intelligence and leadership and included 26,600 individuals. He found that six emotional intelligence competencies and skills consistently emerged as the most powerful predictors of leadership:[21]

- Accurate self-awareness (Self-regard)
- Ability to manage emotions (Stress Tolerance)
- Ability to control emotions (Impulse Control)
- Responsible social interaction (Social Responsibility)
- Optimism and positive thinking (Optimism)
- Happiness and self-motivation (Happiness)

In research conducted by Antoine Bechara, Hanna Damasio, Daniel Tranel, and Antonio Damasio, they found that certain brain-damaged subjects lacked intuition.[22] Thus, they did not have the emotional reaction to help them anticipate consequences of actions. The authors also found that normal participants developed an anticipation of consequences long before they were conscious of it. Similar studies have shown that measuring the emotional responses of people when asked which of two political candidates they will vote for is a better predictor of actual voting behavior than their telling the researcher which candidate they will vote for.

The results discussed in this section provide support for a situationally specific set of emotional intelligence abilities and skills for particular jobs. There is, however, a consistent finding of the core emotional intelligence abilities of Perceiving, Appraising, Motivating, and Acting. The proper use of these four components is required regardless of the job or role level.

Emotional Intelligence and Decision Making: Avoiding the Hijackers

One of the concepts that Daniel Goleman introduced to the world with his book on emotional intelligence was "amygdala hijacking."[23] This results when the amygdala overpowers the PFC and drives not only the decision-making process but also overt behavior. Neuroscientist Joseph LeDoux describes this emotional hijacking as the hostile takeover of consciousness by emotion.[24] The amygdala dominates working memory.

When the hijacking occurs, it sets up an opportunity for your "evil twin, Skippy" (and everybody has one) to come forward. Skippy is the "bad" side of you who says and does things that are uncharacteristic of you. It was not Mike Tyson who bit off a piece of Evander Holyfield's ear during a championship fight in 1997; it was Tyson's evil twin, Skippy.

When the amygdala completely takes over, the person seems to be out of control and behaving outside his character. The person says and does things that he tends to regret later. Let's say a loyal employee, in search of a raise, asks his supervisor at just the wrong moment for a pay increase. What he does not know is that his boss (who is usually fair and reasonable) has just been asked to cut 10 percent of her staff because of an unusually bad third quarter. She is reeling from the news, and then she is presented with an employee's request for more money. "Your timing is awful," she sneers. "A raise? Just be glad I haven't fired you!"

A growing body of emotional intelligence knowledge indicates that emotions and emotional intelligence affect not only the leader's decision-making ability but overall performance as well. We know that the old adages of "check your emotions at the door," and "don't bring your personal life to work" are impossibilities. Knowing how emotions work, their role in emotional intelligence, and the critical role emotional intelligence plays in decision making is essential for making more effective decisions. The trick is to have emotions, not be had by them.

George Loewenstein and Jennifer Lerner write that most decision-making research has neglected to address the influence of the immediate emotions being experienced as a decision is being made: "Immediate emotions can influence decisions indirectly by altering the decision maker's perceptions of probabilities or outcomes or by altering the quality and quantity of processing decision-relevant cues. They can also affect behavior directly. As the intensity of immediate emotions intensifies, they progressively take control of decision making and override rational decision making."[25]

Emotional Intelligence and Rational Decision Making

As we have seen, rational decision making uses a logical, analytical step-by-step process that tends to be driven by the PFC, but emotions tend to be associated with the intuitive decision-making strategy. Do emotions have any association with the rational decision-making strategy? Of course! All decisions involve a blend of cognitive (rational) and emotional components. The PFC, which drives the rational process, also has an attachment to emotions. Whenever a rational decision-making process is running in the foreground, emotions are running in the background, providing a subtle, unconscious influence on the final decision.

Antonio Damasio, physician, scientist, and author, is renowned for his work on the human brain and emotions.[26] One of the points he makes in his book *Descartes' Error* is that you cannot make a decision without emotion.[27] When someone says you need to be "rational," "leave the emotions out of it," or "make a logical analytical decision," you cannot do it. Unless you have brain damage or a psychological pathology, emotions will be present.

Damasio has shown that if emotions are disconnected from the decision-making process, a person can't make a decision. If a person who has damage to the emotional center of his brain, such as Damasio's patient Elliot, is asked, "Which restaurant do you want to eat in tonight?" and then shown a list of restaurants, he can comprehend the information about each restaurant but can't tell you which one he prefers. He can't make a decision. Whenever you make a decision, emotions are involved. Of course, sometimes the emotion can be so strong that you might not make a good decision. Finding the right blend of emotions and logic is key to making effective decisions.

Emotional Intelligence and Intuitive Decision Making

We have already established that intuitive decision making takes place primarily in the unconscious. Now we add to this process the emotional component. That is, intuitive decision making is driven by emotions. The "primed" component in Klein's recognition-primed decision model (examined in Chapter One) comes about as a result of emotional tagging of previous events and solutions. Damasio refers to this emotional tagging as *somatic markers.*[28]

According to the somatic marker hypothesis, events are marked, or linked, to emotions so that when a specific event is recalled, a particular emotion (or emotions) is regenerated. If you had a bad experience at a restaurant, even if the experience had nothing to do with the food—perhaps you became ill after eating there through no fault of the restaurant—every time someone asks if you want to eat in that particular restaurant, you are likely to have an immediate, negative response and say, "No, thank you." Your response may be so fast that you are not sure where it came from. The unconscious emotional decision about eating at the restaurant and the Action of saying, "No, thank you," were made before you were consciously aware of why you did not want to visit that restaurant.

We all have had emotions and feelings occur as the result of experiencing certain sights, sounds, smells, touches, and tastes. For example, you see a spider close to you and experience fear or panic. You hear a song from the past and experience an emotion that has been "tagged" to it. A soldier who has recently returned from Iraq hears a car backfire and ducks before realizing what he is doing. You walk through a crowded room and smell a perfume that your mother used to wear and experience a feeling of warmth and love. When these emotions occur, even intentionally, they impact decision effectiveness.

"What we find is that there are situations that affect all of us in similar ways, leading us to be biased, and that personality doesn't matter in those cases," Jennifer Lerner writes. "It's not so much about finding people with the right personal characteristics as it is changing the judgment and decision context."[29] Table 3.4 summarizes the impact of some emotions on decision making.

One aspect of emotional intelligence is the ability to evoke emotions on demand to facilitate decision making. For example, happiness enhances the creative process. To be successful at using emotions requires knowledge of how emotions work.

TABLE 3.4 Influence of Emotions on Decision Making

Emotion	Influence on Decision Making
Happiness	More use of stereotypes and biased judgments. Sees their possessions as more valuable. More optimistic.
Sadness	Seeks change. Less use of stereotypes and biased judgments. Sees possessions as less valuable and thus might be more willing to sell or buy. Focuses more on one's self. Might be more influenced by anchors and might make worse overall decisions. More pessimistic.
Anger	Increases confidence, feeling of power, and willingness to take more risks.
Fear	More risk averse. Ready to flee.

Source: For happiness research: Lerner, J. S, & Tiedens, L. Z. (2006). Portrait of the angry decision maker: How appraisal tendencies shape anger's influence on cognition. *Journal of Behavioral Decision Making, 19,* 115–137. For sadness research: Cryder, C. E., Lerner, J. S., Gross, J. J., & Dahl, R. E. (2007). Misery is not miserly: Sad and self-focused individuals spend more. *Psychological Science, 19,* 525–530. For anger research: Lerner, J. S., & Tiedens, L. Z. (2006). Portrait of the angry decision maker: How appraisal tendencies shape anger's influence on cognition. *Journal of Behavioral Decision Making, 19,* 115–137. For fear research: Lerner, J. S., & Keltner, D. (2001). Fear, anger, and risk. *Journal of Personality and Social Psychology, 81*(1), 146–159.

Emotional Intelligence Moderating Factors

Numerous factors moderate not only how we use emotional intelligence but how effectively we use it. A few of these factors are considered here.

Age

Age has an impact on the expression of emotions and emotional intelligence primarily from two perspectives, brain development and environmental influence. Various regions of the brain must reach appropriate levels of maturity (cognitive capacity) in order for emotions to develop and for the PFC to provide the appropriate interpretation and control over emotional Appraisals and Actions. Young children are noted for their direct communications. They make comments to each other and to adults that may be considered rude or inappropriate, even emotionally unintelligent. They have not yet developed emotional control.

Research suggests that emotional intelligence might increase until around the age of fifty, then it decreases a little. It should be noted, however, that the newness of the emotional intelligence field has not allowed longitudinal studies of sufficient length to validate that it actually does increase across time and decrease after age fifty. The current research was done by taking snapshots of various age groups.[30] The decline of scores after age fifty could be an artifact of having a large age range in this age group. Another possible reason for the difference in the fifty-year-old group is that they grew up in a different environment from those who are currently in the twenty-year-old group. Thus, environmental influences might account for some of the differences between the groups.

Gender

In general, women score higher on the EQ-i subscales of Social Responsibility, Empathy, and Interpersonal Relationship. Men tend to score higher on Stress Tolerance and Self-regard.[31] Assessments like the EQ-i provide the opportunity to use a "gender norm" when scoring. Using this scoring procedure is sometimes helpful, even though it makes little difference overall, when working with groups of a single gender.

Nutrition

Skipping breakfast tends to make people grumpy. One reason is that the PFC needs energy (carbohydrates) to function at its peak and to be able to control emotions. At the beginning of the day, most people have gone several hours without food. Breakfast provides the needed carbohydrates required by the PFC. As mentioned in Chapter Two, children do not learn as well when they don't have a good breakfast, and now we know they might not function as well emotionally when they haven't had enough to eat or the right kind of food.

Sleep

Lack of adequate sleep may also contribute to grumpiness. Not getting enough sleep, particularly rapid eye movement (REM) sleep (discussed in more detail in Chapter Nine), reduces the effectiveness of the PFC to manage the amygdala and, consequently, the emotions. Cognitively the person will not perform as well and may not perform as well emotionally. Sleep is the brain's time for regeneration and consolidation. Not getting enough sleep tends to have a moderating effect on interpersonal interaction—and emotional intelligence.

Leading by Example: Emotional Intelligence at Work

Dick Yeomans was promoted to director of the Hardwoods Group of one of the largest forest products companies in the world. He hired High Performing Systems to build the leadership foundation for his group. Yeomans began by immediately setting goals for himself—but not for how well he was going to run the organization or profit or production goals. He set three personal goals: stop smoking, lose twenty-five pounds, and become the role model he wanted all the leaders under him to aspire to.

In one of our discussions, he said, "How can I ask my employees to live healthier lives, work safely, and take care of each other if I don't lead by example?" In my thirty years as a consultant, I have never encountered another senior leader more committed to taking care of his people. Employees quickly discovered that he was approachable, likable, and smart and that he knew what he was doing and could be trusted. When he told them he would do something, he did. He led from the heart.

Yeomans turned the Hardwoods Group around, made it successful, and changed the lives of his employees—and their families. When I see or hear the phrase "emotionally intelligent leader," he is one of the first people who comes to mind.

The Takeaway on Emotional Intelligence and Decision Making

Emotional intelligence emanates from and is controlled by the brain, which is why understanding emotions and their sources can help leaders make more effective decisions. Brain studies shed light on that delicate balance between the emotional system and the PFC—the CEO of the brain. A primary function of the PFC is to control emotional responses, but such responses can be transmitted so quickly that they sometimes bypass the PFC, and emotional hijacking takes place as a result; a leader goes from having emotions to being had by emotions. There are also many cases where emotions cause decisions to be made in ways that worsen the problem. The situation goes from bad to worse for the leader, the organization, and any individual (within or outside the organization) affected by the poorly made decision.

Many books have been written about decision-making techniques, on topics ranging from analytical decision making to quantum decision making. What has been missing until now is an understanding of how the impact of stress on the human body and brain dramatically impairs effective decision making. Chapter Four describes what happens when a leader's stress level goes up and lays the groundwork for reducing its negative impact.

4 Stress and Decision Making

Each morning when the sun comes up, the gazelle awakes and knows it must outrun the fastest lion or be eaten.

When the sun comes up, the lion also awakes and knows it must outrun the slowest gazelle or starve. In the end, it does not really matter if you are a gazelle or a lion; when the sun comes up, you'd better be running.

Paul Ekman, the renowned psychologist, was traveling to Papua New Guinea in 1967.[1] It was a long trip, eventually requiring him to charter a small single-engine plane to fly to a missionary landing strip within walking distance of the village where he would be staying. Although Ekman had flown many times before, he had a fear of flying. He was especially concerned about flying on a single-engine plane but had no choice: it was the only way to complete his trip.

He boarded the tiny plane and realized it was being flown by what appeared to be an eighteen-year-old bush pilot. They bounced down the little airstrip and then managed to launch into the air just in time to clear the treetops—barely. Just as it appeared that the worst part was over and they might survive, the young pilot leaned over and said, "We're going to have to turn around and go back. Our wheels fell off when we lifted off the ground. When we land, we'll have to slide in on our belly on the dirt next to the airstrip. I'll put the wheels back on there and take you on to the landing strip."

As the plane turned back toward the airfield, the pilot leaned over to him again and said, "You need to be prepared to jump as soon as we crash. Go ahead and crack your door a little, too. If we hit too hard, the door'll jam into the doorframe and you won't be able to get out if the plane catches on fire." The pilot then said, "Be careful not to let the door swing completely open, because you might be thrown out." And if things weren't bad enough, the plane had no seat belts.

As they got close to the airstrip, Ekman could see the fire brigade pulling onto the field. At this point, he was having a significant emotional reaction, but it wasn't fear. He was disappointed because he realized that he had traveled so far over so many days, to be within one hour of his destination and he might not make it. The whole ordeal seemed "ludicrous," to use his word.

Then suddenly it was over. He had survived. There was no fire. He had no injuries. Fifteen minutes later, he was boarding another plane and taking off. This time he worried that the scene would repeat itself, and he would not survive, but Ekman did successfully complete his trip and became a leading researcher not only on facial expressions but also on the emotion of fear. In a very short period of time, Ekman had been subjected to a wide-ranging batch of emotions, accompanied by extreme stress, where he was being confronted with some life-or-death decision making. Although most leaders won't find themselves in such dire and dramatic circumstances during the average work day, many will experience stress levels that probably come close to Ekman's.

All Stressed Out: Our Way of Life?

Some leaders describe their jobs as being similar to living every day in a blender, waiting for someone to push the "puree" button. Leaders are continually being bombarded by stimuli requiring them to Perceive, Appraise, become Motivated, and take appropriate Action to handle difficult situations. The appropriateness of the Action a leader takes in response to a stressor can affect the lives and fortunes of hundreds, thousands, and millions of people, as we have seen in the past few years.

Leadership is stressful, and not all leaders seem to have the same ability to make successful decisions under high levels of stress.

Though the word *stress* was first used in a nontechnical sense in the fourteenth century to refer to hardship, straits, adversity, or affliction, for over two hundred years it primarily referred to what happened when you put a load on a bridge.[2] Then in the 1920s, physician Hans Selye redefined stress and in so doing created what some have called the "twentieth century disease."[3] Selye, considered a pioneer in the field of stress research, defined stress as *the body's nonspecific response to any demand made on it.* Under this basic definition, whether you win a million dollars or lose a million dollars, you will experience stress. The appropriateness of how you react to stress influences your success and health—and how effectively you make decisions.

Selye made the term *stress* the catchall for anything related to health. "It is as though, when the word *stress* came into vogue, each investigator, who had been working with a concept he felt was closely related, substituted the word *stress* and continued in the same line of investigation," researchers C. N. Cofer and M. H. Appley wrote.[4] Once the term was popularized, we had "stress" surrounding our health, our personal relationships, our jobs, our finances, our children, the state of our world, and much more.

In this chapter, we look more closely at what stress is and how it affects leaders' decision-making ability. The latest neuroscience research offers tremendous insights into how stress changes both the brain's and body's chemistry, which in turn has an impact on the quality and effectiveness of decision making. (The news isn't all bad. You'll see that stress can have a positive impact on decision making.) Getting a handle on how stress works is the first step toward managing this ever-present condition.

The Cost of Stress

During Selye's second year of medical school, he and other young doctors practiced their diagnostic skills on homeless people. It was during this time that he began to notice that all of the homeless "patients" shared some similar symptoms, including a common set of physiological complaints such as general aches and pains, stomach problems, and fevers or rashes.

One day he asked his professor if there might be something like a "just being sick" syndrome. He explained that everyone who was sick seemed to have some of the same symptoms. He related later that this was one of the darkest days in medical school for him, because his professor told him that this "syndrome" was not something he should be thinking about. That kind of thinking work was for "real" doctors (not mere students). He was told to forget about it and get back to his studies.

Selye waited until he graduated from medical school and then published his groundbreaking paper in *Nature*.[5] This set his direction and started him down a path that would define the field of stress. It bears repeating that at the end of his career, he had published over seventeen hundred papers and authored over forty books, and is credited with defining the twentieth century disease that we refer to as "stress."

Selye identified a condition that is of great importance to leaders. In the United States, stress costs industry an estimated $300 billion a year.[6] It is the key factor in absenteeism, lost productivity, accidents, and medical insurance claims, and it causes 75 to 85 percent of all industrial accidents. It is also linked to the six leading causes of death in the United States: heart disease, cancer, lung ailments, accidents, cirrhosis of the liver, and suicide. And it accounts for 66 percent of all visits to primary care physicians, contributes to more than 60 percent of long-term disability, and is the leading cause of lost work hours (headaches). Finally, more than 200 million people take medication related to controlling stress. Everyone—from the youngest infant to the oldest adult—experiences some level of stress every minute of every day. A person's level of stress constantly influences decision making—for instance: "I don't want to eat lunch with my coworkers today." "I'm excited about my daughter's piano recital!" "I'm staying late to finish this report, no matter what." "I don't have time to exercise today." "I'm going to get away this weekend." Stress is not always "bad," but it is always present when we make choices, whether the stakes are large or small.

The Stress Effect: It's Like Taking a "Chemical Bath"

When a stimulus is perceived, the brain's thalamus acts like an air traffic controller, sending information to various parts of the brain, particularly "up" to the prefrontal cortex (PFC) and "down" to the amygdala, part of the emotion center of the brain (see Figure 4.1). If we have the right blend of thinking and control from the PFC with the right amount of emotion from the amygdala, an appropriate Motivation forms, moving the leader to make a decision to execute an appropriate Action to respond successfully to a particular event (Stimulus). If the process is working "correctly," the leader can make effective decisions.

FIGURE 4.1 Stress and the Human Brain

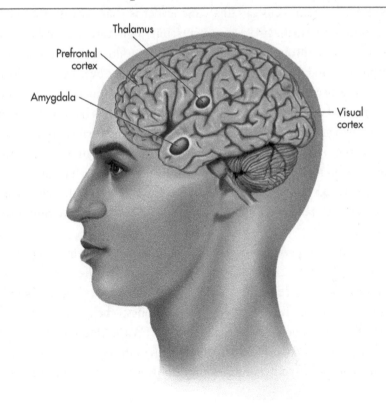

When a leader encounters a stressor, the initial result is a cascade of hormones, such as epinephrine, norepinephrine, dopamine, and cortisol, released into her system. The brain and body experience a "chemical bath" in which these chemicals initiate a series of other chemical changes, as well as physiological, cognitive, emotional, physical, and behavioral changes. Initially these changes tend to be positive and increase the leader's concentration and strength and shorten her reaction time. These stress effect changes are designed to be helpful. Let's say this leader is under a stiff deadline to combine two departments in her division in the upcoming quarter, which means adding staff. Despite the work involved, she is energized by the challenge to build the division and her business because this is a positive development; she makes wise choices, and her goal is successfully realized. Mission accomplished.

However, if stress remains high for an extended period of time, the continual refreshing of the chemical bath will begin to cause damage to the leader's brain. Let's say this same leader is charged with the same task of combining the two departments, but in this case she must reduce the workforce through layoffs, increase the workload of the remaining employees, and find ways to cut costs even further over the next fiscal year. Now her task is unpleasant, it drags out over a much longer period of time, and it will inevitably result in raising the stress levels of the staff she is trying to lead, which deeply concerns her (and further contributes to her stress). She is no longer energized; rather, she is stressed out, and her decision making (as well as her health) may suffer as a result.

Tables 4.1 and 4.2 show additional examples of the chemical, physiological, behavioral, physical, emotional, and cognitive responses to stress.

When we experience stress, a whole internal and external process is launched. Neuroscientist Robert Sapolsky and his colleagues describe stress as taking place in three waves, all of which touch off the body's production of a dizzying array of hormones, chemicals, enzymes, and other substances—especially cortisol.[7] Wave One occurs within seconds. As Wave One kicks off, the changes in the body are minute but immediate. Some people initially may not feel any different as they are

TABLE 4.1 Examples of Chemical, Physiological, and Behavioral Responses to Stress

Chemical Changes	Physiological Responses	Behavioral Responses
Cortisol	Heart rate	Nervousness
Epinephrine	Blood pressure	Aggression
Norepinephrine	Capillary restriction	Forgetfulness
Dopamine	Internal "blood pooling"	Lack of concentration
Glucocorticoids	Gastrointestinal motility	Moodiness
Blood sugar	Pupil dilation	Nightmares
Coagulation factors	Sweating	Rationalization
Corticotrophin-releasing hormone	Dry mouth	Risk taking
	Muscle tenseness	Impulsive
Arginine-vasopressin		

TABLE 4.2 Examples of Physical, Emotional, and Cognitive Responses to Stress

Physical Changes	Emotional Changes	Cognitive Changes
Headaches	Crying	Confusion
Backaches	Fear	Forgetfulness
Gastrointestinal motility	Anxiety	Low impulse control
Sweating	Loneliness	Distracted
Fatigue	Anger	Inability to make decisions
Shaking	Depression	"Freezing"
Sleep problems	Frustration	Loss of logic
Cramps	Panic attack	Inability to track conversations
Vision problems	Withdrawal	Inability to retain information

exposed to stressors, but eventually these changes build into something much larger. No one is immune to the physical effects of stress, although some can mange it better than others.

Wave Two, which begins within minutes after Wave One, primarily involves the release of additional cortisol into the bloodstream, which results in several positive effects: a quick burst of energy, increased memory, enhanced immunity, and a higher pain threshold.

Cortisol, sometimes called the *stress hormone,* is the trigger for the good, the bad, and the ugly of the stress effect. It is a powerful and important hormone in the body, known as a glucocorticoid. It is secreted by the adrenal glands and contributes to glucose metabolism, blood pressure regulation, release of insulin, immune function, and inflammatory response. When a stressor occurs, cortisol is secreted into the bloodstream and interferes with the functioning of various neurotransmitters, some of which influence the ability to recall old memories or form new memories. In other words, our minds go blank.

Chronic stress results in higher and more prolonged levels of cortisol, which produce negative effects: impaired cognitive performance, suppressed thyroid function, blood sugar imbalances, lower bone density, loss of muscle tissue, higher blood pressure, lowered immunity, and increased abdominal fat.[8] High levels of cortisol tend to impair old memories but not recent ones.[9] Chronically high levels of cortisol have been shown to be related to hippocampal shrinkage, resulting in memory loss. A shrinking hippocampus is also related to the early onset of dementia and Alzheimer's disease.[10] Sapolsky also found that exposure to high levels of stress (or cortisol) accelerates the degeneration of the hippocampus.[11]

It is not uncommon for people beyond the age of fifty to lose 20 to 25 percent of their hippocampus cells due to excessive cortisol.[12] Unfortunately, the hippocampus is the brain area responsible for turning off the secretion of cortisol, so the more cortisol that is being secreted, the more damage there is to the hippocampus; and the more damage to the hippocampus, the less ability it has to shut off the cortisol. A vicious cycle is created.

this point the leader has perceived the presence of a stressor but is not yet able to react appropriately. The leader has been caught by surprise.

When Jennifer begins her daily run, she often notices that during the first half-mile or so, her heart accelerates and she begins breathing heavily. The stressor, running, demands more resources than her body has readily available. The sudden increase in physical activity rapidly drains her energy stores. She must also exert more energy than she normally would to run at her current speed. The sudden demand throws her body into the alarm reaction stage. Figure 4.3 shows how her ability to resist stress is rapidly decreasing. She must keep her running speed slow enough so that she does not deplete all of her body's energy before it has time to react. If she maintains the proper speed, she will be able to marshal additional resources to meet the demands of the run.

Most people become distracted when they run. This distraction may hinder a runner's ability to make effective decisions. As the physical stress increases and the PFC's control of the amygdala decreases, Jennifer's emotions are more likely to influence her decisions negatively. Beginning runners, for example, find overcoming negative emotions and the urge to quit (produced by the amygdala) to be very powerful. One of the most difficult parts of beginning an exercise program is overcoming the emotional desire to quit. Whether you are beginning a two-mile run or an exercise program or making a series of stressful decisions (your company is being sold to the competitor and you are being offered a potentially tenuous new position or must go elsewhere), you must overcome the urge to quit before you get to the resistance stage.

It is important to understand that even if the stressor is removed, recovery is not immediate. Once a leader starts down into the alarm reaction trough, he encounters a delay before he can begin coming back up to normal, or toward the resistance stage. His fall down the leading edge of the trough causes him to feel out of control. Nothing seems to be going right. He may feel sick to his stomach and might even begin to panic. The leader realizes he must get control or he will be in too deep to recover. (You are unsure of what to do and don't have enough information to decide whether to take this new job; you are worried about your department; you feel unable to take action.)

While in the trough, he continues to consume many resources. Even when the stressor is removed, there is a delay before he can begin climbing out. If the stressor remains, that is, becomes chronic, the leader might not be able to recover. (If this situation persists where you are unable to get information, you may not feel confident about your decision to stay or to leave.) If Jennifer consumes too much energy too quickly, she will not be able to recover while continuing to run. She will have to stop running and rest in order to recover—and this may allow the saber-toothed tiger to catch her!

Figure 4.4 shows that even if Jennifer stops running, there will be a delay, an "aftereffect," before she begins to climb her way up and out of the trough. There are obviously many factors that influence how long the aftereffect will last, for example, her level of physical conditioning, motivation, age, altitude, and time to climb the exit curve to get back to her original level. Ideally, she would avoid the trough or limit how far she goes down by recognizing what is happening to her—she is having difficulty "getting enough air"—and slows or stops running before she is in too much oxygen debt.

If Jennifer runs at her correct pace, additional resources become available, and she will experience what is commonly called "getting a

FIGURE 4.4 Stress Aftereffects Model

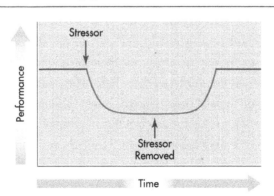

second wind." This means that her body has adapted to the increase in physical activity by increasing the resources available for the run. Breathing becomes easier, the heart rate settles down, and she begins to settle into her rhythm. She begins to experience optimism and enjoyment from both the victory of getting out of the trough and from knowing she is now performing well. She is now in the *resistance* stage of the general adaptation syndrome. During this stage, concentration seems to be easier, she is processing more information, her field of vision is wider, and her hearing is more acute. Now she is beginning to enjoy the run. (You have a breakthrough on getting the information you need to make a decision; you decide to take the new position with the newly merged companies and are excited about the prospect.)

If she runs too far or too fast, she may deplete her available resources for running and, at some point, rapidly descend into the *exhaustion* stage. In a race, Jennifer will try to time the consumption of resources at a rate that allows her to finish just before going into the exhaustion stage. (Similarly, you must learn to pace yourself. In our hypothetical example, you're moving into a new and somewhat risky job, so your self-awareness is vital.) Decision making during the exhaustion stage can be very difficult. Jennifer's extremely high level of stress results in tunnel vision, a significant loss of hearing, and almost no ability to make rational decisions. Her entire body has entered a survival mode.

Excitation Transfer Model (Introducing "Skippy," the Evil Twin)

In graduate school I did extensive research on human aggression, particularly stress and aggressive behavior. One of the most helpful theories I found for understanding how stress builds up across time was researcher Dolf Zillman's excitation transfer theory.[16] Zillman demonstrated not only that stress is cumulative, but that the arousal and emotion from current stress transfers to a new stressor.

A leader has an important presentation to make to the executive team this morning. Unfortunately he oversleeps and is running late. His stress level has just increased. Within seconds his brain and body undergo a chemical bath, and he experiences numerous physiological changes. After reaching a peak response to the stress of being late, he slowly begins to return to normal. This could take three to five hours—provided nothing else stressful happens during that time. (In Figure 4.5, notice how long it takes him to recover to a normal level.)

On the way to work, however, the leader finds himself stuck in a traffic jam. Now he is going to be even later than he had thought, and his stress level rises more, adding to the remaining stress from the first stressor. Just before going in to the executive briefing, he realizes that in his hurried dash out of the house, he left his suit coat at home. This new stress is now added to the stress from the traffic jam.

The CEO does not like the presentation. The feedback the leader receives during the presentation causes his stress level to increase again. Fortunately, the workday is finally over, and he can go home. But when he gets to the parking lot, he finds a dent in the passenger side door of his car with a note on the windshield that says, "I'm sorry." No other information has been provided. His stress level jumps again.

As he walks into his house, his dog runs up to him and jumps up on his pants leg with muddy feet. Normally he might laugh and pet the dog, but at this point, his stress level crosses what I call the "crazy threshold."

FIGURE 4.5 Stress Transfer Model

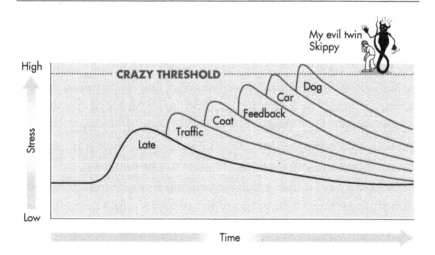

Without thinking, he kicks at the dog. He misses, but the closeness of his kick scares the dog enough to make him yelp before cowering on the floor. That last act seems to be far more aggressive than called for by the dog's actions. The leader's "evil twin Skippy" has gotten loose!

Each time a stressor is encountered, it adds to the stress left over from the previous stressor. Stress continues to build up during the day as additional stressors are encountered. Each time a stressor is encountered, all of the stress built up until that point is attributed to the new stressor.

As stress increases, the ability to use the full capacity of the PFC and cognitive intelligence is decreasing. If enough stress builds up during the course of the day, the leader will eventually be pushed across the crazy threshold. At that point the amygdala takes control, his evil twin Skippy emerges, and he begins to behave in an emotionally unintelligent manner, like trying to kick the dog—or worse.

A senior human resources manager recently confided in me, following a presentation on stress I had given, that her stress level at work had increased dramatically over the past two months. Her department had downsized in people only, so those remaining were expected to continue doing their own work in addition to the work of their former colleagues. She told me that she could literally feel her blood pressure rising as she got closer to her office on her morning commute. By the time she got to the office, she was a different person—she was starting to have conversations as "Skippy."

Two weeks later, she emailed me to say that my advice had been helpful; she had left the company and was searching for another job, her stress level was much lower, and she felt like herself again. (She found a new position and is much happier.)

An important point to remember about the stress transfer model is that stress is additive. That is, if the leader doesn't have adequate coping strategies for reducing his stress as he goes through the day, stress will continue to build up until it significantly interferes with his decision-making capability. And at some point, stress might push him across the crazy threshold.

Stress Comfort Zone Model

A diver stands alone on a twelve-inch-square piece of board attached to a small metal tower ninety feet above a pool of water that is ten feet deep and twenty-six feet in diameter, wearing nothing but a Speedo swimsuit. A breeze is causing the tower to sway. His back is turned to the large Texas crowd below while the announcer builds the anticipation of watching Bill Treasurer complete a dive 50 percent higher than he has ever before attempted.

Bill heard the announcer say, "Ladies and gentlemen, when Bill turns around, let's all put our hands together to wish him good luck on his very first *high* dive." As Bill, both a friend and a colleague, later told me,

> *A flurry of thoughts and feelings bombarded me.* I could die. I could literally be dead in a few moments. Or maybe I will crash hard and be paralyzed. I'll be in a wheelchair for the rest of my life. *The fear was gripping, yet strangely exciting. This was, by far, the greatest risk I had ever attempted. It was a sheer rush, teetering at the far edge of my own potential. It was also humbling. Of all the people who have ever lived, some 100 billion of them, there were probably fewer than 1,000 who had done what I was about to do. In a few moments, I would be one of them—dead, paralyzed, or otherwise.*[17]

Bill thrust himself off the platform and began his rapidly accelerating descent, completed his maneuvers, and braced for the tremendous fifty-mile-an-hour impact with the water. "*Holy* %$&!, I thought as my brain scanned my body through a lightning-fast checklist. *Arms? Check. Legs? Check. Back? Check. Neck? Check.* Everything checked; I was okay ... and profoundly grateful to be alive." He surfaced from the water with his fist raised in triumph. He had faced a secret fear and been successful. In the following months, Bill stretched his comfort zone even further and made his first dive as "Captain Inferno." He wore a protective suit covered with a flammable substance and ignited it just before leaping off the platform—a very dangerous and stressful feat.

When Bill came to work for High Performing Systems in 1992, he had completed fifteen hundred dives, many of them using fire. He told me that just the thought of making a dive like that still "gets my heart pounding." Fear, stress, and comfort zones can be managed. Today, Bill is the CEO of GiantLeap Consulting, a professional speaker, an author, and a retired high diver.

Everyone has a comfort zone in terms of how much stress they can handle, how much they want to handle, and the long-term impact. The HR manager mentioned earlier had been outside her comfort zone too long and had to change jobs to save her health. Figure 4.6 shows a simple depiction of a comfort zone with upper and lower limits. As long as a leader stays inside his comfort zone boundaries, he feels comfortable and can manage whatever stress there is in his life. If his stress level gets so low that he moves across the lower limit of the comfort zone, however, he will become bored. This area of the graph is sometimes referred to as the *rustout* zone. Research shows that too much time in the rustout zone might have worse health consequences than having too much stress and being in the burnout zone.

If a leader experiences enough stress to push him across the upper limit of the comfort zone into the burnout zone, he will experience sensations commonly associated with being extremely stressed: frustration and being overwhelmed. Figure 4.6 shows a bold line moving up and down across the comfort zone. This line represents the leader's

FIGURE 4.6 Comfort Zone

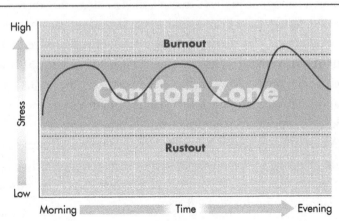

fluctuating stress level during the day. Note that the leader's stress level is not static. It is dynamic and constantly moves up and down, based on the stressors encountered as well as the leader's coping ability. Anything that moves you outside your comfort zone will cause stress. It doesn't matter if it's as simple as spending too much time with people (or not enough), changing your diet, getting a new office mate, or having to learn new software, it might be just enough to push you out of your comfort zone—and this causes stress. Most people find it difficult to read about Bill's experience on the tower as he prepared for his dive without experiencing at least some of the same visceral reactions he was having. (Chapter Six discusses the comfort zone in more detail.)

More Control Equals Less Stress

Robert Sapolsky, author of *Why Zebras Don't Get Ulcers* and *A Primate's Memoir*, has spent decades studying a population of baboons in Kenya.[18] One of his discoveries about baboons is that it takes only a few hours for them to find enough food to eat for the day, which leaves the rest of the day free for them to get into trouble with each other. Each baboon population has an established hierarchy, with the top baboon being aggressive and abusive to the baboons immediately under him. His underlings in turn abuse the baboons under them. This process works its way down through the population. The data that Sapolsky has collected over the years on stress levels within the baboon population reveal that the higher a baboon is in the hierarchy, the less stress he experiences.

Similar results have been found in organizations that have a well-defined hierarchy. For example, the British postal service, a highly structured organization, was analyzed and assessed for stress at the various leader levels. The results were very similar to the baboon population. The higher the leader was in the organization, the lower the stress level compared to other leaders in the postal service.

These results suggest that the amount of control you have over your situation influences the amount of stress you experience. Being a leader in an organization in which you have low control and high stress may lead to significant health problems.

Numerous studies have found a relationship between control and stress. Martin Seligman and Steve Maier found that when two dogs were yoked together and received electrical shocks (of very low voltage), the dog that could prevent the shocks by making a certain body movement developed fewer ulcers than the dog with no control.[19]

Sanderson and his colleagues conducted a similar study with humans using the threat of a panic-provoking agent (no shocks). One group had a dial and could reduce the amount of the agent. This group reported fewer and less severe panic symptoms than the group without the dial.[20]

Michael Marmot and his team of medical researchers found that a person who has both control and some predictability of the outcome experiences less stress.[21] Real people in real work environments have been shown to experience higher levels of stress and more negative health consequences, such as heart attacks, cancer, stroke, and gastrointestinal disorders, when they have less control. Having control over a situation, even if it is only perceived control, tends to help the leader resist stress and remain healthier.

When I was in the military and leading special operations teams on missions deep behind enemy lines, the flight to the landing zone was less stressful once I realized I could request and use a headset. This allowed me to monitor the radio traffic so I knew what was taking place at the insertion point. If it was going to be a "hot" insertion (bad guys shooting at us as we came into the landing zone) or heavy antiaircraft fire on the way out, I could adjust my mindset and initial deployment plan accordingly. This extra information gave me a better sense of control, resulting in less stress, even if it was going to be a hot insertion.

Four Sources of Stress: It's Not Just 9 to 5

How many times have you heard (or perhaps said) that workers should leave their personal lives at home and avoid bringing the stresses of the workplace home at the end of the day? In reality, this is exceedingly difficult. Of course, you can conduct yourself professionally and "leave your personal life at home," but that doesn't mean you won't think about it during the workday. And the same goes for work. You may not lug your laptop home every night, but chances are you'll think about your job at some point after hours. The fact is, home goes to work, and work comes home, and in between are our health and the environment in which we exist. Everything is connected.

Stressors come in all shapes and sizes, and most can be grouped into one of four categories: home, work, health, and environment. The categories and the individual stressors listed in these categories in Table 4.3 have been artificially separated for ease of discussion. In reality, they are all part of an overall system and inextricably linked.

Home

Home stressors are those that are primarily encountered in a leader's home life. There are numerous types of stressors associated with life outside work. I have chosen to focus on a few that I have found garner the most energy during workshops and coaching. The number one stressor for most people is their spouse (unless they do not have a significant other, which is sometimes a stressor as well!). Table 4.3 lists other home stressors, such as children, finances, in-laws, and various

TABLE 4.3 Stressors by Categories

Home	Work	Health	Environment
Spouse	Boss	Nutrition	Noise
Children	Role	Body weight	Traffic
Finances	Communication	Lack of exercise	Temperature
In-laws	Direct reports	Lack of rest	Technology
Time management	Peers	Poor life-work balance	Crowding
Illness	Deadlines	Caffeine	Pollution
Pets	Lack of recognition	Back injury	Global warming
Home maintenance	Job security	Aging	Economy

illnesses. In today's fast-paced, high-stress family life, leaders often find that they have become part of the "sandwich generation." That is, they are still taking care of their own children and grandchildren, but now their parents have reached the age where they too need to be taken care of, placing an additional strain on a leader's resources.

With regard to the category of finances, money is a stressor that easily spans categories in one form or another. Under "work" we discuss "job security," but the size and predictability of one's salary also have an impact on household finances. Money worries can touch the "health" category too; a family member's serious illness can have an impact on household finances, even with insurance. Finally, even when there is enough to go around, money is a sensitive topic that can set off disagreements between many couples, as well as between parents and children.

Work

Work stressors are those that are primarily encountered in the leader's work environment. Until 2008, the stressor identified most frequently in the workplace was the boss. There almost always seemed to be stress associated with interactions with the boss. But in 2008, the boss began to be supplanted by job security. By 2009, the United States was seeing 400,000 to 500,000 jobs lost per month, and with figures like that, it doesn't take long before a leader has lost his own job, knows someone who has lost her job, or is the person delivering the bad news to employees who are losing their jobs. All of this makes job security a powerful stressor. On top of this, many companies have eliminated pension plans, severely reduced 401(k) benefits, frozen salaries, or even asked workers to take salary cuts.

Work itself can be highly stressful (for example, diving off a ninety-foot high platform and hitting the water at fifty miles per hour). Many jobs are physically dangerous (for example, military, law enforcement, roofers, iron and steel workers) as well as psychologically dangerous (air traffic controllers and nursing). Ekman's trip to a remote jungle site, noted at the start of this chapter, was stressful.

Health

Health stressors are centered on a leader's physical and mental health. They range from lack of exercise to being overweight, to medical illnesses. As we age, our concerns increase over affordable health care, long-term care, and disease. Baby boomers are beginning to wonder whether they will be able to experience the "golden years" they have been planning for and looking forward to. Health deterioration raises a leader's stress level, which exacerbates current and future health issues.

Environment

The environment in general continues to be a battleground over global warming, pollution, waste disposal, fuel consumption, recycling, and carbon footprints. Leaders are becoming increasingly aware of the impact of these on a daily basis, along with other stressors such as noise, temperature, and crowding.

One stressor that receives little attention until it actually affects someone is noise. The National Institute on Deafness and Other Communication Disorders estimates that 26 million people between the ages of twenty and sixty-nine have high frequency hearing loss.[22] Not only can noise levels above eighty-five decibels (sometimes referred to as toxic noise) cause damage to the ears, but these can also raise a person's stress level. As noise levels increase, stress levels increase and decision-making effectiveness decreases.

In some training sessions I use two versions of a sixty-second video clip showing people frantically moving about trying to get to work on time, each with a different sound track. The first video has loud traffic noise and the second has Pachelbel's "Canon in D Major." I play the traffic clip first, have participants take a few breaths, and then play the second video. I can see a distinct difference in the group's facial expressions and focus. When we discuss the two videos, most people think the first one is longer, more stressful and that they are in the video. The second video is perceived as shorter, calming and viewers feel like they are observing the people in the video. The perceived noise has a dramatic emotional and stress effect on the participants.

Jamie Rhudy and Mary Meagher are psychologists at Texas A&M University who conduct research on the role of stress and emotion with an emphasis on pain and immune-related diseases. They have found that "women have a lower threshold to experience noise as stressful. Our data suggest that women may be more sensitive to noise stress than men."[23] Women tend to respond to loud noises with an emotional response of fear and men tend to respond with surprise. This supports anecdotal reports that women are less comfortable with high sound pressure levels, for example, those generated by home theater systems, than men.

Following this initial response to noise, women tended to have an increased ability to endure pain, whereas men showed a decrease in pain tolerance. Meagher hypothesizes that if the intensity of noise is increased, the gender effect will probably go away. From a survival standpoint, it makes sense that both genders have an increased tolerance to pain and that women might need to generate this tolerance at a lower level of noise.

In my research at the University of Georgia, I found a causal relationship between the noise level of baby crying and a person's stress level—and decision making.[24] Participants in the study listened to a baby crying at either a low volume level, when the crying sounded cute, or at a high volume level, when the crying sounded angry and irritating (both levels used the same audio recording). Participants listened to one of these two noise conditions (low or high volume) while participating in a competitive reaction-time game with two other people. The loser of each round of competition received a low-level electrical shock to the wrist, with the strength of the shock (level of discomfort) determined by the winner of the round.

Each round required a series of decisions including the shock level each participant should receive if he or she lost. The study found that noise level—and resulting stress level—significantly affected the shock levels set by the participants. The high noise (high stress) group made decisions to set significantly higher shock levels than the low noise (low stress) group. The increased level of stress influenced decision making in a manner such that participants were much more willing to set high shock levels for their competitors when their stress levels were high.

Optimal Performance Zone:
Finding the Balance

In 1908, psychologists Robert Yerkes and John Dodson published the Yerkes-Dodson law, which says that a relationship exists between arousal level and performance level.[25] Graphically this relationship looks like an inverted "U." Figure 4.7, a simple graphic representation of their law, shows an optimal performance curve relationship between stress and performance. As the leader's stress level increases, performance level also increases until she reaches the optimal performance level relative to stress. As stress continues to increase, she goes down the other side of the curve, resulting in a decrease in her performance.

The optimal performance curve is a powerful way of visually depicting the relationship between stress and performance, two different factors that have a special relationship.[26] If the leader's stress level is not high enough, she will not be motivated to perform at her optimal level. But if her stress level is too high, she will not be able to perform at her optimal level. The trick is for her to know what her optimal performance level feels like and how to get herself to that level, regardless of which side of the curve she is on. One characteristic of professional athletes is their ability to recognize when they are "in the zone" and to know how to get themselves into the zone when they are not there.

Let's take the example of giving a presentation. If you are on the left side of the curve (not very stressed or excited about doing the

FIGURE 4.7 Optimal Performance Curve

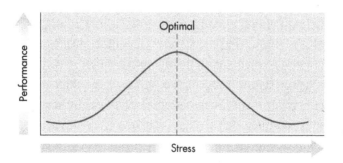

presentation), you probably won't put out much effort to get ready, might not do a very good job presenting, and might be perceived as unenthusiastic, maybe even unmotivated. If you are too far on the right of the curve, you may be so nervous that you overprepare, have difficulty retaining the information, and may get confused during the actual presentation. Being in the optimal range on the curve gives you the best opportunity to perform well.

It's a challenge to stay at the top of the curve, but one simple and important rule is to be aware of the impact that stress has on a leader's performance. "Powering through" various stressors by ignoring them is not a good idea. You should find ways to manage them. The first step is to acknowledge that stress can and will affect your decision making. As we've seen from the way the brain works, the stress effect varies from person to person, though there are some common denominators. In Chapter Nine, we'll look at some techniques for preventing stress from impairing decision making.

Psychiatrists Thomas Holmes and Richard Rahe studied the medical records of thousands of patients and found a way to create a relative score for different types of stressors.[27] For example, of the forty-three items on their scale, death of a spouse receives a score of 100, personal injury or illness gets 53 points, change in living conditions gets 25, and a minor violation of the law gets 11 points. The points are added to produce a total score. Total scores fall into ranges that indicate your chances of illness as a result of the stress in your life. One of the points here is that all stress is not created equal. Some life events (stressors) carry more stress than others, a topic explored in Chapter Six.

The Takeaway on Stress and Decision Making

We've seen that at a minimum, stress has a chemical, physiological, behavioral, physical, emotional, and cognitive impact on us. These changes significantly influence how we make decisions, as well as the quality of those decisions. Chemical changes in the brain influence how the brain Perceives information, Appraises it, and is Motivated by it and the Actions it chooses to implement.

As the stress level increases, there is an overall degradation in the amount and quality of information that we can recall, as well as in our ability to store short-term information. This means that we make many decisions without adequate information, leading to a higher probability of making ineffective decisions.

Information processing slows as stress increases. Any step of the decision-making process that requires the use of the brain's PFC will be degraded. Stress reduces the amount of working memory available to dedicate to decision making. The slowness of the PFC becomes exacerbated. At the same time, the amygdala, which controls emotions, is allowed to contribute more to the overall decision-making process. In some cases, this causes an imbalance between the amounts of cognitive input versus emotional input used in the Appraisal process, resulting in poor decisions.

Stress also tends to "set" the brain, making decision-making processes and identified solutions rigid and difficult to change. A sense of urgency develops to create and implement a decision. The ability to go back and reevaluate a decision or to change how it is implemented becomes increasingly difficult as the stress level increases.

After looking at some of the impacts of the stress effect on the brain and body, we must ask, "What are the specific effects on cognitive and emotional intelligences? Does stress enhance or degrade their functioning? How can I know whether my decisions are being overly affected by stress?"

The next chapter addresses these and other issues as we explore in greater detail a leader's ability to use cognitive and emotional intelligences under stress to make effective decisions.

5 How Stress Leads to Poor Decision Making

If your emotional abilities aren't in hand, if you don't have
self-awareness, if you are not able to manage your distressing emotions,
if you can't have empathy and have effective relationships, then no
matter how smart you are, you are not going to get very far.
DANIEL GOLEMAN

L aw enforcement officers undergo a significant amount of training
on how to make quick decisions under stress. Most go through
extensive training using shoot–no-shoot simulations to help
build the appropriate pattern recognition for high stress split-second
decisions. Yet even with extensive training, some officers manage to
be "had" by stress and find themselves stepping onto a fast-moving
landscape where one bad decision leads to another and another. They
know something is wrong but seem powerless to stop it.

The following story is pieced together from numerous newspaper
articles, TV news reports, and interviews, with the stress effect overlaid
on the various decisions made that night.[1] Just before midnight on
February 3, 1999, Amadou Diallo, a West African immigrant living in
New York City, arrived home from work. He stood on the steps of
his apartment building enjoying the night air. At the same time, an
unmarked police car containing four Caucasian plainclothes police officers turned onto the street and passed in front of his apartment building.
They were part of the New York Police Department's Street Crimes Unit
dedicated to patrolling crime "hot spots" in poor neighborhoods.

When the officers saw Diallo on the steps, his actions fit that of a "push-in robber"—a burglar who pushes his way into people's apartments. He also fit the description of a serial rapist who had been active in that neighborhood the year before and was still at large. They backed up the car; two of the officers got out and started toward Diallo. The officers were big men, wearing baseball caps and armored vests under sweatshirts, making them look even bigger. They were moving toward Diallo (he was about five feet six inches, 150 pounds), shouting something at him. They later discovered that he did not speak English well and that he had a stutter. He might have responded, but they did not hear anything.

At first he froze; then he ran into the vestibule. Two officers ran toward him with the other two following. Diallo reached for the doorknob of the inside door while turning his body sideways and reaching inside his pocket with his other hand. The officers began to yell for him to raise his hands.

We can't know with absolute certainty exactly what those men on the scene were thinking, but based on how the human brain functions, we can make some science-based assumptions. At this point, the brains and bodies of all present were undergoing the chemical bath we learned about in Chapter Four. Heart rates skyrocketed. Norepinephrine, which causes forgetfulness, among other effects, was rampant. The two officers' total attention narrowed to Diallo's hand in his pocket. The situation probably began to take on a surreal quality for all involved, becoming quiet even though the officers were shouting. The only things that existed for the two officers and Diallo were very specific sights and sounds playing out in front of them. In such crisis situations, those involved often comment afterward, "It was like everything began to move in slow motion."

"We were at the top steps of the vestibule trying to get him before he got through that door," the first officer said later. Diallo turned toward them as he pulled a black object out of his pocket. Each officer's amygdala, which responds to threats and creates emotions, instantly "recognized" the fuzzy, incomplete pattern of a gun, and the action escalated. One officer yelled, "Gun! He's got a gun!"

Then the officer opened fire. His partner instinctively jumped back off the top step, firing wildly as he slipped, and fell backward, his bullets ricocheting around the vestibule. The first officer's amygdala instantly processed the ricocheting bullets as coming from Diallo, and his partner went down as if he had been shot. The first two officers emptied their magazines toward Diallo.

When the third officer arrived, he saw the first two officers firing. One appeared to have been hit and was down but still firing. He could see Diallo crouched with his hand out; he could see what he thought was a gun and instantly thought, "My God, I'm going to die!" He began to fire as he tried to jump out of the way of Diallo's fire.

When the shooting stopped and the smoke from the forty-one gunshots cleared away, there was no gun, only a bullet-riddled body with an outstretched hand containing a wallet. Diallo had been trying to get his wallet out to show identification.

When stress suddenly escalates to extreme levels because of fear, the amygdala hijacks the prefrontal cortex (PFC) and all processing changes (see Chapter Three on emotional intelligence and decision making). The brain dramatically filters, reduces, and focuses the data that are perceived; changes how information is Appraised (cognitively and emotionally); and changes the person's Motivation, all of which drive toward different Actions from those that would be taken under normal circumstances. In general, people tend to underestimate how dramatically stress changes their decision-making process. This example shows how one bad decision led to a chain of bad decisions, resulting in a tragic outcome.

How Stress Turns "Normal" into Anything But

Up to this point we have examined the role of cognitive and emotional intelligences in the decision-making process of a leader and the general influence of stress on these processes. Now we turn to the specifics of how stress actually "leads" leaders to make poor decisions. The knowledge of how poor decisions come about will provide leaders with opportunities to avoid the negative impact of stress and even, in some cases, turn stress into an ally.

Making effective decisions can be difficult even under normal conditions. When the additional responsibility and accountability of leadership are added to decision making, it becomes even more difficult. Now let's pile on the impact of stress and time pressure on neurological functioning and you have a recipe for the "perfect storm." Unquestionably, the stress effect changes how leaders Perceive and Appraise, as well as the Actions they choose.

Why It's Not So Easy to "Get a Grip"

A stressor that occurs and goes away quickly, such as a near-miss traffic accident, is typically called an *acute* stressor. A stressor that lasts for a longer period of time—being in a traffic accident that requires hospitalization and causes extensive damage to your car, for example—is a *chronic* stressor. Acute and chronic stressors are very different, but both have some influence on future decision making. The fast driver who nearly plowed through a stop sign and hit another vehicle may learn to slow down more frequently. The injured driver who got broken bones and a totaled car may be too traumatized to drive anywhere for the foreseeable future.

Stress must also be viewed from the perspective of intensity. An extreme acute stressor might result in a permanent change in decision making (no more speeding, ever) while a low intensity chronic stressor might have little effect on decision making (just a fender bender and a sore knee, and the driver is behind the wheel of a rental in no time). Figure 5.1 shows a Grip Meter depicting four intensity levels of stress.

The four intensity levels of stress are labeled low stress, moderate stress, high stress, and very high stress. On a good day, leaders spend 50 percent or more of their time in the low to moderate zone, keeping them within the comfort zone (identified in Chapter Four) most of the time. Crossing into the high stress zone produces noticeable behavioral changes, not only to leaders but to those around them as well. Leaders can easily sense the physiological changes taking place as their mental,

FIGURE 5.1 The Grip Meter

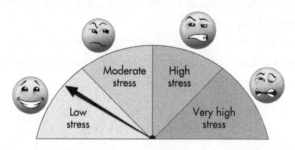

Source: Thompson, H. (1997). Coaching, stress and communication style. *Bulletin of Psychological Type*, 20(4), 19–20.

emotional, and physical resources are being drained. This is not an area where they should spend much time.

When the police officers approached Diallo, they had entered the high stress zone and were primed to react aggressively. Diallo's sudden movement was enough to initiate the officers' aggressive pursuit. When Diallo reached into his pocket to pull out his wallet, the officers' stress levels immediately jumped into the very high zone. They entered a kind of "mental tunnel," where the only thing they saw was a fight for their lives against an opponent. Their emotional systems had created a new reality—and in *this* reality, the bad guy had a gun and was firing at them. Interestingly, all four officers created and shared the same perception of reality. At this level of stress, their brains could not tell the difference between reality and imagination.

When the "danger" (perceived or real) ends, the stress effect does not end. (Revisit Figure 4.4, and notice that when the stressor is removed, the leader experiences an aftereffect that might last for hours.) If the stress level was very high, this aftereffect might be accompanied by nausea, vomiting, weakness, trembling, or other physiological symptoms related to experiencing very high stress.

The Grip Meter can be a useful tool for visualizing your own stress level as well as helping others get a grip on their stress, and their perspective. With a little practice you can develop an awareness of where you are on the Grip Meter at any given time. If you sense that you are about to move beyond the moderate zone, stop, breathe, and take a break if necessary to regain control. Awareness, followed by action, is key to staying in control.

During normal or pressure-cooker moments, where do you travel along the Grip Meter? Where would you like to be? What are techniques you use to control your location?

Decision Making

The decision-making process is about recognizing that a decision needs to be made, gathering information about the decision, using that information to make an Appraisal of the situation, developing the right Motivation, and then choosing the solution (Action) that will be implemented. Although this process sounds simple, there are numerous inherent pitfalls along the way.

All leaders are human and occasionally make bad decisions that they later change or wish they could change. Making a poor decision because of faulty information, lack of experience, or the Peter principle is not necessarily the result of stress. Sometimes leaders make bad decisions as a result of incomplete information, not following a standardized process, or not listening to their "gut" (instinct).[2]

The Perception-Appraisal-Motivation-Action Model Under Stress

As we've seen, the Perception-Appraisal-Motivation-Action model (PAMA) is one of the best general decision-making models, and it works with both rational and intuitive decision-making strategies. Let's look at its various components once again, this time through the lens of stress.

Perception: Avoiding Overload and Misinformation

The first component of the PAMA model to be affected by stress is Perception—the process of recognizing that stress (an event) has occurred either externally or internally, consciously or unconsciously. Perception sets in motion a chain of reactions to PAMA processes already in progress. It may sound trite, but the brain does not "sit idly by" waiting for a Stimulus to occur so that it has something to do. The brain is in constant motion, running numerous PAMA cycles both consciously and unconsciously. When "another" Stimulus occurs, such as Captain Sullenberger's seeing the "birds" or the officers' seeing a "suspect," the new information is added to other PAMA cycles already in progress.

Leaders must be careful in the Perception process not to take in too much information. The PFC is hungry for information and will quickly overload itself. Work by Harvard psychologist Paul Andreassen in the 1980s with MIT students revealed that students who were given too much information for use in making financial stock decisions did not perform as well as students who received less information.[3] When given too many options, the PFC becomes overloaded and has difficulty making effective decisions. This is sometimes referred to as *analysis paralysis.*

Psychologist Barry Schwartz, author of *The Paradox of Choice,* writes: "As the number of choices increases, the autonomy, control, and liberation this variety brings us is powerful and positive. But if the number of choices keeps growing, negative effects start to appear. As choices grow further, the negatives escalate until we can become overloaded. At this point, choice no longer liberates us; it might even be said to tyrannize."[4] When too many choices overload the PFC, it sometimes just picks an option—and it might not be the best one for the situation. Researcher Herbert Simon says that "a wealth of information creates a poverty of attention."[5] The human brain is limited by the amount of simultaneous information it can manage in consciousness at any time.

Having too many options can also slow the decision-making process, often just when an immediate decision needs to be made. During military operations, pilots sometimes find themselves in a "target-rich environment," where it can be difficult to decide which target to engage first, especially when the stress level is already high. Two primary methods are used to help pilots make the best prioritizing decisions in these types of environments. The first is the extensive training pilots receive that is designed to help them develop skills for identifying and prioritizing targets. A second method, available in many attack aircraft, is a targeting priority algorithm built into the onboard software system. Larry Thompson, an Apache helicopter pilot during the First Gulf War and later an Apache Longbow systems simulations manager for Boeing, says that the Apache Longbow's fire control radar can track 255 air targets or approximately 125 ground targets and, based on preprogramming, will prioritize the top 16 targets for a single mission.

Training and tools, when applied appropriately, help leaders improve their decision-making abilities in environments with too many options and high stress. A leader might not have the onboard software system of a fighter plane on her office desktop, but it is possible for her to learn better decision-making skills. Chapters Seven through Nine of this book offer ways to increase stress management capacity and develop both cognitive and emotional resilience.

We Don't See What We Aren't Looking For

A leader is bombarded by approximately 10 million pieces of information per second. Each eye can send a million pieces of information per second to the brain. Table 5.1 shows the most common senses and their functions.

Information goes through a thorough filtering process based on numerous factors. Stress, for example, tends to degrade the ability of the senses to perform their functions. For example, fatigue may slow the focus of the eyes, make them more light sensitive, or reduce acuity. This may degrade the type of information sent to the brain, its accuracy, and the amount—key elements for beginning a decision process. As in proofing, if it is not being done on the original source, false data might be embedded in the process from the beginning, resulting in "garbage in, garbage out."

TABLE 5.1 The Most Common Senses and Their Functions

Sense	Function
Sight (vision)	
Hearing (audition)	
Touch (tactition)	
Taste (gustation)	
Smell (olfaction)	
Vestibular (equilibrioception)	Balance and acceleration
Kinesthetic (proprioception)	Awareness of body positions
Temperature (thermoception)	Sense of heat and cold
Pain (nociception)	Sense of damage or near damage
Internal organs (interoception)	Sense of organs, arousal, bladder pressure

Mental Models: Beware the Blind Spots

Kenneth Craik in his 1943 book *The Nature of Explanation* describes mental models as "deeply held beliefs, images and assumptions we hold about ourselves, our world, and our organizations, and how we fit in them."[6] Each leader has a personal paradigm lens for perceiving the world—both external and internal.

The personal paradigm lens includes filtering components such as age, gender, ethnicity, and other factors that influence how we see the world and make sense of it. During the Perception process, the brain searches for patterns and fills in missing information. When leaders look at Figure 5.2, they typically say they see a dog, a spotted dog, and specifically, a Dalmatian. Most, in fact, become so fixated on what appears to be a dog in the image that they stop looking for other patterns and, consequently, fail to see the firefighter spraying water in the upper left corner. Stopping at the first recognizable pattern is typical behavior, especially under stress. We look for and react to the most obvious patterns and filter out other information. The amygdala uses a

FIGURE 5.2 Pattern Recognition

Source: Gregory, R. L. (1970). *The intelligent eye.* London: Weidenfeld and Nicolson. Copyright © 1970 by Richard L. Gregory. Reproduced with permission.

kind of fuzzy logic. It responds to fuzzy patterns rather than waiting for more information, more clarity. This fuzzy logic reaction was designed to keep us alive. Today we have a much more complex array of stimuli coming at us with many of the patterns being similar. The officers in the Diallo case saw a gun, not a wallet.

Filling in the blanks can also add significant data errors to the decision-making process. Although the image in Figure 5.2 isn't really a dog, many people say that they see a dog among the spots. In eyewitness accounts of accidents or crime scenes, some witnesses "remember" details and specifics they "saw" that may or may not be accurate. Additions or omissions of information have a significant impact on the accuracy of the Perception process.

Decision-making researchers Max Bazerman and Don Moore present data to support a "confirmation trap" in decision making.[7]

This trap is based on leaders' searching for information to confirm what they already believe. The brain's limited capability for conscious searching and evaluation of various alternatives requires leaders to be selective in their search. This selectivity results in a bias toward information that supports the leader's current belief.

This trap is easily confirmed by the audiences of talk shows and cable news shows. These shows tend to be politically biased in the material they present and, consequently, draw audiences that share the same beliefs as those presented on the shows. For example, it is not likely that many people with a liberal political ideology listen to conservative radio talk host Rush Limbaugh on a daily basis. Nor is it likely that many people with a conservative ideology listen to liberal cable network host Keith Olbermann. Audiences tend to be drawn to shows that confirm their beliefs. Carl G. Jung wrote, "It is a fact, which is constantly and overwhelmingly apparent in my practical work, that people are virtually incapable of understanding and accepting any point of view other than their own."[8] This type of bias can have a negative impact on decision making—for example, seeing a wallet as a gun when very highly stressed.

Chapter Seven of Plato's *The Republic,* written as a fictional dialogue between Plato's teacher, Socrates, and Plato's brother, Glaucon, is an allegory about a cave. I have taken liberties with Plato's original story in the retelling that follows.[9] If infants are put near the back of a cave so that they can see only the back wall of the cave and a fire is built behind them so that anything that passes between the fire and their backs casts a shadow on the wall, as they grow older they will think that the shadows are real objects.

When they grow older, if one child is unrestrained and taken to the fire, and then shown that moving an object between the fire and the other children casts a shadow on the wall and that what is real is the object and not the shadow, that child would have an enlightening experience, to say the least. If the goal were to shock the child, he could be taken to the mouth of the cave and allowed to look outside. But for now, the child has seen the fire and understands the difference between the shadow on the wall and the object itself.

If the child is returned to his confined position with the others, once more facing the wall, he would probably tell them about the fire and the shadows. In telling them that the shadows are not real objects, the other children might say, "Where have you been, and what happened to you? Of course, what we see on the wall is real!" In the same way, leaders sometimes tend not to believe what others tell them if they have not validated the information for themselves personally. Leaders "build" their own versions of reality and then interpret all incoming information through their personal paradigm lens, especially when they are stressed.

Figure 5.3 provides an alternative method for discussing shadows. If the light is shining down from above the objects, all three will cast circular shadows. If the only things that can be seen are the circular shadows, a leader might be led to believe that all three objects have the same shape. If the light is moved to the side, all three objects cast different shadows. Moving the position of the light changes what the viewer sees. Changing a mental model changes what a person sees.

FIGURE 5.3 Shadows

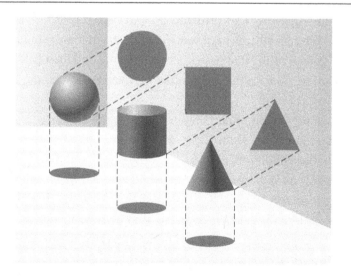

A key point to remember is that *all* models, whether mental, physical, mathematical, or iconic, have blind spots. When you choose a model, you choose your blind spots. A victim Perceives a dangerous situation with a different model than the rescuer. Sharon Patterson, superintendent of Georgia's Bibb County School District, asked me to conduct systems thinking training for her public school principals. After showing the image in Figure 5.2, I was particularly struck by an observation made by a middle school principal. While we were processing the concept of mental models, she made the following powerful and insightful statement about shadows and students: "Sometimes we try to apply the same solution to all students because we see the shadow and we think all the students are the same. If we stand back and look at the shape instead of the shadow, we will see that all students are different. We can't treat the shadow; we must treat the shape itself."

Understanding the concept of mental models (personal paradigm lens) and their impact on our Perception gives insight into René Descartes' statement, "We do not describe the world we see, we see the world we can describe," and Gareth Morgan's statement, "Think 'structure' and you'll see structure. Think 'culture' and you'll see all kinds of cultural dimensions. Think 'politics' and you'll find politics."[10] Mental models or the personal paradigm lens define Perception, and Perception defines reality. Stress narrows and redefines our reality.

Over the years I have worked with many law enforcement agencies. John Bredehoft, a game warden in Colorado who has attended several workshops I conducted, described one of the differences in how game wardens and local police use search patterns when approaching someone. When a police officer approaches someone who looks suspicious, the search pattern includes looking for possible weapons. If the officer spots a weapon or something that looks like a weapon, it triggers a particular set of responses, including stress. When a police officer finds someone with a weapon it usually means trouble.

When John, the game warden, approaches someone in the woods, most of the time that person will have a gun and perhaps a knife because they are typically hunters, and hunters carry these weapons. Looking for a weapon is nevertheless still part of the game warden's search pattern, but seeing one does not tend to trigger the same stress response as it does when a police officer encounters someone with a weapon.

The examples thus far show how confirmation traps, mental models, and the personal paradigm lens influence people to see what they "want" to see. Other factors cause leaders not to see things they aren't actually looking for.

In 1992, psychologists Arien Mack and Irvin Rock coined the term *intentional blindness*.[11] One of the most famous series of experiments on intentional blindness was conducted by Harvard University psychologists Daniel Simons and Christopher Chabris.[12] Research participants were asked to observe a basketball game between two teams. One team wore white T-shirts and the other team wore black T-shirts. Their task was to count the number of times the ball was passed among members of the white team and to remember the count.

During the time the research participants were counting the passes, a person dressed in a gorilla suit walked through the middle of the players. In some versions of the video, the gorilla actually stopped, turned, faced the camera, and beat on its chest before continuing across the field of view. In another version, a woman carrying an umbrella walked through the game. After watching the video, the research participants were asked if they noticed anything unusual during the game. In most groups, less than 50 percent of participants saw the gorilla or the woman with the umbrella! They were so focused on counting the passes of the ball that they did not see anything else. After you see the gorilla, it seems impossible for someone not to see it—but most people don't.

I have used this video many times. When I induce stress into the exercise by having groups compete to get the correct number of passes, 10 percent of participants or less see the gorilla the first time they watch the video. Even when they view the video a second time and are not counting the ball passes, some do not see the gorilla. When participants who missed the gorilla the first time see it the second time, they typically say that the second video is different from the first. Having shown this video in a variety of settings, I am always surprised by how many people do not see the gorilla.

Stress focuses a leader's attention and might cause him to miss vital information needed in his decision-making process. Consider the following example when a business owner's personal stress caused him to lose his focus—and a sale.

One Saturday, Charles took a break from bush-hogging (clearing land by dragging a special mower device behind a tractor) and drove his old truck to a nearby town in Mississippi to purchase a used refrigerator. He was still dressed in overalls and his old baseball cap when he made his first stop at a locally owned appliance store.

He found a used refrigerator that he thought would suffice, even though its white door had been replaced with a green one, and asked the store owner, who appeared to be in a bad mood, for the price. The owner told him it was $150. Charles considered this and asked him if he would replace the green door with a white one. The store owner looked Charles over and said, "I'll tell you what, son. Why don't you go back home and see if you can raise $150 cash, and come back and we'll talk." The store owner had become so distracted by his stereotypes and Charles's attire that he could not see that Charles was bright, articulate, knowledgeable, and friendly. There was a distinct incongruence between the clothes and the person talking—but the store owner could not see that, and he lost the sale.

Shortly after becoming CEO of a large chain store corporation in the late 1980s, Charles had purchased a 350-acre property, mostly wooded, to be his "farm." He built a lodge deep in the woods that he could use for weekend relaxation and for company retreats and meetings. Charles found it relaxing to get on his tractor and bush-hog the fields and cut trails into the woods. He purchased an old, somewhat beat-up pickup truck to use around the farm.

That weekend, Charles, using his high emotional intelligence, simply turned and walked out of the store with the knowledge that he could have written a personal check large enough to purchase the man's entire business. Then he drove to another store down the street and bought a *new* refrigerator.

"Who Is That?" My Experience with the Confirmation Trap

Several years ago while serving on a conference committee, I volunteered to pick up one of the keynote speakers at the Atlanta airport. I was particularly tired, but I was the only committee member who had actually met the speaker in person and would recognize her in the crowded airport. It was Friday evening, and the airport was standing room only, so I waited for the speaker at the top of the escalator coming from the concourses.

Having traveled through this airport many times, my experience led me to determine that she had had ample time to travel from her concourse to baggage claim, and I was concerned. I had seen everyone who stepped off the escalator. She could not have gotten past me. As my concern grew, a voice behind me said, "Hi, Dick. I didn't see you when I came off the escalator." As I turned around, my internal intuitive voice said, "Who is this lady?" before realizing it was the keynote speaker. She was taller than I remembered, had a different hair color, and was not wearing glasses. Obviously my memory was wrong. I had selectively eliminated anyone from my search pattern who did not fit my mental image of the speaker. Fortunately, when she looked around, she recognized me. My moderate to high level of stress had caused me to retrieve the wrong information.

Appraisal: Beginning to Filter Data

The Appraisal phase of the PAMA model is designed to begin the process of evaluating and Appraising the Stimulus data as soon as they are Perceived consciously or unconsciously. Many parts of the brain are involved in data collection and interpretation. The "Chief Appraisal Officer" in this case is the PFC. It has the responsibility for pulling in data from numerous brain regions, then synthesizing and interpreting the data that will eventually lead to a decision or, more likely, many decisions.

Anything that interferes with processing in any brain region and with communication among the regions, especially when the PFC is involved, will degrade the overall decision-making process. Even on a good day, some interference will occur during the Appraisal process. When a stressor is encountered and chemicals are released into the bloodstream, the Appraisal process takes on a whole new look as we saw previously.

Three key areas of Appraisal are affected by stress: working memory, cognitive intelligence, and emotional intelligence. We will look at each in turn.

Working Memory Under Stress

Imagine that a leader has been working at her computer most of the day. She has spent a significant amount of time surfing the Web looking for information. The computer has probably picked up numerous cookies and spyware, each of which tends to degrade the performance of the computer. Microsoft Word, PowerPoint, and Excel are open and using a significant amount of the available working memory (RAM). The computer's processing speed has continued to slow all morning.

Think of the spyware and programs as stressors. Every time a program is opened, the computer enters Selye's alarm reaction stage and struggles to climb back to the resistance stage. If action is not taken to free up some system resources, it is possible that the computer will eventually experience the dreaded "blue screen of death" as the system enters into the exhaustion stage and crashes.

When a leader's brain gets overloaded and stressors continue to be added to her system, her processing speed slows. The ability to retrieve information becomes more difficult and takes longer; the accuracy of the information being retrieved is questionable; thinking itself becomes a chore; and it becomes difficult to maintain focus, clarity, and the motivation to continue.

Two key components of the Appraisal process that require adequate amounts of working memory are the leader's cognitive and emotional intelligences. Stress has a significant impact on how well these two critical components perform and on the appraisal process.

The Impact of Stress on Cognitive Intelligence

Not surprisingly, the slowdown of PFC functioning and reduction of working memory due to stress decreases cognitive intelligence. As cognitive intelligence declines, the Appraisal process becomes confused. Retrieving information takes longer, is more difficult, and the accuracy and quality of information deteriorate. With the loss of processing speed and working memory, manipulation of information gets more difficult. Even the storage of short-term and long-term memory becomes degraded.

As the stress level increases, a notable decline in a leader's ability to process complex information and handle ambiguity occurs. This loss results in simpler and less ambiguous thought contributions to the Appraisal process.

The PFC (and, consequently, cognitive intelligence) tends to take on a more concrete and short-term perspective. The long-term planning ability of the PFC is lost with increased stress. As stress increases from low to moderate to high, time horizons continue to become shorter. The leader begins to operate in the "now." (Think of the police officers. At the peak of their "now," all they could anticipate was the next moment; all they could process was a suspect reaching for a weapon.)

A study by researchers Bernard Brown and Lilian Rosenbaum of Georgetown University looked at four thousand seven year olds and compared children who were under stress to those who were not according to their Stress Index scores. They found that low stress children scored 13 percent higher (104) on the index than high stress children (91) did.[13]

Researchers Poonam Malik and Shanti Balda found that the academic achievement of high IQ adolescents (110 and above) was negatively affected by stress. They assessed mental stress using the Bisht Battery of Stress Scale, which tests seven types of stress: existential, achievement, academic, social, institutional, financial, and vocational. Student academic achievement was based on an average of the students' last three academic examinations. Malik and Balda conclude:

> *A person under stress needs to fight the stress in order to survive. Adolescents whose minds are full of apprehensions are not free to use their energy and ability. Their foremost priority is to nullify the effects of stress over their mind and they have to spend a major part of their energy in this task. Hence a lot of highly intelligent children who are under mental stress give poor performance in academics.*[14]

This study adds validation that stress at any age has an impact on cognitive performance.

Researchers and psychologists Kasey Saltzman, Carl Weems, and Victor Carrion found a link between IQ and post-traumatic stress disorder. Their work suggests that leaders with relatively high IQs might hold up better than those with lower IQs; in other words, they may be more resistant to the long-term effects of very high stress.[15]

Baba Shiv, a professor at Stanford University who teaches decision neuroscience (the study of how the brain makes decisions), and his colleague Alexander Fedorikhin conducted an experiment on memory recall of digits.[16] They divided research participants into two groups and asked one group to remember two digits and the other group to remember seven digits. Both groups were told to walk down the hall to another location, where they would be required to say their digits to one of the experimenters. Along the way, they passed a dessert table that had two types of desserts: a fruit cup and a decadent chocolate cake. They were allowed to choose one of the desserts and continue to the other room.

Participants in group one had to remember only two digits, not a very demanding cognitive task. Group two had to remember seven digits, which borders on the average digit memory span for most people and fits the seven-plus-or-minus-two hypothesis. Shiv's primary focus was not on the participants' ability to remember digits but on which dessert they selected. The hypothesis was that the more distracted the PFC became trying to remember digits, the lower control it would exert over emotions. Overloading the PFC with excess information such as spreadsheets, charts, graphs, and minute details might predispose a leader to use a blend in decision making that includes a higher level of emotion than might be desired.

Shiv believed that most people would see the fruit cup as a healthier choice than the chocolate cake. If the PFC and impulse control were working properly, participants should choose a fruit cup. If, however, the PFC had temporarily lost control of the participants' emotions, they would be more likely to choose the chocolate cake.

It turned out that 59 percent of participants trying to remember seven digits chose the chocolate cake compared to only 37 percent of participants trying to remember two digits choosing chocolate cake. Shiv interprets this as evidence that the effort required for the PFC to process and maintain the additional five digits in working memory was enough to allow the emotions to overpower the PFC and for participants to choose the chocolate cake over the fruit.

The fact that 41 percent of participants who were trying to remember seven digits did not choose the chocolate cake suggests other factors might have been influencing the decision. This possibility is also supported by the fact that 37 percent of those who had two digits to remember also chose the cake. The bottom line is that this study and similar ones suggest that as working memory is consumed, the ability of the PFC to control emotions is decreased. If remembering seven digits is enough to cause someone who would normally choose a fruit cup to make an emotional response and choose chocolate cake, then it is highly possible that high levels of stress might have a significant impact on access to cognitive intelligence and emotional intelligence.

How Stress Changes Emotional Intelligence

Emotional intelligence as I have defined it in this book is a leader's ability to exert enough control over his emotions to allow him to manage his and others' emotions in a way that promotes well-being and successful relationships with others. An emotionally intelligent leader must be aware of his emotions; he must also be able to choose when, where, and how to use emotions to bring about his own emotional well-being, as well as positive relationships with others. Anything that interferes with this ability, such as stress, will tend to degrade his application of emotional intelligence.

One of the critical functions of the PFC, the CEO of the brain, is the control of emotions. Stress has been shown to degrade the performance of the PFC and, consequently, the ability to control emotions. Without the controlling influence of the PFC, the amygdala and other components of the limbic system have more freedom to drive decision making. In other words, the balanced blend of cognitive and emotional intelligences begins to shift toward decisions that are emotionally driven. (Think of the example of the study participants: those who chose the chocolate cake were making emotionally driven decisions. They were distracted from having to remember the digits, and when their PFCs began to go on the blink, their amygdalae took over.)

Under normal circumstances, the emotional system has the ability to transmit signals almost four times as fast as the PFC. Without the control of the PFC, the emotion center can operate at full speed. When the emotion center begins to operate on automatic pilot, previous decisions and data that have been emotionally tagged or primed as in Klein's recognition-primed decision model (addressed in Chapter One) now become the uncontested decision choices. This increases the chances of making a less than effective decision compared to those that are made with input from the PFC and cognitive intelligence.

As the emotional system assumes more control of the decision-making process, the focus becomes even more immediate. Decisions are being made in the "now." (We saw this in the Diallo example, with the "now" decisions the officers made.) Everything becomes short term, with little consideration for unintended consequences. The working memory available to conduct the mental simulations used in the recognition-primed decision model becomes inadequate and may cause the simulations to be skipped altogether. When the brain fails to perform these mental simulations, the chance of making effective decisions drops.

The CEOs discussed at the beginning of this book who led so many organizations into failure made many decisions in the "now" with no regard for the fallout or the long-term global consequences.

The Influence of Emotions on Decision Making Under Stress

Deborah Richardson and I conducted a study at the University of Georgia looking at what I called the "rooster effect." Anyone who has raised chickens (at home, not in commercial chicken houses) can tell you that having one rooster in the chicken pen is good; having two results in a lot of fights between the two roosters. They compete with each other for the hen harem. On the human level, the rooster effect most visibly plays out with the love triangle. Two men (roosters) fight for the affection of a woman (hen). It also occurs when two women fight over a man. Richardson and I were looking at the effect this phenomenon has on the opportunity to behave aggressively toward the other "rooster" and the "hen."

In the study, two men and a woman, all alleged strangers, met together briefly.[17] The woman, a confederate (someone who pretends to be a research participant but is actually working with the researcher), chose one of the men, also a confederate, over the second man, the actual research participant, to form a two-person team to compete against the research participant—the hen chose the other rooster.

They were notified that the losing team for each round of the competition would receive an electrical shock administered to their wrists by the winning team. Having the woman choose one of the men (in this case, the confederate) created a significant amount of stress in the research participant. All variables measured, including the electrical shock levels delivered to the two-person confederate team by the research participant and the interaction that followed, were significantly affected by the induced stress and resulted in aggressive and emotionally unintelligent behavior on the part of the research participant. Rooster effect situations occur on a daily basis whether with strangers or friends, and the result is an elevated level of stress that affects decision making.

Imagine a leader being faced with a stressful decision. Let's say she has been tasked with choosing a new manager to be put in charge of an important growth initiative and has two candidates to choose from. (It will be a plum assignment for whoever gets promoted, though much is riding on the performance of this person.) This boss usually conducts herself in a fair and impartial manner, but she is bothered by a sarcastic comment one candidate made in a meeting, which embarrassed and irritated her since her boss was present. She can't get it out of her head, and although he is the better person for this particular job, she picks a less qualified staffer.

*Who Made Skippy CEO? When Stress Shuts Down Cognitive
and Emotional Intelligences*

As we know, when a leader's stress level rises, access to both cognitive intelligence and emotional intelligence decreases, resulting in his making less effective decisions. Because decision making is a key component of effective leadership, an increase in stress tends to result in a decrease in leader performance. A leader who has no skills or techniques for handling stress simply "can't think straight" when his cognitive and emotional intelligences are under fire.

Every leader has a range of cognitive intelligence capped by a maximum level. For example, a leader might have an IQ of 110. If this is the best cognitive performance the leader is capable of, this would be that leader's maximum level of cognitive intelligence. The leader typically would operate near this maximum level. When under stress, the leader's ability to reach his maximum level of cognitive functioning decreases. The higher the stress level, the further below the IQ of 110 this leader would operate.

The same concept applies to emotional intelligence. As the leader's stress increases, emotional intelligence decreases. If the leader's maximum level of emotional intelligence is 110, he would operate below that level when stressed. A drop in emotional intelligence is also associated with a drop in leader performance.

One way to visually conceptualize this interaction between stress and these two intelligences is to use a version of catastrophe theory.[18] Figure 5.4 shows an example of a three-dimensional *leadership performance response surface* created by using leader performance (success or failure), stress (low to extreme), and cognitive and emotional intelligences (low to very high).

Think about the response surface in the figure as a sheet of paper that has a fold on the near edge. The axis along the left edge of the paper is the cognitive-emotional index (CEI), and the axis along the back edge of the paper is stress. The left half of the response surface represents successful leader performance, the right half represents a lower performance state, and the right front quarter of the response surface represents leadership failure. As stress increases, a leader moves from

FIGURE 5.4 Leadership Performance
Response Surface

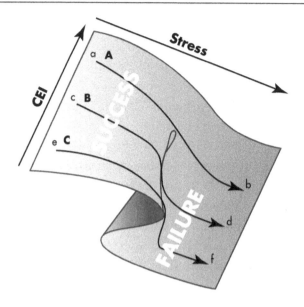

left to right across the response surface. Leader A, for example, who has a high CEI, moves along line ab on the back part of the surface, which shows some moderate decline in leader performance as stress increases.

Leader B has a medium CEI and moves along line cd, showing a sudden significant drop in leader performance as he crosses the leading edge of the fold. Leader C, with a low level of CEI, moves along line ef, exhibiting a catastrophic change in leader performance as he falls over the edge of the fold and drops immediately into the failure zone.

It is important to keep in mind that I am not suggesting that leaders A and B are immune to catastrophic failure, but rather that leader C is in a more vulnerable position. He is already aligned with the catastrophic edge, which means it will not take much stress to push him over the edge. Note that as the stress level increases, leaders A and B are not only pushed along their respective lines (ab and cd) toward the right edge of the surface, but also downward toward the catastrophic cliff. If their stress levels become high enough, they could be pushed to the spot where leader C goes over the edge.

When catastrophic leadership failure occurs, it is sudden and causes a catastrophic change in the leader's ability to perform successfully. The leader will exhibit some or all of a characteristic set of behaviors:

Not listening	Rationalizing
Overanalyzing	Self-satisficing
Failure to make decisions	Hedonism
Low-quality decisions	Denial
Emotional decisions	Inattentional blindness
"Flip-flops"	Fear-based decisions
Short-term decisions and focus	Anger-facilitated decisions
Reactive decisions	Automatic decision making
Defensiveness	Mental paralysis

As we saw in Chapter One, CEO Jimmy Cayne admitted that he was paralyzed with indecision and did not know what to do to turn Bear Stearns around.

In a scene from the movie *Pirates of the Caribbean 3,* a ship's commander needs to make a critical and immediate decision during a life-threatening situation. He stands looking over the rail of his ship, staring blankly ahead, while his crew members are asking, "What do we do? Make a decision! What do you want us to do?" He just stands there, cognitively and emotionally paralyzed, unable to function as a leader—experiencing catastrophic leadership failure.

Sometimes catastrophic leadership failure results in hedonistic decisions—the leader takes care of himself. The CFO says, "We can set up several shell companies in Bermuda and flow a few million dollars into them, make millions of dollars ourselves, and not pay tax." During catastrophic leadership failure, this might sound like a good idea to the CFO because his PFC has stopped working and IQ and emotional intelligence have dropped dramatically.

The evidence suggests that a high stress environment might restrict leaders' access to their full potential of cognitive and emotional intelligences. A reasonable prediction based on current research would be that the lower the leader's starting emotional intelligence, the faster he will fail under high stress. A corollary is that the lower the leader's starting emotional intelligence, the less stress it will take to produce catastrophic leadership failure. Leaders must be aware of where they are on the "surface" at all times and be ready to take action to stay on the high side of the surface.

Examples of corporate leadership failures in which catastrophic leadership failure might have played a role include Enron, WorldCom, and Tyco.

Motivation: The Hard Part

The Motivation component is focused on using the Appraisal information to set a goal and make a decision on how to reach that goal. Keep in mind the Yerkes-Dodson law discussed in Chapter Four. A leader must be Motivated to accomplish the goal or she will not put forth the effort to make it happen. In some cases, she will not even put forth the effort to decide what should be done. And just because a leader has the Motivation to accomplish a goal does not mean that she will attempt to accomplish it. Ideas tend to be easy; implementation tends to require more effort.

Three key factors drive what the Motivation component does with the information from Appraisal: risk, emotions, and "What's in it for me?" The "what's in it for me" factor contributes to part of the goal-setting process: "What is my goal? To survive? To have a relationship? To lose weight?" The answers to these questions go back to the personal paradigm lens in terms of the impact of those factors on a person's Motivation.

Some leaders seem to be constantly driven toward goal accomplishment. Others seem to be less motivated; perhaps they appear scattered and may be less focused on accomplishing goals. The impact of a leader's drive for success strongly influences her motivation, goal setting, and execution. T. Boone Pickens says, "Be willing to make decisions. That's the most important quality in a good leader. Don't fall victim to what

I call the 'ready-aim-aim-aim-aim syndrome.' You must be willing to fire."[19] There is an old saying that a good plan well executed is much better that an excellent plan poorly executed—or not executed. Decisions have to be made and action taken.

Risk

Every decision poses some degree of risk. Motivation is influenced by the assessment of the current risk level associated with a particular decision. When time permits, always explore the unintended consequences of decisions. For example, how might this decision affect how the leader's boss will perceive her significance, competence, or likeability? She may have thoughts like these: *If I present this idea for spinning off this division into a separate company that I could run, will he think it's a ridiculous idea or a brilliant one? I'm confident it's a winner, but what if he thinks I'm dead wrong and it's a money pit? And what if he's right and I'm wrong? My reputation and my job could be on the line! What should I do?* The risk posed and possible outcomes will influence the decision the leader makes.

Emotions and Motivation

Emotions create goal-oriented behavior. If a leader has an opportunity to accept or reject an idea presented by a direct report and he is experiencing the emotion of anger, he is more likely to reject the idea. If the leader is experiencing the emotion of happiness, he is more likely to accept the idea.

With the emotion of fear, there is a tendency for him to become more risk averse. Fear causes leaders to be more cautious in making decisions. Anger creates the opposite effect. An angry leader tends to downplay the risk and might even become overconfident in his ability to succeed.

Emotions tend to play a role in how motivated a leader is to set goals, the type of goals he sets, the level of risk he's willing to accept, and how he perceives the value of the decision to himself. As emotions change, so might his decision in a particular situation. When the boss's secretary says, "I would not ask him for a raise today. He is not in a good mood," the wise leader would take this information to heart and perhaps ask for the raise another day.

Action: Not Quite the End

Action is about executing the decision made during the Motivation process. It turns thinking and goal setting into movement. Sometimes the leader is aware of the process behind the Action and sometimes is not.

Sigmund Freud once suggested that approximately 95 percent of our behavior is driven by the unconscious. Much of Freud's work, and particularly this hypothesis, was discounted by psychologists during the late twentieth century. As neuroscience continues to discover how the brain works, however, it lends credence to some of Sigmund Freud's thoughts about the unconscious: "When making a decision of minor importance, I have always found it advantageous to consider all the pros and cons. In vital matters, however, ... the decision should come from the unconscious, from somewhere within ourselves. In the important decisions of personal life, we should be governed, I think, by the deep inner needs of our nature."[20]

As discussed in Chapter One, we make most of our decisions unconsciously. And high levels of stress tend to cause even more decisions to be made in the unconscious and to be made more quickly. When a leader is asked about how a particular decision was made, he tends to make up a rational, conscious, and deliberate process for how the decision was made.

Stress focuses Actions on the short term. As the stress level increases, Action becomes more short term and simpler, and these solutions in many cases turn out to be temporary bandages rather than substantial solutions. If this is the case, the leader will be solving the same problem on a regular basis. A quick fix may work for now, but it's not the end of the Action process.

How Do You Behave?

Fight, freeze, flight, adapt, and tend and befriend are the five basic responses to stress, but each seems to attract distinct personalities. For example, some people tend to be more predisposed toward a fight response. As their stress level increases, they become more aggressive. Other leaders might move quickly toward adaptation. To some degree, motivation will also play a role in the strategy adopted by the individual leader.

Laurence Gonzales studies who survives and who dies in survival situations. He says, "At least 75 percent of people caught in a catastrophe either freeze or simply wander in a daze .... They can't think, they can't act correctly."[21] Even when they are motivated by survival, if people can't manage severe stress, they might make the wrong choices.

Stress causes us to go into a defensive mode. Will Schutz, the creator of FIRO (fundamental interpersonal relations orientation) theory, identified several defensive behavioral responses typically used by people under stress.[22] Jim Tamm and Ron Luyet, two of his long-time students and colleagues, have expanded on these defensive behaviors.[23] Stress tends to bring out these behaviors in most leaders. The impact of these behaviors is driven by the intensity of the stress and the rigidity exhibited by the leader. Just glancing at the list of behaviors that follows will probably get you thinking about how you behave in stressful situations and what responses stress evokes in you or your colleagues:[24]

Aggression	Playing "poor me"
Loss of humor	Sarcasm
Taking offense	Blaming
Wanting to be right	Eccentricity
Wanting the last word	Being too nice
Flooding with information to prove a point	"It's my personality; it's just the way I am."
Holding a grudge	Trivializing with humor
"I know that."	"Don't lecture me."
Jealousy	Inappropriate laughter

Being aware of our own behavior is extremely valuable in managing stress.

The Takeaway on Stress and Poor Decision Making

Although the decision-making process sounds simple (the PAMA model is very straightforward), you've now seen numerous inherent pitfalls along the way, particularly when stress is introduced.

All leaders make some less than optimal decisions. Some leaders, however, make more than their fair share of bad decisions. Although lack of information, low skills, and little experience contribute, this chapter has shown that stress is a major contributing factor, especially if the leader has a relatively low IQ and/or low emotional intelligence.

Yet we've now seen that all aspects of decision making are affected by stress at both the conscious and unconscious levels. Decision making is a systematic process, and all the parts interact. When stress increases, cognitive and emotional intelligences are compromised. Perception changes and in many cases becomes less accurate and more biased. This sets the stage for less effective Appraisal, which changes Motivation, and Motivation changes the Action. All of this can lead to leadership (and organizational) failure.

I have laid the foundation for the "what" and "why" of the stress effect. Now let's explore an important "how": How do we most effectively deal with stress and prevent it from short-circuiting good decision making? The answer may lie in increasing our capacity to manage stress.

6 Increasing Stress Management Capacity

We find that people's beliefs about their efficacy affect the sorts of choices they make in very significant ways. In particular, it affects their levels of motivation and perseverance in the face of obstacles. Most success requires persistent effort, so low self-efficacy becomes a self-limiting process. In order to succeed, people need a sense of self-efficacy, strung together with resilience to meet the inevitable obstacles and inequities of life.

ALBERT BANDURA

For almost two years, I had been training to lead a special operations team into combat. During those two years, I had successfully completed U.S. Army Ranger and Special Forces training and had become a member of the most elite military force in the world. When I got to base camp in Vietnam in 1968, I erected a six foot tall two-by-four board in the dirt and wrapped hemp rope around the top eight inches of the board to provide a striking surface. Every day in camp, I pounded the striking pad with my fists and my feet, continuing to improve my accuracy and power. I had been trained in Ranger and Special Forces hand-to-hand combat and had earned a black belt in the Korean martial art of tae kwon do. I had become an expert with all special operations weapons as well.

I quickly found myself deep inside enemy territory, leading my elite team of three Americans and four mercenaries on a classified mission.

Every human within a hundred miles was the enemy. The temperature was 110 degrees, and the humidity was 100 percent. The salt from our own perspiration constantly burned our eyes. Mosquitoes swarmed. Each of us carried thirty-five to forty pounds of ammunition, grenades, and water on our load-bearing harness and a seventy-five-pound rucksack on our back. No one wore an armored vest or a helmet because these would add too much extra weight and would be too hot. We were operating under triple-canopy jungle that allowed very little light to come through and no air movement. It rained every day; everything was wet. The bushes and the ground were covered with small leeches that began to move up and down frantically when they sensed our body heat, thinking they might have a meal soon. They attached themselves to us without our noticing them. The next day we would find them on our faces, chests, arms, and legs, filled with blood and the size of our thumbs. The physical and mental stress was very high.

This type of mission required complete silence. No talking for days, just hand and arm signals or notes. There could be absolutely no noise while moving. We were traveling along at a snail's pace of a hundred yards (the length of a football field) an hour. Every step and every foot placement were preplanned. Toe down first and then slowly the heel. This technique was designed to muffle the noise of any small branches that might be broken if we accidentally placed our weight on them. Each team member had an area of responsibility for maintaining vigilance as we moved. We were always looking for booby traps, ambushes, enemy personnel, poisonous snakes, and tigers—we couldn't forget the five hundred pound hungry tigers! We knew a large North Vietnamese Army force was very close to us; we just didn't know exactly where.

We spent most of the day moving up to the top of a ridge, one step at a time, without making a sound. Just as we neared the top, the point man signaled to us to halt and get down. He could hear a large group of enemy soldiers just over the ridge. Our hearts began to race and adrenaline spiked. Our seven-man team was about to come face to face with over a hundred highly trained North Vietnamese Army soldiers. Our stress levels soared, and our attention became focused. We knew everything could literally explode at any second. The closest help was an hour away. We could make no mistakes, and we could not be discovered.

I moved forward into a position to observe the enemy soldiers, who were less than forty yards down the other side of the ridge from our location. They appeared to have finished eating and were getting ready to move up the ridge toward our location. I signaled the team that we needed to move quickly. Although the ground was muddy, slippery, and steep, we tried to move as quickly and as quietly as possible. It was going to be very difficult to avoid contact with them, and contact would be deadly. I was about twenty feet behind the point man, moving deliberately, tightly gripping the handle of my CAR-15 submachine gun with my right hand while using my left hand to steady myself by grabbing bushes as I moved. It started to rain hard, making it even more difficult to get help if we were discovered.

We could hear the enemy talking on the other side of the ridge. Then, out of nowhere, I was hit so hard from the high side of the ridge that my weapon was knocked out of my hand, my feet left the ground, and I was falling backward down the side of the steep ridge. Instinctively, I grabbed my attacker as I fell and took him with me. My stress level was so high that all my hand-to-hand combat training automatically kicked in. As I tumbled down the incline in the rain and mud, I literally ripped my attacker "limb from limb," biting, pulling, and breaking any part I could get my hands on. I used every deadly move I knew and actually heard the sounds of bones breaking.

Although the entire event lasted only a few seconds, it appeared to pass in slow motion. A stream of thoughts and questions went through my mind. Where did this guy come from? How did I miss seeing him? Does he have a knife? How can I get my knife? Is he alone? Will he call his comrades before I can silence him?

Then it was over as quickly as it began. We were wedged hard against a large tree that stopped our tumble down the ridge. The impact momentarily knocked the breath out of me. The attacker was not moving; apparently I was the winner. All my hand-to-hand combat training had paid off!

Looking up the ridge, I saw some of my team members looking down at me with sheer horror and shock on their faces. *It must have been almost as terrifying for them as it was for me,* I thought. Everyone's life hung in the balance, but I had won the fight, *mano a mano.* I had saved the team!

As I began to untangle myself from my attacker, the world suddenly came back into focus. Now I had the same horror and shock on my face as my team members did: I had just used all my expert hand-to-hand combat techniques on a banana tree! In that part of the world, worms eat around the bottoms of banana trees, which weakens them and causes them to fall without warning. I was "lucky" enough to be in the right place at the right time to be blindsided by a falling banana tree.

Fortunately, two components to this event ultimately saved us. First, I was hit so hard and unexpectedly that my weapon was knocked out of my hand, preventing me from firing at the tree and giving away our position. Second, it was raining so hard that the enemy soldiers did not notice the commotion. We completed our mission and returned to Vietnam unharmed—except for my ego. I have heard, however, that banana trees in that part of the world still tremble at the mention of my name.

The Stress Resilient System:
Fitting the Pieces Together

Resilience is the ability to continue to move forward, even when encountering adversity. For me, back in Vietnam (banana tree aside), resilience would prove to be a powerful weapon for managing the nonstop stressors my teams and I faced. For leaders in high stakes, high stress situations, where decision making is everything, resilience is an extremely desirable quality.

Years ago a friend of mine was placed in a situation where his resilience as a leader made all the difference in the world. He took over as CEO of a large organization during a tumultuous time, when he had no choice but to embark on downsizing and store closings in order to save what business and jobs he could. It was a dark and difficult period for employees at all levels, but my friend stayed level-headed and persevered, encouraging and motivating workers to stay the course. The key was his realism. He did not act as if there were no worries; he told it like it was. But he did so with the confidence that at some point, the situation would improve. He and his workforce made it through the bad patch, and eventually he turned the organization around so that it was profitable once more. This is resilience: the ability to confront reality and find a way to persevere.

Figure 6.1 depicts how Stress Management Capacity, Cognitive Resilience, and Stress Resilient Emotional Intelligence all work in unison to reduce the likelihood of experiencing a catastrophic leadership failure. The three major components, depicted as circles, come together to form the Stress Resilient System, the subject of Chapters Six through Eight.

FIGURE 6.1 Stress Resilient
System Model

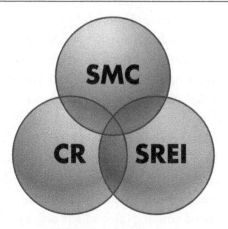

Note: Stress Management Capacity (SMC);
Cognitive Resilience (CR); Stress Resilient
Emotional Intelligence (SREI).

Building Stress Management Capacity

Adequate stress management capacity, which refers to the total ability the leader has to manage stress, is crucial for preventing the negative impact of stress on decision making. This capacity is finite because each leader has only a certain amount to draw on, and the amount varies from person to person. "Current ability" is the amount of stress management capacity a leader can access at a given time. If the leader's stress load exceeds this capacity, there will be a deleterious effect on the leader's cognitive and emotional performance, decision making, and, in many cases, his health.

Chronic stress is a constant drain on a leader's overall capacity. Accidentally leaving the car lights on begins to drain the car's battery. When the battery's charge is drained, the car will not have enough power to start the engine. Similarly, if chronic stress drains enough of a leader's capacity, she may not be able to cope with the next stressor, especially if it is major or if she is already near the crazy threshold (see Chapter Four for this threshold). Fortunately, the capacity to manage stress can be significantly improved for most leaders, teams, and organizations. One effective method is to "stretch" the comfort zone.

Life in the Comfort Zone: Highs and Lows

The comfort zone, introduced briefly in Chapter Four, defines the amount of stress a leader is comfortable working with. What happens when someone is working inside the zone? And what happens when she gets pushed out of the zone? That is, how much stress is enough to keep the leader motivated to perform well without being so high that it starts to have a negative effect on her overall performance?

There are at least three key components to the comfort zone: the top and bottom levels of stress the leader is comfortable with and the relationship between stress level and performance. Figure 6.2 shows the comfort zone band running horizontally and a performance graph running vertically. The comfort zone is bounded on the top by a line

FIGURE 6.2 Stress Level, Time, and the Comfort Zone

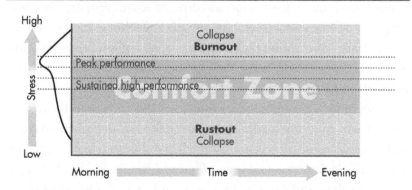

that indicates the maximum level of stress the leader is comfortable with on a sustained basis. If the leader experiences stress levels above this line for an extended period, the result will most likely be burnout.

The line just above the maximum comfort zone line indicates the maximum peak performance level of stress. This represents the maximum level of stress in relation to the leader's maximum performance. It might seem strange that working in a stressful environment can enhance leader performance, but as previously mentioned, within a certain range of intensity, stress is a motivating factor. Peak performance lies outside the comfort zone, indicating that a leader who operates in this area for an extended period of time will experience burnout. The leader will be able to perform at a higher level than by staying in the comfort zone but will not be able to sustain peak performance for very long. We take a closer look at this in the next section.

The further the leader moves into the burnout zone, the faster he will experience burnout. His performance, job satisfaction, interpersonal relationships, motivation, and health will begin to deteriorate. This typically results in the leader's changing his work habits, finding another job, or perhaps becoming a dysfunctional leader and increasing his likelihood of making bad decisions.

The lower edge of the comfort zone marks the lowest level of stress the leader is comfortable working with. If stress becomes low enough, the leader's motivation and drive to accomplish the work may drop to a dysfunctional level. The comfort zone model suggests that as long as leaders stay within their comfort zones, without dropping below the bottom edge of the zone, they should be able to operate within a comfortable level of stress.

Dropping below the comfort zone takes the leader into the rustout zone. There the leader will experience boredom, loss of motivation, and lowered sense of purpose. Initially, the leader may search for additional work, find a new sense of purpose for current work, or look outside work to find a use for his energy and passion. Operating in the rustout zone may be more harmful to the leader's health than operating in the burnout zone.

It is not uncommon that people who are strongly identified with their work find retirement stressful. They may even experience retirement as being in the rustout zone. Without the daily, weekly, and monthly goals provided by work, they become more susceptible to health issues such as heart attacks. There is substantial anecdotal and documented evidence of people dying within twelve months after retirement. For example, legendary football coach Paul "Bear" Bryant died less than a month after his final game and retirement from the University of Alabama.

In a study of Shell Oil employees, Shan Tsai, a researcher at Shell Health Services, found that people who retired at the age of fifty-five tended to die sooner after retirement than those who retired at the age of sixty-five. "This difference could not be attributed to the effects of gender, socioeconomic status, or calendar year of the study, although the poorer health status of some early retirees may play some part," notes Tsai.[1]

Tsai's study is just one of many; however, the jury is still out on the relationship between retirement and death. Other studies have produced opposite findings, suggesting a positive change in both stress and health after retirement. The findings vary perhaps because so much depends on an individual's attitude toward a particular work environment. In some cases, it seems likely that retiring from a dysfunctional organization would lower stress and increase overall well-being.

The "Peak": Hard to Maintain

The vertical graph on the left in Figure 6.2, showing the relationship between stress and performance, reveals a small peak starting at the upper limit of the comfort zone. This vertical graph is based on our observations and experience over the years and tends to support Peter Nixon's human function curve.[2] The peak suggests that a leader could operate at a higher performance level if his stress level were increased; but increasing his stress level to get a rise in performance takes him into the burnout zone. For short periods of time, this tradeoff might be worth it. Leaders regularly demonstrate the ability to create a performance surge when required to complete a project or overcome an obstacle. The surge comes at a cost, however: resources are consumed, and this can result in burnout or exhaustion. Einstein wrote his four critical papers, including his doctoral dissertation, over a four-week period in 1905. He was totally consumed during this time, hardly eating or sleeping. The results were phenomenal, but he spent the next two weeks in bed recovering. He had totally exhausted his physical and mental capacity and had to go into a recovery phase.

Extending the Comfort Zone:
Pushing at the Edges

The size of the comfort zone varies from person to person. Nevertheless, there seem to be consistent factors that influence its size. (We've discussed some of these concepts already, such as motivation and awareness. Others will be explored more fully as we work through this chapter.) These factors include *commitment* (the ability to feel deeply involved in the activities of life), *control* (the belief that you can control or influence stressful factors in your life), *motivation*, awareness, reality (the ability to confront it without distortion), sensitivity or reactivity to stressful situations, natural capacity for stress, coping strategies for stress, and finding meaning (having a greater purpose than coping with the immediate situations).

Like all other biological processes in the body, the comfort zone does not like change and attempts to maintain homeostasis. The most dramatic change that takes place inside the comfort zone occurs along the boundaries between comfort and burnout and between comfort and rustout. When a leader crosses into the burnout or the rustout zone, the change in physiological performance and behavior tends to be dramatic rather than slow and gradual. The easiest way to extend the comfort zone is to work along both the top and bottom edges of the zone, where it is most unstable. It's not hard to imagine working along the top edge near the burnout boundary, pushing one's self to the limit. However, leaders sometimes work along the bottom edge, just above burnout. For example, a colleague recently found herself unexpectedly without her laptop for nearly a week. She had limited Internet service and access to work files and was forced to slow her pace—and to think about becoming a Luddite. She was at the very bottom of her comfort zone and stressed that the work week would be lost. But then she turned to other ways to be productive: working the "old-fashioned way" and writing on hard copy and making phone calls instead of relying on email. Though she pushed at the lower boundaries by slowing down, she avoided total rustout because she still felt that she was being somewhat effective at work.

However, as with working at the very top of the zone, this is not a position anyone should maintain for long. You will either find yourself slowed down by all the "rust" that accumulates or by the exhaustion that accompanies burnout. The longer you stay below your comfort zone, the more difficult it is to break free from the rust and get moving again.

Stress Capacity and Decision Making

Imagine that a bucket holds the capacity available to a leader to apply toward managing stress. The bucket has resources flowing into it and a drain that allows capacity resources to flow out of the bottom of the bucket when needed. As long as there are enough resources (capacity) in the bucket to meet the demands, the comfort zone remains stable and the leader is able to manage stress.

Stress management capacity influences a leader's ability to make effective decisions. The higher the stress is, the more likely the leader is to be "pushed" out of the comfort zone and begin making less than optimal decisions. Let's look at a few situations where people are regularly forced out of their comfort zones, either on purpose or because that's what happens when they are on the job. With adequate training that increases their capacity for stress, they can function at a high level and make good decisions in tough situations.

Special Operations: Pushed to the Brink

I spent over ten years training and leading special operations forces in the U.S. military. Receiving a military qualification in special operations requires passing the qualification program for the particular service (U.S. Army Ranger or Special Forces, Navy SEAL, or Air Force Air Commando). For example, the U.S. Army Ranger school is sixty-one days of extreme mental and physical endurance conducted in three phases: the woodland terrain (Fort Benning, Georgia), the "mountain phase" (Dahlonega, Georgia), and the "Florida (swamp) phase" (Eglin Air Force Base, Florida). Students train approximately twenty hours per day, consume two or fewer meals per day (around 2,200 calories), sleep approximately three and a half hours per day (extra sleep is allowed prior to parachute jumps for safety reasons), and carry sixty to ninety pounds of combat gear while patrolling more than two hundred miles over various types of rugged terrain.

Students are pushed to the brink of physical and mental endurance and are tested each day, mentally and physically, on their ability to make tactically sound decisions. Each Ranger student has a "Ranger buddy." They are responsible for taking care of each other during the training—they share any morsel of food they find and keep each other awake, safe, focused, and motivated. Teamwork helps get them through the training. Never leave your Ranger buddy and never let your Ranger buddy get more than an arm's reach from his weapon. (All students use a "dummy cord" to attach their weapon to them so they cannot walk away from it—but by the mountain phase some manage to become separated.) By the time students get to the Florida phase they are beginning to hallucinate—my Ranger buddy kept seeing dogs, angry dogs.

When you get that tired and sleep deprived you find yourself in situations where the Ranger instructor is talking to you and, in what seems like the middle of his sentence he says, "Wake up, Ranger!" And you wonder who he is talking to. It couldn't be you. You have been standing in front of him the whole time. Ranger students learn to sleep standing up, as well as many other techniques for operating for long periods without sleep.

Needless to say, the graduation rate is low. For example, my Ranger class began with 248 students; only 75 of us received the coveted Ranger tab. Each special operations qualifying course has its own brand of physical and mental endurance requirements, focused on the type of military missions graduates will be required to accomplish when they join their special operations teams.

Navy SEAL (Sea, Air, Land) training extends across twenty-five weeks and incorporates extreme physical and mental demands on students (sailors), the first of which is to survive the training. Students receive extensive training on how to make quick, effective decisions under all types of situations, life and death. Building stress management capacity is crucial for the students to complete the course.

SEAL trainees learn four key techniques—self-talk, setting short-term goals, mental rehearsal, and arousal control—that teach them to survive and be successful, minute by minute, hour by hour, even when cold, tired, and sleep deprived. (The implementation of these four techniques increased the SEAL graduation rate from 25 percent to 33 percent.) A one-day goal is too long. Trainees must learn to live in the present. In general, leaders need to think beyond the present to be successful, particularly at higher role and complexity levels. In some high stress situations like special operations training, survival is the main goal, and this requires short-term thinking to complete the training.

As the sailors endure long runs and even longer swims in very cold water—they are always wet and cold—and complete myriad additional exercises, they use these techniques to get them through. During hell week, they endure a 120-hour exercise with less than four hours of sleep. The end result is a highly trained, skilled, and competent group of SEALs, equipped to do their jobs better than anyone else in the world. The effectiveness of SEAL training was demonstrated on April 12, 2009, when a SEAL team killed three Somali pirates and freed Captain Richard Phillips, captain of the American cargo ship *Maersk Alabama*, who had been held captive at gunpoint for five days in a life boat.

Special operations training is a laboratory for seeing just how far the human mind and body can be pushed and still function. Most students find their minds and bodies cannot meet the challenge of special operations training.

Air Traffic Controllers: The Need for Focus

The PFC is limited in how much information it can effectively track. Anything that distracts the PFC, such as a personal phone conversation, reduces a person's ability to focus on his primary task. In today's fast-paced environment, it takes only a second of distraction to create a catastrophe.

Air traffic controllers have an extremely stressful job, guiding aircraft around the sky with thousands of people's lives in their hands every day. One wrong decision can turn into a disaster. On August 13, 2009, while an air traffic controller at Teterboro Airport carried on a conversation about a dead cat, a small plane he was responsible for collided with a sightseeing helicopter over the Hudson River, killing all nine people aboard the two aircraft. No one will ever know whether the disaster would have been avoided if his mind had been focused on his area of responsibility—but it might have.

A similar incident occurred in Chatsworth, California, on September 12, 2008, when a train engineer who was sending and receiving text messages missed seeing a critical warning signal seconds before crashing into an oncoming train. Twenty-five people were killed and 135 injured in the worst U.S. train crash in fifteen years.[3]

Law Enforcement: Stress, Emotion, Danger

Law enforcement is a high stress job. Officers go to work every day not knowing if they will find themselves in a life-threatening situation. When the danger increases, stress increases and decisions become more automatic. When officers travel in pairs, they are more likely to receive complaints of excessive use of force than when operating alone. Anger, stress, and aggressive behavior are exacerbated when more than one officer is present. An officer traveling alone is more likely to slow down, think, and not rush in on a suspect. The emotion of fear makes him more risk averse.

When there are two or more officers, the emotion of fear transitions to anger, and aggressive behavior typically follows. Almost annually you see this played out on TV news. The news helicopter follows a high speed car chase, with what looks like every police car in the county in pursuit, until the car eventually crashes. Then all the officers who have been in pursuit jump out of their police cars and run to the driver—and every year or two, emotions are so high, they all physically attack the driver. Their PFCs have been emotionally hijacked.

Captain Justin Gregory, a police officer with the University of Georgia Campus Police and a fourteen-year veteran with the Athens–Clarke County Police Department, created, using his own time and money, a Use of Force Decision-Making Lab for training police officers on how to choose the "right" (and legal) level of force (a continuum, ranging from the act of talking on one end to deadly force on the other) to use in a variety of situations while under stress. One key difference in Gregory's Lab is that it has a series of simulations that require the officers to use their actual "Batman Belt" with all of their tools (pepper spray, baton, Taser, cuffs, and pistol).

Gregory's training is also "live fire"; the officers use their actual duty weapon to fire live ammunition, not a laser or paintball gun. This is more realistic and it raises the officers' stress level dramatically. A paintball or laser gun cannot compare to the adrenaline rush that comes from making a split-second decision to unholster a loaded weapon, take aim, pull the trigger, feel the recoil, hear the explosion, see the fireball and smoke, smell the burned powder, and almost instantly repeat the process and know that you have just sent two lethal bullets speeding toward a target. To add to the stress, officers are being evaluated on the appropriateness of their response and their combat firing technique. Having situations where the officers actually fire their weapons increases their stress level considerably, which supports the decision-making philosophy of training to make decisions in as near-real environments as possible.

On the Ropes: Leadership Reaction Courses

Fort Benning, Georgia, has one of the best leadership reaction courses in the world. The course, created by the U.S. Army for use by members of the military, is constructed as a series of events or obstacles that take place in "cubbyholes" built over a large pool of water. Each problem space is hidden by walls that prevent other teams from seeing how to negotiate a particular obstacle before arriving at the site.

When arriving at the cubbyhole, each team is given a quick briefing on its mission, materials, safety, and the amount of time to solve the problem. The teams quickly go into the problem-solving process, gathering information, examining the materials available to help negotiate the obstacle, creating a plan, and beginning to execute the plan. It is a fast-moving process full of deception and requires creative thinking, teamwork, and effective decision making.

The exercises are performed over water to help protect team members if they fall off the obstacle. In summer, the water helps to cool the teams on hot days. In winter, the cold water below adds additional stress as team members try to stay dry and warm.

Ropes courses, a similar concept, became popular in the 1990s with civilian and business groups. Team members negotiate various types of obstacles within short time limits, testing their ability to work together, apply creativity, and learn from failure. Ropes courses can be valuable tools for organizations seeking to help employees develop leadership skills as well as a sense of teamwork.

Capacity-Building Techniques:
From Stress to Relaxation

Training, learning, and practicing in high stress environments help build stress management capacity, as we've seen in the examples from the military and other fields. Navigating leadership reaction courses and going through rigorous physical training isn't just about "toughening up" physically and mentally; it's about learning to create a *dominant response hierarchy* in which a leader is equipped to choose the right course of Action when stress kicks in. (The concept of the dominant response hierarchy is explored more fully in Chapter Eight.)

In the business world, scrambling over high walls and racing through booby-trapped obstacle courses aren't the usual modes of career preparation. However, completing an M.B.A. and then working as a consultant for an organization like the McKinsey Company, which specializes in placing new consultants into fast-moving, demanding client teams surrounding high stress situations, provide an excellent training ground for gaining experience quickly. Interestingly, such education and work experience tests and develops the same leadership skills that are so desirable in the nonbusiness examples above. In other words, you don't actually have to experience "hell week" as a Navy SEAL might, though you may find yourself tested with another kind of hell week during the course of your career! But such examples are instructive.

Yet another example is a leader deciding to throw his body out of a perfectly good aircraft while in flight, definitely a high stress environment. In fact, just thinking about jumping out of an airplane raises most people's stress level.

The U.S. Army's Airborne School at Fort Benning, Georgia, is one of the best examples of building stress management capacity for a specific high stress task that I have personally experienced. "Jump school" is three weeks long, with an intense focus on one thing—getting students out of an aircraft while in flight and onto the ground safely. The first week is basic parachutist training, combined with intense physical exercise.

Students learn everything about a parachute—how to wear it, inspect it, sit in the aircraft with it, and get safely out the door of the aircraft—and they learn to be pros at executing the parachute landing fall (PLF). The PLF allows the parachutist to execute a controlled, seamless fall and roll that spreads the force of the impact with the ground along the side of the body.

The first week also introduces the students to the thirty-four-foot mock tower where jumpers practice exiting an aircraft in the correct body position, experiencing the sensation of "falling" and "counting."[4] (These are short bungee jumps.) The height of the tower was selected because it intensifies the psychological perception of height. The jumpers are slowly building confidence in their ability and overcoming any fear of heights.

Week 2 reinforces the first week's training, continues to be physical, and introduces more advanced training processes such as the swing landing trainer (a device that swings a jumper back and forth a few feet above the ground, then drops her to the ground), more PLFs, more tower jumps, practice recovering from being dragged by the wind, more emergency procedures practice, and a free-drop from a 250-foot tower. By now the students have practiced jumping and have heard the commands so many times that the whole process has become automatic. All the jumper needs now is to see a "green light" come on, and she will be moving toward and out the door. The jumpers have developed an automatic response (a dominant response hierarchy) for jumping out of an aircraft.

Week 3 is jump week. Training is over, and today is the real thing. So much excitement surrounds the first jump that the students are almost in a daze. They hear the roar of the engines and the wind going by the open doors at 150 miles per hour. They sense a slight smell of engine exhaust and the swaying and bouncing of the aircraft as the pilot fights against the updrafts and winds at a low altitude (1,200 feet) to keep the plane level and on track. When they near the drop zone, they hear and see the command from the jumpmaster to "get ready!" This command is followed by a series of others, but once the students hear "Get ready," the amygdala kicks in, and everything is automatic from that point on.

The jumpers form single lines on each side of the aircraft, pressed tightly against each other while performing equipment checks, static line checks, and struggling to keep their balance. Inside their brains, the chemical bath is in full swing as they get another shot of epinephrine (sending blood pressure up and triggering an aggressive response to get out the door) when they hear the next-to-last command: "Stand in the door!" The first person in each line moves into the door opening and assumes the "door position." All eyes are on the red lights over the doors, waiting for them to turn green. The lights turn green at the same time the jumpmaster shouts, "Go!" All the jumpers begin shouting "Go! Go! Go!" as they shuffle to the door. One by one the jumpers alternate going out the doors on each side of the plane, each one taking up a tight body position and starting to count, "one-one thousand, two-one thousand . . . "

From personal experience, I can say that when a jumper hits the slip stream (the air coming down the side of the aircraft), it knocks his socks off. Then, everything goes deathly silent. By the count of "four-one thousand," the jumper is suspended under the parachute canopy descending to the ground (or begins executing an emergency procedure). He executes a perfect PLF when he hits the ground, rolls up his parachute, and realizes he is on his way to becoming a qualified parachutist. As parachutists increase their number of jumps and experience, they also build stress management capacity that allows them to focus on the mission rather than be distracted by the jump.

The Importance of Training: Do It; Then Do It Again

Studies of how experts become experts indicate that becoming a world-class expert in a particular field requires approximately ten thousand hours of training. This equates to approximately twenty hours per day over a period of ten years. Experts tend to make decisions based on the intuitive rather than the rational strategy. Their knowledge and experience allow them to use the intuitive strategy, which in their case is much faster and more accurate than the rational strategy.

A novice in a particular field should use a rational strategy for decision making. In the rational strategy, the PFC follows a logical, structured process that allows the novice to think through his decisions. A novice does not have the knowledge, skill, or experience level required to make effective decisions intuitively.

If an expert is asked to describe the process he uses just prior to using that process, he might not be able to use the process as effectively. Making the process conscious for him may disrupt the automatic, unconscious flow of execution. If basketball legend Michael Jordan is asked to do a layup, he will do it perfectly. If he is asked to sit down and explain step by step how to do a layup, then get up and do one based on what he just said, he will probably find it much more difficult to do. He has executed layups so many times over the years that the "how-to" resides in his unconscious memory.

Experts build up massive knowledge bases around a particular area. This gives them more information and more previously successful solutions to draw from when making a decision than a novice. Their experience with the tasks also contributes to certain decisions having emotional somatic markers.[5] These "marked" decisions are primed and ready to come forth intuitively to solve a particular problem.

An abundance of information clearly shows that stress management capacity can be increased for most decision makers. Selye's general adaptation syndrome describes how a leader's system goes into shock when a stressor is encountered. Resources are marshaled to counter the stressor and develop resistance. If the stressor goes away before the resources have been expended, the leader returns to normal; otherwise, the leader moves into exhaustion.

In 1985, I adapted components of the general adaptation syndrome concept to train individuals, teams and organizations under the name StressTrain.[6] The idea was to intentionally stress a person, initiating a progression through the alarm and resistance stages. If adequate resources are provided during the resistance stage, it becomes the new norm. Once a person's stress capacity renorms, it is stressed again. During each cycle, the person declines in performance and then moves up to resistance. This cycle is repeated numerous times. Each iteration moves the person to a higher state of performance. This is analogous to what happens in weight training. As an athlete's muscles increase in strength, additional weight is added. The athlete becomes stronger each time the cycle of "stress and adapt" is repeated.

Overlearning helps build stress management capacity. The more times a leader can perform a task under the same conditions she will have to perform the task at work, the easier it will be to perform the task under stress. Michael Jordan has performed free throws, layups, and other moves so many times that the stress of the game has little impact on his performance.

Another technique for maintaining stress management capacity is rest. A tired brain does not perform well cognitively. It becomes confused easily, has difficulty focusing on the task, and loses its working memory. As the PFC becomes tired, emotions begin to take over, reducing stress management capacity. (Rest techniques are discussed in more detail in Chapter Nine.)

Risky Business: I Can Beat the Train—Almost!

Part of developing stress management capacity is having full access to the PFC, but unfortunately, the PFC is the last part of the brain to develop. Having an underdeveloped or immature PFC is similar to being stressed: a person under stress does not always make good decisions and tends to take more "dumb," uncalculated risks. The lack of maturity often exhibited by teenagers comes from the underdeveloped PFC and results in too many incidents like the following.

On July 9, 2009, in Canton Township, Michigan, one teen made a tragic decision. He thought he could go around the cars waiting at a railroad crossing, swerve around the crossing gate, and get across the track before the train reached the crossing. This would scare his four passengers and show how cool he was. Unfortunately, his flawed decision-making process resulted in the brutal deaths of five teenagers.[7]

Even under the best of circumstances, the young, not yet fully developed PFC can struggle to make the "right" decision. With the presence of others in the vehicle, teen drivers often make poor, sometimes deadly, decisions. Many parents of adolescents, teens, and those who are in their twenties who do risky things or make bad decisions (leaving an unlocked bike outside that is stolen, going to the ball game instead of studying for the big exam, not following up for a summer internship) get frustrated and admonish their kids, "Grow up!" It turns out that growing up involves maturing of the PFC, and that doesn't happen overnight. In fact, for most people, their PFCs do not fully mature until their late twenties or early thirties.

Many young leaders have PFCs that are still developing. (Research shows that in most people, the PFC continues to develop through the twenties and for some people into their thirties.) Former Bear Stearns CEO Jimmy Cayne turned a blind eye when $10 million was handed over to an inexperienced twenty-two-year-old employee to start a hedge fund. Risk led to more and bigger risks, and eventually the hedge fund imploded. This event played a pivotal role in the collapse of Bear Stearns. This isn't to say that young leaders can't do a fine job, but it's worth remembering that experience may not be the only thing they lack. A fully mature PFC may also be missing from the résumé.

Bubbles and Bubble Poppers: Start Small for a Big Boost

One technique I have used for many years for stress management is to think of stressors as bubbles that are pushing up your stress level (see Figure 6.3). If the bubbles push your stress level above your upper comfort zone limit, you will experience very high stress. To get your stress level back inside your comfort zone, you have to "pop" some of the bubbles. Most of the time people tend to try to reduce their biggest, most painful stressor (bubble) first. Not only do the big bubbles tend to be the most difficult to pop, but you are consuming so many resources trying to survive your overall high stress level that you do not have the ability to successfully overcome the biggest bubbles.

FIGURE 6.3 Bubble Model of Stress Management

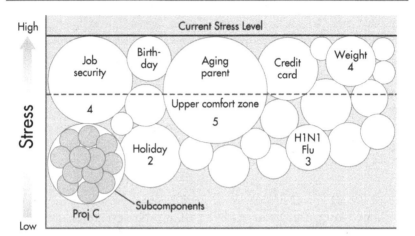

One strategy is to go after the smaller, easier-to-pop bubbles first. Each bubble popped, even small ones, reduces the overall stress level because all bubbles are exerting an upward force on your overall stress level. As your stress level starts going down, you will find it easier to deal with the larger bubbles. The objective is to get your stress level well within your comfort zone.

Each bubble represents a specific stressor. Most are chronic, but a few are acute and will pop on their own. Chronic stressors are difficult to pop and stick around for a while. Notice that all bubbles in Figure 6.3 are not the same size. The size of the bubble represents the magnitude of the stressor. The bubbles should be labeled as they are drawn and labeled as to their difficulty to pop. Figure 6.3 uses a scale of 1 to 5, with 5 being extremely difficult to pop.

Big bubbles are really combinations of smaller bubbles. A technique for attacking big bubbles is to go after the smaller bubbles that make up the big bubbles. This is known as the Swiss cheese approach—punching holes in the big bubble by popping its smaller bubbles. For example, a CEO told me that one of his biggest stressors (bubbles) was the number of key leaders he was losing during the economic crisis. He rated this bubble a 5 in difficulty. Our strategy was to break the big bubble down into smaller bubbles of recruiting, development, and retention, each of which was broken down into smaller bubbles. This allowed for creating plans to quickly begin popping some of the smaller bubbles. Once the plans were in place and working, his stress level began to drop.

Identifying your major stressors and using this model to visualize them makes it easier to identify stressors (bubbles) that you might be using as distracters from other stressors. There are times when you need a break from a powerful stressor and can use work or focus on another stressor to accomplish this. For example, when lack of sales is a major stressor, changing focus to a supply chain stressor can bring a welcome . relief, especially if it is a bubble that can be popped.

The bubble graph can be quickly hand drawn and labeled. (Some people do it mentally.) Once it's on paper and you can see it, plans emerge. Try it on work or personal stressors. You will be surprised at how effective it is at helping you reduce stress.

The Relaxation Response: Releasing Stress on Demand

In the 1960s, Herbert Benson discovered that the hypothalamus, which plays a significant role in the body's stress response, also produces a counterbalancing action that he named the *relaxation response*.[8] The relaxation response puts the body into a state of deep rest, essentially the opposite of the stress response. This state of relaxation tends to produce a decrease in metabolism, slowing of the heart rate, muscle relaxation, decreased blood pressure, and increased levels of nitric oxide. Benson also discovered that the relaxation response can be evoked on demand. That is, a leader can learn to generate a relaxation response whenever she feels excessive stress. This provides a relatively simple method for adding more resources to the stress capacity bucket.

According to the Benson-Henry Institute for Mind Body Medicine at Massachusetts General Hospital in Boston, the relaxation response can be completed in ten to twenty minutes and requires two essential steps: the repetition of a word, sound, phrase, prayer or muscular activity and the passive disregard of everyday thoughts that come to mind. Following is the general technique:[9]

1. Pick a focus word.
2. Sit quietly in a comfortable position.
3. Close your eyes.
4. Progressively relax the muscles, working from feet to head.
5. Breathe slowly saying your focus word (silently) as you exhale.
6. Assume a passive attitude.
7. Continue for ten to twenty minutes.
8. Do not stand immediately. Sit quietly for a few minutes, allowing a slow transition back to your surroundings.
9. Practice the technique once or twice daily.

Benson says that "repeated activation of the relaxation response can reverse sustained problems in the body and mend the internal wear and tear brought on by stress."[10] There is ample evidence to suggest that this technique will also increase stress management capacity.

The Takeaway on Stress Management Capacity

Stress is not just a nuisance designed to frustrate humans and shorten their lives. Quite the opposite. The purpose of stress is to help people increase their odds of survival by providing quicker response time, more alertness, and an ability to focus more narrowly on the environment. The trick is to keep stress as an ally, not an enemy. We've seen numerous examples in this chapter of individuals who are put into stressful situations for a purpose: when they truly find themselves under fire—whether it's in enemy territory or in the boardroom—they will be equipped with enough resources in their stress capacity bucket to react and to decide in a smart way.

Building stress management capacity, understanding how the comfort zone operates, and having the awareness and impulse control to use this knowledge can help leaders perform much more effectively by enabling better decision making.

Increasing your stress management capacity takes work; but it's worth it, because it means that you will always be armed with enough resources to cope with critical stressors. Unlike the car battery that gets drained of energy over time when the lights are left on too long, leaders with adequate resources facing stressor after stressor have the energy to face the next test. But in order for them to truly function at an optimal level, their stress management capacity must be strengthened with two additional key components which complete the triad of the stress resilient system. Chapter Seven describes how developing one of these, cognitive resilience, enables you to maintain access to your cognitive functions during high levels of stress.

7 Developing Cognitive Resilience

More than education, more than experience, more than training, a person's level of resilience will determine who succeeds and who fails. That's true in the cancer ward, it's true in the Olympics, and it's true in the boardroom.

DIANE COUTU

Viktor Frankl, an Austrian neurologist, psychiatrist, and founder of logotherapy, is best known as a Holocaust survivor.[1] Frankl was a successful neurologist and psychiatrist at the "suicide pavilion" of General Hospital in Vienna from 1937 to 1940 and was head of the neurological department of Rothschild Hospital from 1940 to 1942.

He married Tilly Grosser in 1941, and in 1943, he, his wife, and his parents were taken to concentration camps. In *Man's Search for Meaning*, which he wrote after he was freed from the death camp, Frankl gives example after example of his standing in line with hundreds of other victims waiting to be sorted into two groups. Each time he got to the front of the line, the German sitting at the table sent him to one group or the other. Each time he watched as the other group—the group that, for some mysterious reason, he had not been placed in—would be marched into the gas chambers. In the preface to *Man's Search for Meaning*, Gordon W. Allport says,

> As a long-time prisoner in bestial concentration camps he [Viktor Frankl] found himself stripped to naked existence. His father, mother, brother, and his wife died in camps or were sent to gas ovens, so that, excepting for his sister, his entire family perished in these camps. How could he—every possession lost, every value destroyed, suffering from hunger, cold and brutality, hourly expecting extermination—how could he find life worth preserving?[2]

Yet Frankl later wrote these words:

> There is nothing in the world, I venture to say, that would so effectively help one to survive even the worst conditions, as the knowledge that there is a meaning in one's life.[3]

In his story, Frankl tells of the turning point in his life. He began to think about life after the concentration camp, about giving lectures to the medical community after he was free. He began practicing these lectures with anyone who would listen. He continued to practice medicine by taking care of his fellow prisoners and helping people survive. In this way, he found meaning in his life. He wrote:

> Ultimately, man should not ask what the meaning of his life is, but rather he must recognize that it is he who is asked. In other words, each man is questioned by life; and he can only answer to life by answering for his own life; to life he can only respond by being responsible.[4]

Frankl was obviously a man of great intellect who was able to maintain a high level of cognitive functioning under the most horrible circumstances. He was able to bend when he had to bend, adapt when he had to adapt, and recover from an incredibly traumatic life experience. He reintegrated himself back into society and not only continued his work, but took it to new levels as a result of what he had learned about himself and others during the Holocaust. Frankl had an ability that allowed him to move beyond his dire circumstances: he possessed *resilience*.

In the preceding chapters, we saw the influence of stress on a leader's brain, decision making, and general overall performance. We also discussed how the Stress Resilient System (combining stress management capacity, cognitive resilience, and stress resilient emotional intelligence) can protect the decision-making process. Chapter Six focused on building stress management capacity—how to manage stress in general. This chapter examines resilience and developing cognitive resilience—the ability (resilience) to ward off the negative influences of stress on the cognitive aspects of decision making.

Resilience: The Core of Stress Management

The concept of resilience might bring to mind images of palm trees, cacti, crocodiles, and cockroaches—things that seem to survive extremes by bending, adapting, and recovering as much as possible wherever an opportunity presents itself. *Human resilience is similar and can be described as having the agility, strength, and flexibility to adapt effectively to sudden, enormous stress and change, and recover quickly.*[5] This definition is descriptive of Frankl's experience. He was able to bend, adapt, and successfully recover.

Diane Coutu wrote one of the most frequently searched *Harvard Business Review* articles on resilience.[6] Her studies led her to believe that resilience can be boiled down to three factors: facing down reality, the search for meaning, and ritualized ingenuity.

Facing down reality is about asking yourself, "Do I truly understand the reality of my situation? Am I ready to allow another version of reality to pass through my personal paradigm lens?" Can I see what I have been blocking out, especially when stressed? *My experience has been that to confront reality, I must know what reality is. My internal and external reality help shape my reality.*

No one exemplifies Coutu's *search for meaning* more than Viktor Frankl. She uses examples from Frankl's book to make her point that meaning is critical to being resilient. You must have some purpose greater than the immediate situation that motivates you to do whatever it takes to survive that situation.[7]

Ritualized ingenuity refers to being able to use whatever is at hand to help you survive your current situation. Recall Tom Hanks's character in the movie *Castaway*, stranded on a remote, deserted Pacific island for four years. Using a soccer ball and charcoal from the fire, he fashioned a "friend," Wilson, to have someone to talk to in order to keep from going crazy. The resilient person is always moving, innovating, and finding new ways to do things to improve his situation.

When Martha Stewart was convicted of making false statements during an insider trading investigation and sentenced to five months in prison and an additional five months of house arrest, the world seemed to divide into two camps: love her or hate her. No matter the camp chosen, no one can deny that this very savvy businesswoman and entrepreneur has resilience. Stewart, who handed out lemons to reporters, vowing to make lemonade, had this to say to Barbara Walters prior to her sentencing: "There are many, many good people who have gone to prison . . . look at Nelson Mandela." Stewart told a press conference, "I know I have a very tough five months ahead of me, but I understand, too, that I will get through those months knowing that I have the ability to return to my productive and normal life, my interesting work and future business opportunities."[8]

Following a two-and-a-half-year legal battle and serving time in 2004–2005, Stewart's popularity and bank account have continued to climb. In 2005, she made her first appearance on *Forbes* magazine's list of billionaires.

In his book *Good to Great*, Jim Collins coined the term "Stockdale paradox," which refers to the discovery Vice Admiral James B. Stockdale made during his almost eight years as a prisoner of war in North Vietnam.[9] As the senior ranking officer in the infamous Hoa Lo Camp, dubbed the "Hanoi Hilton," he was responsible for providing leadership and guidance to his fellow prisoners. One of the innovations he implemented was a tap code for communication. The code, similar to Morse code, allowed the POWs a clandestine way to communicate health status, questions, and answers among themselves and to get guidance from Stockdale.

When Collins asked Stockdale which POWs didn't make it out, Stockdale responded, "That's easy. The optimists." The optimists were the prisoners who believed and would say that the North Vietnamese were going to release the POWs by Christmas. When it did not happen by Christmas, they would say it was going to happen by Easter, then by Thanksgiving. Eventually the optimists would die of a "broken heart."

The solution according to Stockdale is that you must never confuse faith that you will prevail in the end—which you can never afford to lose—with the discipline to confront the most brutal facts of your current reality, whatever they may be.[10] (Optimism and Reality Testing are two of the EQ-i subscales and are related to resilience.)

Collins found that the leaders of the "great" companies in his study exhibited the characteristics Stockdale described: optimism blended with the ability to confront reality. Great leaders are optimists, but they also confront reality, even though it can be brutal to have to do so. The Stockdale paradox also supports Coutu's "facing down reality" component of resilience.

Elizabeth Edwards has experienced a significant number of tragedies in her life in the public eye and has shown amazing resilience. She is the wife of former U.S. Senator John Edwards, a one-time presidential hopeful. Her son Wade was killed in a car accident at the age of sixteen. She survived breast cancer (2004) and her husband's public infidelity. Since 2007 she has battled the return of breast cancer and continues to share messages of hope and courage with others. In her book, *Resilience: Reflections on the Burdens and Gifts of Facing Life's Adversities,* she inspires readers with her story of rebounding from setbacks and tragedy.[11]

Psychological Hardiness: The Scientific Foundation of Resilience

In the 1980s, I worked at the Center for Army Leadership at Fort Leavenworth, Kansas, as a subject matter expert on leadership and stress on the battlefield. In addition to teaching leadership to mid- to senior-level military officers, I conducted research on stress, taught classes on managing stress, and briefed military staffs from other countries, such as the British Army Staff, on how to extend human performance, particularly during stressful operations.

While working on how to extend human performance under stress, I came across Suzanne Kobasa's work on psychological hardiness. Kobasa, with her colleague Salvodore Maddi, conducted research suggesting that some people were much more resistant to the negative effects of stress than others. They referred to this ability to resist stress as *psychological hardiness*.[12]

Their initial research indicated that people high in psychological hardiness differed from people with low psychological hardiness in four primary ways: a stronger commitment to self, an attitude of vigorousness toward the environment, a sense of meaningfulness, and an internal sense of control. Continued research narrowed these differences to three factors:

- Commitment: the ability to feel deeply involved in life's activities
- Control: the belief that you can control or influence stressful events in your life
- Challenge: the anticipation of change as an exciting challenge for further development

Paul Bartone, a leading researcher on hardiness and resilience, created an assessment for measuring psychological hardiness.[13] A partial listing of the positive effects of psychological hardiness Bartone reported includes the following:

- More robust immune system responses to infection
- Better peripheral vision in football players
- Better decision making in police shoot–no-shoot scenarios
- Higher performance in rugby players
- Better retention rates among West Point cadets
- Success in the U.S. Army Special Forces selection course

Research on Kobasa and Maddi's psychological hardiness model has identified numerous connections among commitment, control and challenge, and stress management, health, and resilience. Mihaly Csikszentmihalyi's flow model, Viktor Frankl's logotherapy, and Diane Coutu's three resilience factors all have some overlap and close linkage to Kobasa and Maddi's model.[14]

Most people who study resilience agree on a core set of common factors: flexibility, adaptability, meaning, value, determination, strength, and recovery. Other factors affecting resilience can be divided into cognitive and emotional categories. Table 7.1 presents a way that I have found useful to think about resilience from both cognitive and emotional perspectives.

The comparison of cognitive and emotional functioning in Table 7.1 aligns with the types of functions associated cognitively with the PFC and emotionally with the limbic system. Information in this table is not intended to be exhaustive, but rather a starting point for thinking about how to enhance and maintain resilience, using these two perspectives as a starting point.

TABLE 7.1 Cognitive and Emotional Attributes of Resilience

Cognitive	Emotional
Think	Meaning
Plan	Personal value
Integrate	Commitment
Logic	Determination
Challenge	Energy
Innovation	Intuitive
Abstract reasoning	Self-esteem
Flexibility	Significance
Long term	Short term

Cognitive Resilience

Albert Einstein, one of the greatest minds in history, was known for his ability to sit in his chair for hours without getting up, engrossed in thinking and taking notes on a pad. He had the ability to block out his surroundings and totally focus on his thought processes.[15] This allowed him to use all of his cognitive resources without distraction for thinking.

One of the keys to human resilience in general and cognitive resilience in particular is awareness. Awareness allows a leader to know how well he is functioning cognitively. With this knowledge, he has the capability to make adjustments in areas where he is not functioning well. It would be impossible to monitor all of the cognitive functions of the brain and have any working memory left to use for decision making; therefore, awareness must be focused on those critical functions affecting cognitive ability.

The Cognitive Functioning Dashboard: Check Your Levels

The dashboard concept was popularized in the mid-1990s by Robert Kaplan and David Norton with their balanced scorecard process.[16] A dashboard (imagine the dashboard, or instrument panel, of a car) is designed to provide the most critical information about how well a process is functioning at a particular level and in real time. The captain of a cruise liner, for example, does not need to constantly monitor engine RPMs, temperature, or hundreds of other processes taking place on board the ship. Critical pieces of information might include location, speed, direction, estimated time of arrival, and weather along the route. If a problem occurs with any of these indicators, he will drill down to the next level of information, which is monitored on additional dashboards by the next level of crew below him.

The dashboard concept can be applied to monitoring cognitive resilience by identifying the most critical performance indicators involved in the cognitive aspects of resilience. The dashboard in Figure 7.1 shows the four critical indicators of cognitive resilience—*processing speed, information retrieval, available working memory,* and *planning*—and a rating for *overall* cognitive functioning that I have found to be key to monitoring cognitive functioning.

FIGURE 7.1 Cognitive Functioning Dashboard

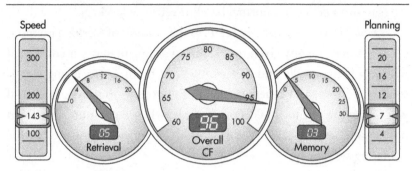

The idea here is to combine awareness with a mental dashboard that gives you a status update on how well you are functioning. How well you are performing varies from day to day as well as during the day. For instance, at work you may find yourself having difficulty following sales numbers being presented in a meeting so that you have to ask a colleague to repeat what she just said because you were not able to track it. Later in the day, you may be drawing a blank when someone asks you a question. On the way home, perhaps you are unable to remember what you are supposed to pick up at the grocery store. When things like this happen, it means your overall cognitive resilience is operating at a mid to low level. A quick mental evaluation using the cognitive functioning dashboard will allow you to identify where the major problem area may be. Identifying which of the four areas is suffering the most gives you the information to recover the lost ability.

Each leader's brain has a maximum processing speed that is related to the leader's cognitive intelligence. The faster she can process information required for making calculations and decisions, the stronger her ability to adapt will be. Keep in mind that as the leader's stress level increases, her ability to maintain processing speed decreases, as does her ability to adapt.

The speed, accuracy, and completeness of information retrieval determine how much of the leader's knowledge and experience can be accessed. Even under low stress levels, everything that has been learned or experienced is not retrievable (unless you have a photographic memory). When stress increases, however, the leader's retrieval ability tends to drop below her normal baseline retrieval level.

Available working memory refers to the amount of working memory a leader can use at any given time. Some working memory is consumed with just being awake and conscious. Your brain is processing sights, sounds, feelings, and other information, flooding your system even if you are trying not to think. For example, when a computer is on but not "doing" anything, some of its working memory is being used by the operating system.

Planning is about integrating information about the past, what is happening now, and what might happen in the future into an action sequence that can be used if certain events occur. For example, I can create a plan now for what to do in the event that a tornado occurs in the middle of the night. I could purchase a weather radio, store emergency supplies in the basement, keep a flashlight on the nightstand, and practice moving from the bedroom to the basement in the dark. If I have already developed contingency plans, I do not use valuable time and resources deciding what to do if the emergency occurs. Even if I am stressed, which I probably will be if I hear a tornado approaching, I only have to make simple, automatic decisions.

A cognitive functioning dashboard can be created using the four factors noted as the critical variables to provide feedback to a leader on how well he is doing in these different areas. (To build your own dashboard, visualize the illustration in Figure 7.1 with your own levels plugged in; some people even make a rough drawing of a dashboard and keep it handy until they get used to mentally "checking the dash" through visualization.) If he finds that his performance is dropping in any of the critical areas, he can implement predetermined actions to try to recover the lost ability. If his processing speed, for example, seems to be dropping rapidly, he can conduct a quick evaluation to determine whether he is allowing outside information and thoughts to interfere with his focus. If this is the case, he can put more emphasis on focusing on the task at hand.

**Stress and Cognitive Resilience: Protect What You Have;
Develop What You Don't Have**

The date is August 16, 2009, the final round of the Ninety-First Pro Golf
Association Championship. Tiger Woods, one of the best golfers ever
to play the game, has a commanding lead and is expected to win the
championship easily, adding to his impressive record. Sports columnist
Jay Mariotti describes what happened next:

> It was the moment that couldn't happen, the day [Tiger] Woods
> relinquished a 54-hole lead in a major, the one place in time when the
> greatest golfer of his generation—prepare yourself for what I'm about to
> drop here—CHOKED AWAY the 91st PGA Championship and let a
> hungrier, more focused, more composed golfer kick the stuffing out of him.
> His failure led to an epic milestone in the sport's history, the rise of
> Yong-Eun Yang as the first Asian-born player to win a major, with his
> native South Korea quivering in euphoric pride upon learning that their
> self-described "Average Joe," in an all-white outfit that smacked of a '70s
> disco king, outdueled the great Woods at Hazeltine National.[17]

How does this happen? How does someone like Tiger Woods with
legendary golfing skills, ability, and years of championship performance
under pressure suddenly self-destruct? If stress can find a small crack
in a leader's resilience armor, if it can get inside just a little and create
a small amount of doubt, bring what should be automatic behaviors
into consciousness, and make the leader begin to question and analyze
processes, he can literally watch himself spiral out of control. It's as
if he is watching someone else and has no control over the outcome;
the harder he tries, the more mistakes he makes. Maybe Woods was
distracted by events happening off the course.

Most of what Tiger Woods does during a golf tournament is
automatic, unconscious, and intuitive. The techniques and processes he
uses for the most part have been overlearned and require little or no
thinking once a tournament starts. He uses conscious thinking to assess
the lay of the green, the wind, and other environmental factors that have
an impact on how he performs a particular technique. The actual swing of

the club, for example, is automatic. The stakes are high in a professional golf tournament—not only a lot of money, but the golfer's reputation.

Even if a professional like Woods makes a mistake, his stress level increases dramatically. Allowing overlearned, unconscious processes into consciousness can result in a significant degradation of the decision-making process and potentially cause serious negative consequences. Thinking too much about how to execute a process can result in what is commonly called "choking." One of the problems with thinking too much about how to execute a process is that it leads to more mistakes. If Woods, for example, allows emotional, nongolf thoughts to invade his consciousness while he is trying to let his unconscious drive the process, it can be as harmful to his game as thinking about executing the golf technique. Soon he is in a downward spiral, similar to what Woods experienced on that Sunday afternoon in August. *Expert golfers like Tiger Woods need to execute, then think; novice golfers need to think, then execute.*

This book is about smart leaders making dumb decisions. As it is going to press, Tiger Woods is in the news again. This time not for choking on the golf course, but for making numerous "dumb" decisions off the course. It is alleged that Woods has been involved in a number of extramarital affairs. Since becoming a professional golfing sensation, Woods has lived in a high profile, high stress environment where access to almost anything he wanted (good or bad) was just a smart or dumb decision away.

Amy Arnsten, a professor in the Department of Neurobiology at the Yale University School of Medicine, refers to the inability to perform under stress as the "biology of being frazzled."[18] During one of Captain Sullenberger's interviews, he said, "The adrenaline rush shot straight through my heart. I had to block out everything except flying the plane."[19] Part of his resilience strategy was to block out his fear, all thoughts about the crash, all thoughts about the passengers, and all thoughts about dying. His focus had to be on finding a place to put the plane down safely and getting it there before he ran out of time. Total concentration and focus on the task at hand were paramount.

There is a saying that "the last thing that a fish discovers is water." Sometimes stress is so ubiquitous that it tends to be invisible. In some cases, the leader might choose not to acknowledge the stress and its impact on her performance.

Sometimes being put on the spot will have a negative impact on cognitive resilience. One of the cardinal rules for being a corporate trainer is, "Don't do math in public!" Even if you have outstanding math skills, when you are working a simple math problem on a flip chart in front of a group under time pressure, you may quickly be taken back in your mind to Mrs. Johnson's eighth grade algebra class where you had to factor equations on the board in front of the other students. Stress has just gone up, especially when one of your "classmates" points out a mistake. It's downhill from there as cognitive functioning deteriorates rapidly.

The PFC tends not to do math well even when it is not under stress. At High Performing Systems, we tell our trainers to put their math problems on a PowerPoint slide and animate it to bring in the answers that they have worked out in advance. A technique I use to "stress" research participants is to have them do math in public. For example, I might ask them to count backward (in public) by 17 from 1,000, making sure to let them know that they are responding too slowly and when they make mistakes. It is easy to overload the PFC, and the result is stress.

Sleep Loss: A Major Enemy of Cognitive Resilience

Sleep loss is one of the invisible stressors that people experience on a regular basis without realizing the impact it has on their cognitive functioning. Humans require a certain amount of sleep every day in order to regenerate and maintain their functionality. In addition, each leader has a personal requirement for sleep in order to function effectively. Part of awareness is learning how much sleep you require, the warning signs of not getting enough sleep, and the overall impact it has on your performance. The following are some examples of the impact of sleep loss on a leader's cognitive performance and decision making, sometimes with deadly consequences.

Pilots: Asleep at the Wheel—at 40,000 Feet

As a survivor of a military helicopter crash in my younger days, I've always felt a little anxiety when boarding any type of aircraft. In fact, people who know me often ask, "Since you don't like to fly and you don't like to wear neckties, why would you choose a career that requires you to do both?" I usually say that as I've gotten older, I am required to tolerate neckties less frequently. Until the last few years, however, flying has been a necessity for my career. Over the years, I have applied many of the techniques in this book to minimize my discomfort of flying. (I've made over one thousand parachute jumps, some in excess of 25,000 feet, logging over a thousand more takeoffs than landings.) But now, it seems, I need to be concerned not only about bird strikes but whether the pilots are awake!

The U.S. Federal Aviation Administration (FAA) has strict guidelines about the number of hours pilots can fly, as well as the number of hours of rest required prior to flying. It appears that in many cases, pilots are not getting enough sleep during their rest periods to remain awake while flying their aircraft. Even if they can manage to keep their eyes open, research indicates that lack of sleep will significantly decrease their cognitive functioning. In one of my sleep-loss studies, I found that twenty-year-old college students lost as much as 25 percent of their ability to do simple addition problems after twenty-four hours without sleep.[20] Flying a commercial airliner requires much more cognitive ability than simple math.

On June 4, 2008, an Air India plane flew 359 miles past its destination, Mumbai Airport. Air traffic control could not contact the pilots. It appears now that both had fallen asleep at the controls. On February 13, 2009, Go! Airlines Flight 1002 left Honolulu on a scheduled thirty-minute flight to Hilo. The plane overshot Hilo by fifteen miles, and the pilots were out of communication with air traffic controllers for twenty to twenty-five minutes. Eventually the plane turned around and landed without incident. Authorities suspect that both pilots fell asleep during the thirty-minute flight. They were later suspended from flying.

The National Transportation Safety Board has identified pilot fatigue as a factor in numerous crashes, including the February 13, 2009, Continental Flight 3407 crash near Buffalo, New York, that killed fifty people. The investigation of Flight 3407 brought to light the serious problems with pilots not getting enough sleep, especially with small airlines where pilot pay may be so low that pilots and first officers might need to have second jobs to support their families and often live in cities other than where their airlines are based. All of this adds up to tired, sleep-deprived pilots behind the controls.

Not getting enough sleep confuses the PFC and silently interferes with effective decision making. As part of a negative reinforcing loop, not only does lack of sleep cause stress, but stress also makes you sleepy, which can be particularly important to know if you are the pilot of an aircraft.

On October 21, 2009, Northwest Flight 188 with 144 passengers on board went silent for one hour and eighteen minutes while flying 150 miles past its intended Minneapolis destination. The pilots could not be raised on the radio, the White House Situation Room was notified, and National Guard jets were on standby to intercept the plane. The pilots claim they were "distracted" by working on their laptops. Who was flying the plane? These kinds of events seem to be occurring on a more frequent basis.

The FAA is currently reviewing proposals by pilots and airlines to allow pilots to take naps during the cruise portion of flights, citing that naps will improve pilot alertness during the more critical parts of the flights such as landings. Many pilots report that napping is already a common occurrence on longer flights. (Napping and guidelines are discussed in more detail in Chapter Nine.)

As I was talking to Jeff Parker, CEO of Airborne Tactical Advantage Company, about this incident, he pointed out the importance of situational awareness (think about the gorilla from Chapter Five). Jeff is also a jet fighter pilot and knows that a pilot must be aware of what's going on in and out of the cockpit—especially in Jeff's case where he regularly exceeds Mach 1 (the speed of sound) and has flown at Mach 1.85. The pilots of Northwest Flight 188 lost their licenses because of a lack, or even total disregard, of situational awareness. He also emphasized that maintaining situational awareness takes effort and diligence; it doesn't just appear. People who have a natural ability to sense their immediate surroundings, or natural situational awareness, have half the battle won; the rest becomes an exercise in task prioritization and continuous assignment of priority to the correct task at the correct time to maintain overall situational awareness.

Medical Interns: Sleepwalking While Treating Patients

Stories abound about the lack of sleep medical interns get. Given the current body of knowledge about the impacts of sleep loss, the increased level of stress resulting from sleep loss, and its negative impact on cognitive functioning and learning, it is surprising that the medical community, of all places, would tolerate the practice of sleep deprivation for interns or other employees. After all, these interns, and for that matter, nurses, provide medical attention for patients.

Vineet Arora, Emily Georgitis, James Woodruff, Holly Humphrey, and David Meltzer conducted a study at the University of Chicago of eighty-one medical interns from July 2003 to June 2005.[21] The purpose of the study was to determine if the Sleep, Alertness, and Fatigue Education in Residency (SAFER) program was effective in helping interns get the recommended amount of sleep. The results indicated that the SAFER program did not keep interns from becoming sleep deprived and, thus, risking their health and safe patient care. Lack of sleep is a continuing problem during both medical training and medical practice after graduation.

The medical community recognizes that lack of adequate sleep is an issue for interns and has established guidelines, such as requiring five hours of sleep after sixteen hours at work, well below the eight hours research says is required for effective cognitive functioning. But so far, evidence suggests that the medical authorities have not put teeth into an enforcement program. Arora's study found that despite the

Accreditation Council for Graduate Medical Education and the SAFER program residents continue to be sleep deprived.

Successfully completing medical school requires a high level of performance on the cognitive functioning dashboard components. Interns have been operating at a high level of fatigue during school and during their internships. Being an intern requires fast processing and retrieval of specific information from a large, complex database. Adding long shifts and heavy patient loads might not be the best way for interns to learn or to ensure the safety of their patients. Becoming a physician in this type of environment contributes to a belief that operating with little sleep and at a fast pace is acceptable.

Drivers: Sleeping, Speeding, Crashing
Studies and surveys conducted on the frequency with which people doze off while driving estimate that as many as 2.3 million drivers fall asleep behind the wheel of a moving vehicle each year. This number is probably very conservative. The number of fatalities each year linked to tiredness is continuing to climb. Estimates suggest that sleeping drivers may actually kill more people annually than drunk drivers do.

The National Highway Traffic Safety Administration conservatively estimates that 100,000 police-reported crashes are the direct result of driver fatigue each year. This results in an estimated 1,550 deaths, 71,000 injuries, and $12.5 billion in monetary losses. These figures may be the tip of the iceberg, since currently it is difficult to attribute crashes to sleepiness.[22]

A study by the Ford Motor Company found that a driver sleeping 2.5 seconds in a car traveling 70 mph covers the length of one football field (100 yards). This provides a significant opportunity for the driver to run off the road or, worse, cross into the lane of oncoming traffic.[23]

Stress and Sleep
It is not just sleep loss that makes you sleepy; stress does also. When I was a young soldier, I saw other parachutists sleeping on the plane as we flew toward the designated drop zone. The ride was noisy, bumpy, and crowded, and military parachutists, unlike sport parachutists, wear a lot of uncomfortable equipment. How these people could actually fall

asleep on a forty-five-minute flight to make a parachute jump, I could not understand!

Later, however, I discovered that one of the side effects of stress is sleepiness. Stress was making their bodies work harder and use more resources for several hours prior to making the parachute jump. Combine this with the physical exertion of putting on all that heavy equipment and standing for long periods of time in the hot sun, and it is easy to understand how a parachutist can be ready to sleep on a plane.[24]

Although the examples have been about pilots, drivers, and doctors, sleep loss affects all leaders and all cognitive tasks (and as Chapter Eight will show, emotional response). It's not just someone asleep at the wheel. It's also a sleep-deprived leader misreading financial data and then making a decision based on incorrectly processed information. It's a leader pulling long hours before a major presentation and then performing poorly at the crucial meeting with the board of directors. It's an exhausted leader in a decision-making role, with many other members of the organization depending on his abilities, who chooses poorly—and drags everyone down.

Measuring the Brain's Workload in Real Time

Neuroscientist Jason Augustyn, at the U.S. Army Natick Soldier Research Development and Engineering Center, has designed a device and process for measuring the brain's current cognition load—in other words, how much working memory is available and how much processing capacity the brain is using on a real-time basis. Augustyn's work falls under the heading of "augmented cognition": the use of computational technology to enhance human performance.

Augustyn's project uses functional near infrared spectroscopy (FNIR) to shine infrared light into the brain (PFC), where it measures the level of hemoglobin in the blood. Hemoglobin carries oxygen, and the higher the mental workload, the more oxygen is required to function properly. His FNIR sensors are being designed to fit inside a soldier's helmet and connect to a small computer that transmits the PFC's current workload back to the soldier's leader. As you can imagine, combat is extremely stressful and quickly overloads the entire brain. If a leader can have access to his soldiers' brain workload, it might enable him to help the soldiers make better decisions as well as help him deploy his soldiers more effectively.

Soldiers are placed in computer simulations where they have to perform tasks of varying complexity while their cognitive load is being measured. Performance is displayed on a dashboard, showing the overall workload on a dial that goes from zero to one hundred. Preliminary research suggests that when the soldier's workload reaches 80 percent, performance drops off rapidly. The work at Natick incorporates research presented in this book. The military is only beginning to discover the many uses for Augustyn's work.

Source: Augustyn, J. (2009, September 9). The future of combat, augmented cognition segment. *Popular Science.*

Developing, Enhancing, and Maintaining Cognitive Resilience

Numerous techniques can be used to develop cognitive resilience and we look here at some of the best ones. Keep in mind that it will require work to make these techniques part of your unconscious functioning. Leaders must always be aware of how well they are performing. This is why being able to "check the dash" is so important. By monitoring each of the dashboard areas—speed, retrieval, memory, and planning—leaders can apply appropriate techniques to improve performance whenever the levels need adjustment.

Maintain Your Awareness (Always at the Top of the List)

Being aware of cognitive functioning is one of the most important techniques for developing and sustaining cognitive resilience. Awareness begins with education to learn what awareness is, what processes should be monitored (the four dashboard areas), how the different levels of performance look and feel, and what happens when automatic processes move into consciousness. Awareness takes practice, practice, and more practice.

Have Respect for Rest and Recovery—Especially Sleep

Getting adequate sleep and rest are two critical steps in maintaining cognitive resilience. Situations requiring cognitive resilience are characterized by intense demands on cognitive, emotional, and physical resources. As has been shown in previous chapters, as fatigue increases, cognitive performance goes down. Even short power naps (discussed more in Chapter Nine) can significantly improve cognitive function. The rested mind performs much better cognitively than a fatigued mind.

Engage in Overlearning and Chunking

Overlearning happens when a process is repeated over and over until a neural superhighway has been built. Harry Chugani, a professor of neurology at Wayne State University Medical School, says, "Roads with the most traffic get widened. The ones that are rarely used fall into disrepair."[25] Once the superhighway has been built, that particular process becomes "procedural" and can be performed with little thought. As we saw in Chapter Two, Clive Wearing's ability to play the piano is based on procedural knowledge. His amnesia prevents him from doing anything from the past that he has to think about and remember. Procedural steps, however, take place unconsciously.

Michael Jordan's layup, Tiger Woods's golf swing, a military parachutist's jump process, and Admiral Stockdale's codes are examples of overlearned processes. Aside from being able to perform processes faster and more accurately, overlearning can take a complex set of knowledge, skills, and action sequences and convert them into one chunk. The PFC no longer has to use resources to think about and control all the steps in the chunked process. In most cases, the PFC has little to no involvement with the process.

Babies learn to roll over, get on their hands and knees, crawl, stand, take steps, and eventually walk. They become better walkers and are soon running as the individual tasks of walking become chunked and less conscious. Business leaders start at the Tactical level and work their way up as they learn what and how to chunk. This is one reason that experience is so valuable for a leader's development.

Once an overlearned process becomes a chunk, it can be streamed with other chunks, thereby greatly increasing conscious capacity. Consider, for example, this seemingly complex statement by the eminent scientist Stuart Kauffman:

> *If we should find the final theory—perhaps superstrings embedded in 10-dimensional space with 6 dimensions curled in on themselves, and the remaining 4 whipped into some topological foam of quantized space-time, allowing gravity and the other three forces to fit into one conceptual framework—if we should find the final theory, we should have only begun our task.*[26]

Kauffman streams together a series of information chunks into one statement. Granted, one must be knowledgeable about these particular chunks in order for his statement to make sense. The point is that by chunking information or processes, we can make decisions faster, more accurately, and more effectively—even under stress.

When Michael Jordan starts down the basketball court, everything becomes automatic. He sees the position of the players, openings, and patterns in an exceptionally fast-moving, dynamic landscape. If he had to use his PFC to process all that information and make the number of decisions he does during those few seconds, time would expire before he could move.

Overlearning is also a critical process for accelerating performance. Not only does it allow processes to be chunked, these chunks can now be moved into the unconscious, freeing up more room in working memory while significantly boosting the execution speed of the chunks. The unconscious is four times (or more) faster than consciousness.

Because military parachutists tend to be under a significant amount of stress when they jump out of an aircraft, the jump itself, and especially emergency procedures, need to be overlearned. Overlearning enables the parachutist to respond appropriately with minimum cognitive effort, even in an emergency.

When Admiral Stockdale was shot down in 1965, the U.S. military operated under a strict "Military Code of Conduct," of which Article 5 stated, *When questioned, should I become a prisoner of war, I am required to give name, rank, service number, and date of birth. I will evade answering further questions to the utmost of my ability. I will make no oral or written statements disloyal to my country and its allies or harmful to their cause.* It did not take Admiral Stockdale long to realize that in order to survive the brutal torture administered by the North Vietnamese guards, his fellow POWs needed permission to give more information than name, rank, service number, and date of birth *and* a process for selecting the information to share. Every person eventually succumbs to the pain of torture—either talk or die!

Stockdale developed a step-by-step system for responding to torture that would allow the enemy to stop the torture before the real information was revealed or the person died. This process consisted of short-term goals with general times, for example, "After x minutes you can say Y, then after x more minutes you can say Z." These short-term goals are similar to the goals in SEAL training described in Chapter Six. Short-term goals play a critical role in maintaining cognitive functioning in survival situations.

Use Performance Aids (Smart Leaders Use Idiot Lights)

An effective technique for maintaining cognitive resilience during stressful periods is the use of performance aids. The story goes that a young boy once asked Einstein for his phone number. Einstein replied to him that he did not know it; in fact, he never tried to remember things that he could look up. Einstein used performance aids.

A checklist is an example of a performance aid. Recall the US Airways Flight 1549 cockpit conversation between Captain Sullenberger and First Officer Skiles when they were completing the After Takeoff Checklist. Whether you are packing to go on vacation or a business trip, preparing to fly a plane or go into combat or running a business meeting, checklists are invaluable cognitive tools.

When Bill Treasurer hit the water at fifty miles per hour in his dive (see Chapter Four), he immediately began going down a mental checklist: *Arms? Check. Legs? Check.* He used a performance aid, a checklist that he had used so many times that it was automatic. The information gained from this checklist could mean the difference between living and dying if something had gone wrong, like a broken back, for example. Performance aids are critical in high stress situations.

Checklists can aid in problem solving, decision making, or remembering important dates. Today's smart phones make it easy to carry checklists for just about everything and add no noticeable weight to the phone. Checklists provide a method for ensuring that you go through a particular sequence in the right order without skipping steps. When the stress level goes up and there is more confusion in the PFC, having a checklist to follow really helps. Some insurance companies provide an accident checklist to carry in your vehicle that walks you through what to do in the event of an accident—they realize that accidents are not an everyday occurrence and that your stress level will be high even if you are not injured.

Have you ever wondered why cars have idiot lights built into their instrument panels? These are performance aids that provide information you need in case of a potential problem with the vehicle. In past years, cars had individual gauges for engine temperature, oil pressure, and battery charge. These gauges required you not only to look at them on a regular basis, but to know what an acceptable measurement was, adding an additional cognitive load to driving.

The inclusion of warning lights, such as the check engine light or oil pressure light, takes that additional cognitive load off the driver—unless a symbol appears on the instrument panel and you don't have a clue what it means! The lesson here is that you must practice using a checklist *before* the event occurs for it to be effective.

There are numerous types of warning lights and alarms in the cockpit of a commercial aircraft. After the bird strike, the US Airways Flight 1549 cockpit recording contained numerous alarms and warning sounds, especially as the aircraft got closer to impact. These audible performance aids were designed to provide Captain Sullenberger with critical information without requiring him to constantly watch the gauges.

Make Decisions in Advance

One of the abilities of the PFC is future planning. Planning ahead allows decisions to be made now that can be implemented in the future, as we saw earlier with the tornado emergency plan. Contingency plans are techniques for making and chunking a large number of decisions while in a low stress environment that can be quickly executed in high stress environments in the future. Table 7.2 shows a short list of preplanning topics that most leaders will face at some point in their lives.

A death in the immediate family is traumatic, and most families avoid talking about topics like death and, especially, final arrangements. When I was a teenager, two elderly sisters, Mrs. Montgomery and Miss Hunsinger, lived across the street from my family. They had moved in together after Mrs. Montgomery's husband died and Miss Hunsinger was recovering from a broken hip. As they grew older, a recurring conversation during my visits would be: "I told Pearl [Miss H.] we don't have much time left. We could go any day! She needs to get ready. I have

TABLE 7.2 Selected Preplanning and Performance Aids

Vehicle Accidents	Deaths	Neighbors
License number	Notification list	Phone number
Registration	Pastor	House key
Insurance	Funeral home	Travel plans
Fire/Burglar	**Funerals**	**Financial**
Alarm	Arrangements (now)	Bank accounts
Brief guests	Service desires	Investments
Safety plan	Donations	Insurance
Weather	**Wallet Cards**	**Business**
Radio	Emergency identification	Emergency work number
Flashlights	Allergies	Supervisor number
First aid	Who to call (contact)	Direct reports' numbers
Food and water	Emergency numbers	Emergency procedures
Medical Emergency	**Smart Phone**	**Family**
House address	Checklist	Social security number
Personal medical information	Phone numbers	Phone numbers
Insurance	Emergency information	Emergency information
Family doctor information	Speed dial	What to do
Medical history	Extra battery	Medical histories

picked out and paid for my casket and have my funeral service planned, including the songs and who will sing them. Pastor Smith will perform the service. I have finished [sewing] my burial dress, and I'm ready to go. Pearl, on the other hand, refuses to even talk about it. If she goes first, I'll have to figure out everything for her." In the background, Miss Hunsinger would be saying over and over, "I don't want to talk about it. Let's not talk about it now."

Mrs. Montgomery had chunked a set of difficult decisions several years before they had to be made. When she passed away, her plan was carried out automatically. Family members were spared the difficult process of making funeral arrangements—and Mrs. Montgomery got exactly what she wanted.

Table 7.2 lists both events and preplanning and performance aids to facilitate the decision-making process and take some of the load off the PFC. Decisions are made more accurately and efficiently using preplanning and performance aids. The biggest obstacle to using Table 7.2 is executing the decision to preplan and set up performance aids. It's like the story of five birds sitting on a limb. Two of the birds decide to fly to a neighboring tree. How many birds are left on the limb? The answer is five. The two birds only *decide* to fly to a neighboring tree; they did not execute their decision. The world is full of leaders who have decided but not executed their decisions.

Every year people die of heart attacks with a cell phone in their hand. Dialing 911 can be too complex when experiencing this level of stress. Put 911 on the speed dial of both your home and mobile phones as the number one! As trivial as this might sound, overlearning to speed dial 911 and say your location could be critical for your survival. If you have children at home, even toddlers, train them to dial 911. There are numerous stories every year of children as young as two calling 911 and saving a parent's life. Most of the mobile phones in the United States today send your phone coordinates to the local Public Safety Answering Point when you dial 911.

During the last few days of the final edit of this book, Haiti experienced a devastating earthquake that may have killed over 200,000 people and left millions of Haitians without homes or afraid to go inside the homes they have. Trying to get immediate rescue teams, food, water, and medical aid into the country has been difficult because of the single airport, no electricity in the beginning, and traffic jams in the air, on the ground, and in the streets. The government in Haiti has been ineffective at trying to organize the aid effort. Haiti is an example of an extremely stressful environment in which an army of individual heroes are making life and death decisions while sleep deprived, fatigued, and mentally and emotionally exhausted.

On a global level, Haiti shows again what happens when the world's leaders are not prepared to handle catastrophes on this scale. Leaders at all levels must be prepared for disasters and the ensuing high stress and chaos that follow. This type of preparation is LTG Honoré's calling and what he is dedicating the "second half" of his life to accomplishing.

Wake Up Your Brain with Novelty

When a task gets boring, cognitive resources begin to drain away. Novelty stimulates the brain's reticular activating system, the center of arousal and alertness, and helps a leader become more attentive to the task at hand. Just the act of getting up and walking around the room before sitting back down at the workstation will increase attention span by a small amount. Doing this for at least five minutes once every hour helps to stimulate blood flow. Some organizations have workers get up and swap jobs with other workers for thirty minutes to an hour so that they are actually performing a different task. This enhances their ability to remain alert and attentive in their work.

The Takeaway on Stress and Cognitive Resilience

Stress can significantly reduce cognitive ability and cognitive resilience. Table 7.3 presents a summary of techniques for maintaining cognitive functioning under stress in four critical areas. These techniques can be instrumental in the process of enhancing and sustaining cognitive

TABLE 7.3 Techniques for Maintaining Cognitive Functioning

Processing speed	Practice Repetition Get faster	Overlearning Awareness Feedback
Information retrieval	Practice/rehearsal Overlearn Mnemonics Performance aids	Divide tasks Double-check The critical few Feedback
Working memory	Avoid distractions Block out everything Chunk	Focus Only the critical few Feedback
Planning	Preplan KISS (Keep it simple, Stupid) War game Rehearse plans	Plan triggers Performance aids Overlearn Feedback

resilience. Using these techniques is not an easy task. It will require additional learning, training, practice, more practice, and the determination to use them until they become automatic.

Cognitive resilience is a powerful tool that enables leaders to resist the impact of stress on cognitive functioning. Two of the three components of the Stress Resilient System have been introduced and discussed. It is now time to put the last member of the triad, stress resilient emotional intelligence, into place. As we have consistently seen throughout this book, emotions play a major role in decision making; therefore, we need to find a way to protect them from high levels of stress. Chapter Eight takes us deeper into the world of emotions, emotional intelligence, stress, and resilience.

8 Building Stress Resilient Emotional Intelligence

*Emotional competence is the single most important personal quality
that each of us must develop and access to experience a breakthrough.
Only through managing our emotions can we access our intellect and
our technical competence. An emotionally competent person performs
better under pressure.*

DAVE LENNICK, EXECUTIVE VICE PRESIDENT, AMERICAN EXPRESS
FINANCIAL ADVISERS

I n the spring of 2003, the invasion into Iraq was moving at a hot,
dusty, and rapid pace, faster than the TV pundits and armchair
quarterbacks could imagine or understand. U.S. Army Captain
Chris Carter, commander of Alpha Company, 3rd Battalion, 7th Reg-
iment, 3rd Infantry Division, was leading his company toward its
objective.[1] Iraqi forces were firing machine guns, AK-47s, and barrages
of rocket-propelled grenades at his unit as they moved into position
to secure a bridge leading into the town of Al Hindiyah. It had been
a miracle that only one of Carter's armored vehicles had been hit
by a rocket-propelled grenade during their run to the objective. Alpha
Company's objective was to secure the near side of the bridge, inspect
the bridge for explosives, then move across and secure the far side of the
bridge—all while under heavy fire from the enemy on the far bank of
the river and the surrounding area.

The soldiers under Carter's command had been engaged in three
months of intense training while in Kuwait—training that was designed

to make as many aspects of combat as automatic as possible during their preparation to make this surge into Iraq. Now the time had arrived; Carter's men were ready to launch. Everyone was on an adrenaline high as they fought their way to the objective.

The adrenaline high is not the result of fear alone. Extreme excitement builds up during training and mission preparation. It is like the kickoff of the championship football game; the anticipation and excitement are beyond anything you can imagine if you haven't been there. There is such a rush from the experience that some soldiers become hooked on adrenaline—they essentially become adrenaline "junkies."

Upon arriving at the bridge, Carter deployed Alpha Company to protect its flanks and rear while engaging the enemy around his position and on the far bank of the river. While the battle was going on, a car began to cross the bridge from the other side, heading toward Alpha Company. The car was hit by enemy fire and exploded. An Iraqi woman could be seen lying on the bridge next to the burning car. It was not clear whether she had been a passenger in the car or a bystander who was wounded when the car exploded, but she was waving and calling for help, caught in the crossfire between the enemy and Carter's soldiers. After receiving a call about the situation, Captain Carter asked the platoon sergeant to keep an eye on her while he moved toward the bridge.

As Carter approached the bridge, the platoon sergeant reported that she was no longer waving and appeared to be dead. During this conversation, the enemy from the far-side bank continued to place heavy fire on Alpha Company and Carter's new position. Suddenly the woman began waving and calling for help again. Carter immediately made the decision that she must be moved from the bridge and taken to the rear for medical treatment. He asked for a few volunteers to go out onto the bridge with him to retrieve the wounded Iraqi civilian. He asked for volunteers because going out on the bridge was extremely dangerous. He immediately had more volunteers than he needed. He chose four and directed the driver of his Bradley Armored Fighting Vehicle to slowly move onto the bridge toward the woman.

The plan was for the rescue force to walk behind the Bradley, letting it provide armored cover for them. The back door of the Bradley was left open in case the rescue team began to receive overhead fire and needed to move quickly inside the Bradley for overhead protection. When the enemy saw the Bradley moving onto the bridge, they zeroed in on it. The bullets hit the Bradley like a hail storm, making loud metallic clanks and bouncing off. The hundreds of bullets missing the Bradley were making the unmistakable loud crack of a projectile traveling at supersonic speed.

Several other important concerns were in the back of Carter's mind while the rescue was under way. The bridge had not been inspected for explosives at this point. There was no way to know if it had been rigged to explode before Alpha Company could cross it. The enemy could detonate the explosives while Alpha Company was on the bridge, thus destroying the bridge and Alpha Company simultaneously, or the enemy could allow Alpha Company to cross the bridge and then destroy it, trapping Alpha Company on the far side with the enemy (it was not clear at this point if there was a much larger enemy force hiding on the far side).

Another important concern was that this appeared to be a relatively large Iraqi woman wearing the traditional burka, which covered her from head to toe. She could be booby-trapped with enough explosives to annihilate the entire rescue team when they got close to her. Carter was well aware of all of these.

The rescue team continued to move toward the wounded woman until they could see her clearly. They had her move around enough to convince Carter that she was not booby-trapped. (At this point in the war, explosive suicide vests, especially on women, were not much of a threat.) The Bradley provided cover while the rescue team moved her inside, and she was slowly transported back to a safe location, put into a medical vehicle, and transported to the rear.

The rescue team had voluntarily risked their lives to save an Iraqi woman. Morally it was the right thing to do in their minds. Even under the high level of stress, Captain Carter and his men made the right decision. When asked why they performed the rescue mission, every man, including Carter, had a rational explanation for their Actions. Listening to their stories, however, one can begin to hear an automatic, emotional decision-making strategy based on their value systems, somatic markers, and overtraining. (Damasio's somatic marker hypothesis, explained in Chapter Three, suggests that certain experiences become linked to specific emotions; when reminded of that event, a person will regenerate that emotional response.)

As Carter described to me what had happened that day, I could hear the excitement in his voice, as though he was crouching on the bridge once again. But he was also very humble about the whole experience and praised his men for what they did and God for protecting them. His story included the time dilation, tunneling, and audio exclusion experience that happens when time begins to slow down. Their focus narrowed to the woman on the bridge. The sounds of bullets hitting the Bradley or "cracking" as they flew past them disappeared. It became relatively quiet as they exposed themselves to enemy fire and recovered the Iraqi woman. In the high stress of a moment like this, the world becomes surreal.

Captain Carter talks about the event as just one of many that day—and every day during the surge into Iraq. Some were more exciting (stressful) than others; but when streamed together, his actions demonstrate highly developed stress management capacity, cognitive resilience, and stress resilient emotional intelligence.

Combat situations like the one Captain Carter and his soldiers experienced and those experienced by anyone else involved in combat are extreme tests of human resilience. Almost daily we are reminded of the heroic soldiers who were pushed so far out of their comfort zones that they did not have the resilience to recover. The highest casualty rates in any war are not physical; they are mental—and for the most part, invisible.

Stress Resilient Emotional Intelligence

The preceding two chapters focused on the stress management capacity and cognitive resilience components of the Stress Resilient System. This chapter examines the best practices for building the third component, stress resilient emotional intelligence (SREI)—*the ability to resist the negative influences of stress on the emotional aspects of decision making by flexing and adapting to sudden change.*

In Chapter Five, we briefly examined the impact of stress on emotional intelligence from a decision-making perspective. Now we will focus on what SREI is, its components, and techniques for building it. Stress has been shown to predispose the leader to experience negative emotions. Negative emotions in turn affect how leaders make decisions by changing what is Perceived, how it is Appraised, the resultant Motivation, and the ultimate Action or decision—the PAMA model. Building SREI is about protecting emotional intelligence from stress.

In several studies I conducted looking at the impact of stress on emotional intelligence, I found that as the stress level goes up, particularly toward the extreme level, people lose access to their emotional intelligence. To a significant degree, the leader's ability to manage emotions and behave in an emotionally intelligent manner is degraded. We have already determined that cognitive ability goes down as stress goes up. That is bad enough. Now we can see that access to a leader's full emotional intelligence ability is also reduced by an increase in stress. A simple and often overlooked fact is that when stress goes up, emotional intelligence drops.

People do not lose their emotional intelligence; they just cannot fully access what they have. Key aspects of emotional intelligence are the abilities to be aware of your own emotions and how they are affecting you, to control your emotions, to accurately assess other people's emotions, and to choose appropriate Actions to influence their behavior in a positive way. Here we have another reinforcing loop. As stress increases, cognitive intelligence goes down, which causes emotional intelligence to go down, which causes stress to increase, which causes cognitive ability to go down—you get the picture. The leader is in a downward spiral.

Stress temporarily takes away a leader's ability to Perceive accurately, thus causing him to interpret incorrectly his own and others' emotions. Armed with an incorrect assessment, the leader applies incorrect control and influence to his Actions. As a result, he does not behave in an emotionally intelligent manner.

Just before the executive meeting, Mark, the CEO, receives a report from the chief financial officer saying that for the second week in a row, the company's stock price has dropped 10 percent. The company is doing much worse than expected, even in the down market. Prior to the meeting, Mark is aware that his face feels flushed, he is angry and frustrated, and he is now experiencing fear over not knowing what to do about the falling stock price. Everyone is on time for the meeting except John, the chief marketing officer, who is habitually late to meetings.

When John enters the meeting fifteen minutes late, Mark immediately confronts him in front of the group. Mark's fear and anger turn to blaming John for the drop in stock prices. He charges that John's cavalier attitude, disregard for others, lack of customer focus, inability to control his salespeople, and disrespect for his peers have allowed the company to get into financial trouble. Mark's angry outburst at John is not characteristic of him. Everyone is shocked at Mark's behavior, including Mark himself.

As Mark's stress level mounted, he was pushed out of his comfort zone. As he approached the upper level of his comfort zone, he seemed to pick up speed, moving toward the crazy threshold. Suddenly his evil twin, Skippy, not Mark, is sitting at the head of the conference table in charge of the meeting. From Mark's perspective, it was like being an observer of the meeting. He could see himself racing toward the crazy threshold but seemed powerless to stop. He could hear the words coming out of his mouth but could not put on the brakes. The amygdala had sent Skippy out to take over the meeting.

There are numerous reasons why this happens. The PFC is the primary agent keeping emotions under control. As stress goes up, the PFC's ability to maintain control is degraded. In a sense, this leaves the amygdala in charge of the emotions, and the amygdala "enjoys" sending Skippy out to deal with the world. The result is not a pretty sight.

Stress changes the emotional landscape so that information coming into a person's system is Perceived differently than when the person is not stressed. We saw in the Diallo incident in Chapter Five that as the officers' stress levels went from normal to very high, their world became very small and tunnel-like, and their interpretation of the information coming from their senses was different from what would have been perceived in a low stress situation.

If Diallo had spoken to the officers or acted friendly and waited for the officers to come to him instead of running, their stress levels might have stayed in the midrange, enabling them to perceive Diallo as less of a threat. If Diallo and the officers had co-created a less stressful and more emotionally intelligent landscape, the outcome might have been different.

When SREI is being used, someone in the police car might say, "He does look suspicious, but let's all take a couple of deep breaths—remember our tactical breathing. He could be enjoying the night air." Sometimes if only one person in the group uses SREI, it can help manage everyone else's stress level. The fundamental rule all SCUBA divers learn to use in an underwater emergency is: *Stop. Breathe. Think.* This technique also works on the surface. It is a technique leaders at all levels need to know and use.

Behavioral contagion is a powerful effect. The brain contains mirror neurons that enable us to imitate behaviors we see, similar to the way our reflection in a mirror imitates our movements. When we see other people behaving in a particular manner, whether happy, sad, angry, or aggressive, the mirror neurons automatically encourage us to behave in the same way. If you are friendly to me, I'll be friendly back to you. If you are aggressive toward me, I'll respond in kind, especially if my stress level is high. Think about rush-hour traffic. Research shows that most people's stress level increases as soon as they enter traffic. The worse the traffic is, especially bumper-to-bumper and stop-and-go traffic, the higher the stress level soars. As numerous news reports have shown, increased stress can lead to road rage.

Recall the stress transfer model from Chapter Four. Now I'm in rush-hour traffic, my stress level oscillates from moderate to high. In fact, I'm stuck at the top of my last stress curve—like being stopped on top of a Ferris Wheel at an amusement park—except I am not amused. Now some idiot cuts me off. I blow the horn, throw up my hands, and make several expletive-type comments about the other driver's ancestors. Traffic is not moving, my stress is climbing into the very high zone—and Skippy is coming out.

Then I notice something out of the corner of my eye and think, "What is this *other* idiot next to me doing? Wow! She is an attractive young lady. What is she doing? Is she trying to signal me? She's smiling at me. I should smile back. Wait! What is she holding out her car's moon roof? Is that a teddy bear? It appears to be talking to me! How funny. If I'm going to be stuck in traffic, this isn't a bad place to be. I'm feeling better. What a nice person. I wonder if she does that to other stressed-out drivers like me?"

In this case, my mirror neurons picked up and imitated the positive, friendly, silly, de-stressing behavior of the other driver. However, mirror neurons also have a dark side that can be seen in mob behavior. The trick is to recognize when the dark side is pulling you toward it and use the stress management techniques from Chapter Six. You might consider digging out your old teddy bear (your mother probably still has it in a closet).

The woman with the teddy bear was Tricia Evert Welsh, one of High Performing Systems' senior consultants at the time. Tricia used her teddy bear and other techniques on the way to and from work each day to bring a little stress relief to those stuck in Atlanta traffic with her. She is now the CEO of Kideopolis and continues to reduce stress in people's lives through her work.

If building SREI was simple, everyone would be getting along: there would be no conflict, no wars, no starving people, no destruction of the planet. Everyone would be working together for the good of all humankind.

No Access: When Stress Blocks the Way to Emotional Intelligence

When you build SREI, some aspects of emotional intelligence may be left unprotected. Some emotions might be so strongly marked with negative outcomes that you do not take the time and energy to reprogram them.

These emotional areas are the Achilles' heel of your SREI and vary by individual. Each of us has built up an emotional system over our lifetime. Some people have phobias, for example, that they might never overcome. They must learn how to build containment around them by using the techniques in this book to reduce the negative impacts of stress.

In working with leaders over the years, I have observed their fluctuations in stress and the corresponding changes in emotional intelligence. Some leaders have higher stress management capacity than others, perhaps due to innateness, training, experience, or some other factor. To test these differences empirically, I administered the EQ-i, an emotional intelligence assessment, to a group of people who were in a non-stressed mindset. Later, they completed the assessment in a stressed mindset. I found a significant difference in the scores between the two administrations: same people, same assessment, but significantly different scores. The only difference between the two testing sessions was the level of stress. The high stress mind-set resulted in people scoring much lower on emotional intelligence than when they were not stressed.

When these participants were in a stressed condition, they responded differently to the questions on the assessment. They also validated that their responses were consistent with their actual behavior during stressful situations. When leaders are on the edge of the crazy threshold, it is difficult to apply the emotionally intelligent behavior they know they should be using. Even people who "teach" others about emotional intelligence find it extremely difficult to "practice what they preach" when their stress level is high.

Since the EQ-i is a self-report instrument, people report how they *think* they behave in different situations; consequently, it is possible that they might not be truthful in some cases. I also conducted a similar study using the Mayer-Salovey-Caruso Emotional Intelligence Test (MSCEIT).[2] This study was almost identical to the EQ-i study except the MSCEIT is an abilities test of emotional intelligence. Unlike the EQ-i self-report, the MSCEIT measures the ability to select the correct answer in a series of situations. One must identify the various emotions on faces and in pictures and demonstrate an understanding of how emotions form blends and how to apply emotional intelligence. I found the same drop in emotional intelligence ability between a normal and a stressed mindset using the MSCEIT as I found with the EQ-i.

The results suggest that a leader's total emotional intelligence changes under stress. If stress reduces access to the leader's full emotional intelligence ability, his behavior will become less emotionally intelligent. A safeguard against this loss of access to full emotional intelligence ability is to build SREI.

Stress resilient emotional intelligence helps leaders maintain emotionally intelligent behavior even when situations become stressful. A leader with high SREI can keep his value system and morals intact even under high stress levels. Under the stress of combat, Captain Carter's moral system not only knew that the right thing to do was to retrieve the Iraqi woman from the bridge, but enabled him to act on his values at great risk to his own life.

From the opening example, it is evident that Chris Carter is a leader with a high level of stress management capacity, cognitive resilience, and SREI. The supervisors, peers, and soldiers under his command, as well as his family and friends, have watched him demonstrate the power of his Stress Resilient System numerous times. Whether on the battlefield or in his personal life, Captain Carter exemplifies what true leadership is all about.

India-born Indra Nooyi is the chairman and CEO of soft drink giant PepsiCo. She is known for being a savvy deal maker and negotiator. Nooyi promotes the concept of "performance with purpose" and is leading changes to make Pepsi more socially responsible as well as to expand healthy food offerings. In 2009 she was ranked number 3 by *Forbes* magazine in its annual list of the 100 Most Powerful Women.

Making tough decisions is part of her job. In October 2008, PepsiCo cut over three thousand employees globally as part of the company's efforts to restructure in the face of an impending downturn. "While we can't control the macro economic situation, we can enhance PepsiCo's operating agility to respond to the changing environment," she said in a statement.[3]

She is not only a bright and values-driven leader, but also demonstrates a high level of emotional intelligence, especially empathy. In April 2009, in an interview with India news agency Rediff, Nooyi went on to say, "To me it was not 3,000 heads, but 3,000 families whose lives would be impacted by the decision. It was a very, very painful decision and the most difficult decision to make in the past five or six years."

Nooyi was named 2009 CEO of the Year by the Global Supply Chain Leaders Group for her contributions, which include promoting and supporting socially responsible business practices.

Must-Have Components of SREI

As with cognitive resilience, several key components seem to drive a leader's ability to have Stress Resilient Emotional Intelligence. A number of them could be included on this list. The following are those I have found to be the most important.

Awareness: Look for Early Warning Signs
Awareness is a ubiquitous factor that makes repeat appearances on any list of important stress resilience components and plays a significant role in SREI. Knowing what is happening to affect the brain, body, and behavior gives a leader necessary feedback to interpret his current functioning and make decisions on which corrective actions to take to optimize SREI. (This is why this book contains so much scientific information on brain function; having such knowledge is part of having awareness.)

Captain Sullenberger was aware of the adrenaline that shot through his heart. This information alerted him to his dangerous situation and triggered a "marked" response that told him to "block out everything not critical to quickly finding the safest place to put the plane down": block out the fear, but maintain a sense of urgency. Jimmy Cayne's self-admitted response to his awareness that Bear Stearns was failing rapidly was to continue to play bridge and cash in a large amount of his stock. Cayne's responses are indicative of a leader with low SREI.

The brain and the body are like a car. When something is not right, they turn on idiot lights to create awareness of a problem. Being aware of what is happening in your brain and body can warn you early on of a pending problem. Signals such as elevated blood pressure, difficulty with cognitive tasks, difficulty tracking conversations, avoiding meetings, and putting off decisions are the warning lights that give you an opportunity to take action before it is too late—provided that you see them.

Somatic Markers: Understand What's Behind Your Responses

Somatic marking primes the emotional system to respond quickly to perceived events. These responses are normally so fast you don't realize that decisions have been made and options eliminated. When the human resources manager tells you he would like to move Barry to the Jacksonville office, your immediate response is, "Jacksonville would not be a good fit for Barry. Let's leave him where he is." Because your response was so quick, you were unaware of the almost instant and unconscious decision-making processes going on simultaneously: *I don't like Barry, and Jacksonville is a great assignment for someone wanting to move up in the organization. I don't want Barry to get that chance. He will make a better contribution to the company where he is now.* You are aware of only the response you voiced, not the marked emotion (personal dislike of Barry) behind it. And once you said it, you created a rationale for your decision that most likely has no relationship to the intuitive, somatically marked decision-making process that was actually used.

Somatic markers can't be discussed without returning to the topic of awareness. Awareness can be a powerful tool to help identify situations in which decisions are made by somatically marked events in the unconscious.

Response Hierarchy: Why You Respond to High Stress the Way You Do

Somatic marking contributes to establishing a response hierarchy. As stress increases, our responses become more automatic. Making decisions and executing behaviors automatically require some type of ordering of the responses to the situations. For example, if someone suddenly flicks a hand toward your eyes, your instinctive reflex is to blink or close your eyes. If each time something came toward your eyes, instead of closing them, your mouth flew open or you put your hand on your stomach, you would probably sustain eye injuries—and swallow a lot of bugs. The brain is prewired with a set of survival instincts.

In the banana tree example in Chapter Six, I was operating in a hypervigilant state when "attacked" by the banana tree. My response to the attack was instantaneous with the impact of the tree. Unconsciously, I knew this was a life-or-death situation requiring hand-to-hand combat. My amygdala triggered the dominant (top) response in my response hierarchy as an immediate response to the threat. As I mentioned in the story, had my weapon not been knocked out of my hand, my dominant response would have been to shoot the attacker—a very inappropriate response given that the attacker was a tree.

Our thoughts and behavior reflexes come about through connecting information and behavior (the Perception-Appraisal-Motivation-Action model) across time. Somatic marking makes these connections and significantly speeds up processing time, because once marked, decisions are already made (like the blink); they just need to Perceive the Stimulus.

Across time we build a dominant response hierarchy that we use in decision making. Under low stress, we have more flexibility to override some automatic decisions. As stress increases, the dominant response hierarchy takes over. The higher the stress, the fewer the number of response options are available. Whatever is at the top of the hierarchy—the option most strongly marked—becomes "the" option. For most people, seeing a snake near their feet evokes a startled response that causes them to jump quickly backward and away from the snake. Sometimes the jump is accompanied by colorful language. In the case of snakes, this response is already marked at the top of the hierarchy. This response can be replaced, however, if you decide to become a herpetologist (people who specialize in working with amphibians and reptiles, such as snakes) and are willing to put forth the effort to change it. If this strongly marked response to snakes can be replaced in the hierarchy, a leader should be able to replace almost any response with one more appropriate to her needs. This will be covered in more detail below.

Performance Indicators: Check the Dashboard and Recalibrate
The dashboard concept can be applied to SREI by identifying the most critical performance indicators concerning the emotional aspects of resilience. One such dashboard is shown in Figure 8.1. There are four critical factors to be aware of and monitor at this level: *energy, mood, time focus,* and *control.* The combination of these factors produces an overall emotional functioning rating.

Energy is about the leader's energy level, excitement, and enthusiasm for daily challenges and the work she is doing. This is not necessarily characterized by jump-up-and-shout, high-five, expressive, talkative behavior. Leaders with introverted personality preferences, for example, might be doing cartwheels on the inside while appearing very calm on the outside. This is similar to the duck on the pond: on the surface, it appears to be just floating along, but under the surface, its feet are paddling like crazy. Energy is a driving force, and without it, the leader will soon give in to stress.

Mood represents a combination of emotions (happy, sad) and feelings (depressed, optimistic) that creates a lasting state. For example, a leader in an optimistic mood tends to remain optimistic over a period of time. Minor setbacks tend not to cause large swings in mood. If

FIGURE 8.1 Emotional Functioning Dashboard

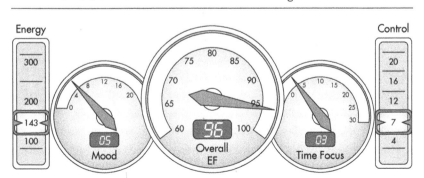

a leader does experience large, frequent mood changes, it might be indicative of a need for professional help.

Time focus is strongly influenced by the PFC-amygdala balance. The PFC prefers to look at the big picture and the long term, while the amygdala is myopic and looks at right now. The shorter the time focus, the more emotions are driving decisions. This puts the leader at risk for emotions to hijack the PFC.

Control gives an indication of emotional stability. The more that emotions take over consciousness, the more out of control and fearful the leader feels. As long as there is a good balance of cognitive and emotional functioning, the leader will feel in control of the present and the future.

An emotional functioning dashboard can be created using these four factors as the critical variables that will provide feedback as to how well the leader is doing in these different areas. (As I suggested in the previous chapter, you may visualize it based on the illustration in Figure 8.1 or make a rough drawing to refer to until you fix it in your mind.) If performance is dropping off in any one or more of the critical areas, predetermined Actions can be taken to try to recover lost ability. If energy, for example, seems to be dropping off rapidly, the leader can do a quick evaluation to determine the source of the energy drain. Then the leader can put more emphasis on preventing the drain.

Building Stress Resilient Emotional Intelligence

While techniques can be used to build SREI, the bottom line is it takes skill and effort to make these techniques part of your unconscious functioning in stressful situations. Because we cannot see inside the unconscious, it is difficult to control what goes on there. Learning to control the unconscious is like learning to fish for bass with a plastic worm. Imagine that you have a boat, rod and reel, fishing line with a hook at the end, and a plastic worm for bait on the hook. There is a lake and, you hope, some hungry and not-too-smart bass. The outcome you want is to get the bass in the boat.

The lake is like the unconscious. You cannot see what is in it, only what comes out of it. When you cast your plastic worm out as far as you can and let it sink below the water's surface, you can no longer see the worm, but you still have to move it through the water near the bottom of the lake (that you cannot see) in a lifelike fashion to trick a bass into believing it is real. At the same time, you are trying not to hang the hook (with the worm on it) on tree limbs, stumps, or whatever else is down there. Since you cannot see anything, you have to imagine what is going on under the water and be aware of any signals you receive and interpret them. "Do the bass see the worm? Are they laughing? What kind of decision strategy do bass use?"

Suddenly you feel a slight tap on the line. Did the worm bump into a tree limb or stump? You feel another "tap, tap" and decide to jerk really hard to try to set the hook, just in case the tap was a signal (like Stockdale's codes) from a bass that it has the worm and hook in its mouth. With practice you will learn to distinguish a "stump tap" from a "bass tap." The line does not give. In fact, it is going away from you. You have a bass! Now you have to get it into the boat without losing it.

Working with the unconscious is similar to bass fishing. You prepare what you are putting into the unconscious so you can get out of it what you want. For example, you work to create a particular emotional response in your dominant response hierarchy for certain events. You receive "taps" throughout the day alerting you that something is going on "in there." Knowing how to create or suppress the right response at the right time takes practice and awareness. You must learn to read those taps and be aware at all times.

Awareness (It's Still Number One)

Leaders must always be aware of how well they are functioning in the different SREI areas and using appropriate techniques. Being aware of emotional functioning is a critical piece in decision making and sustaining SREI. Awareness begins with learning what SREI is, what processes should be monitored, how different levels of performance look and feel, and what happens when automatic processes move into consciousness. Like fishing for bass with a plastic worm, awareness takes practice.

Thinking About Emotions: How Do You Really Feel? (Be Honest)

Another technique for building SREI is thinking about emotions, which requires leaders to step back from what they are experiencing and identify their current emotions and feelings. Stepping back initiates a change in perspective from being "had by emotions" to "having emotions," which gives the leader the ability to extract emotional information. If emotions are, as Damasio believes, conduits of information between the body and the brain that provide a current status report on the body, then thinking about emotions provides a process for gathering information and reengaging the PFC.

Monitoring Emotional Sensations and Physiological Responses: "Tap" In

Emotions, visceral sensations, and physiological responses are linked. Each emotion has a characteristic set of sensations and physiological responses. Anger, for example, is accompanied by flushed skin, increased energy, and specific facial expressions. It is not uncommon for others to notice a leader's physical symptoms of emotions before he does. I used to conduct interviews of college scholarship applicants, a process that they seemed to find somewhat stressful. They would quickly exhibit symptoms such as perspiration, blotches on their necks, eye twitches, and a pulsing vein at their temples, among others. These are examples of "taps" that leaders can use to evaluate their own and others' stress level and its impact on decision making and then use this information to determine the appropriate intervention.

Rest and Recovery—Especially Sleep: Don't Skimp on It

Research linking emotions and sleep continues to mount. Getting adequate sleep and rest are two critical steps in maintaining SREI. One of the characteristics of situations requiring SREI is the intense demands on emotional and physical resources. As has been shown in previous chapters, as fatigue mounts, emotional performance goes down.

The National Training Laboratories Institute T-group sessions of the 1960s and 1970s used lack of sleep and fatigue to "free the emotions."[4]

Tired, sleepy people find it difficult to control their emotions and, consequently, tend to speak and behave emotionally in ways they would not under rested circumstances. A technique for working with a team in conflict is to deprive the team of sleep a little to make it easier for team members to have the difficult discussions, usually involving emotions, that the team normally tries to avoid.[5] Leaders should learn to recognize their primary emotions, their most common emotional blends, and the symptoms of these emotions and to use appropriate interventions.

To "sleep deprive" here refers to working the team into the evening until around midnight or later. On the second evening, the effects of sleep loss on the team members will become evident as they find it easier to express their feelings about the team and interpersonal issues they may be experiencing. Only a trainer with a lot of experience facilitating conflict in teams should use this technique.

Rest also includes vacations, breaks, walks, and other activities that give the brain and emotions a rest from work or other stressful activities. Leaders must always be aware of when they need to rest and do it! All high performing systems need downtime to regenerate, and leaders are no exception. Numerous historical leaders have been famous for napping. For example, Napoleon was famous for sleeping very little at night and taking several twenty-minute naps during the day. (More details on napping are presented in Chapter Nine.) The old saying that sometimes you have to go slow to go fast certainly applies to rest. Decisions made when a leader is overly tired tend to be poor ones. As paradoxical as it might seem, taking the time to rest can actually speed up the overall process.

Performance Aids: Find What Works for You

Performance aids for cognitive resilience were discussed in detail in Chapter Seven. The same concept applies with SREI. Any aid that can assist in maintaining control of the emotions, focusing emotions in a positive manner, and using the information emotions provide will help to develop and maintain SREI.

SREI performance aids can be grouped into at least two categories: emotional control aids and emotional intelligence aids. Like their name implies, emotional control aids focus on keeping emotions under control. The first column in Table 8.1 lists examples of aids in this category. They help keep emotions under control by providing reminders, logical speed bumps, musical interludes, and monitoring techniques. The last item on the list, ARSENAL, represents the seven best practices for developing all three components of the stress resilient system and will be presented in detail in Chapter Nine.

The emotional intelligence performance aids assist with managing and enhancing emotionally intelligent behavior under stress and include checklists, awareness, feedback, working with others, ARSENAL, exploiting emotional intelligence strengths, and containing weaknesses.

Richard Boyatzis and Annie McKee suggest in their book *Resonate Leadership* that it takes more than just "rest and relaxation" to sustain emotional resilience. They suggest that rest must be supplemented with

TABLE 8.1 SREI Performance Aids

Emotional Control	Emotional Intelligence Enhancement
Pocket cards	Headphones
Screensavers	Physical location
PDA reminders	Dashboard
Breathing steps	Training
Math exercises	Partner
Puzzles	Containment
PDA games	Exploitation
Music	ARSENAL
Biofeedback	
Dashboard	
ARSENAL	

actions such as openness, curiosity, and helping others. What they call resonant leaders utilize these behaviors to sustain emotional resilience.

Training: Bring in the Pros

Leaders learn SREI through experience, and training can jump start the development of SREI. A training program for SREI must include opportunities for leaders to experience emotions, not just read about them. The overlearning techniques discussed in Chapter Seven must be used. Emotions sneak up on you because they form in the unconscious. By the time you realize an emotion "has you," it already has momentum and is difficult to manage. Building an unconscious emotional control center through quality experiential training allows you to exert control before you experience the full effects. Like great bass fishers know, you have to learn how to control the plastic worm in a world you can't see.

Desensitization: Overcome Your Fears

Desensitization is about bringing powerful emotional responses under control while in low-stress environments. The example of training parachutists involves a desensitization of fear associated with the dangers of making military parachute jumps. Joining Toastmasters is an excellent way for young leaders to overcome their fear of public speaking and develop their skills. Similarly, allowing young leaders to attend high-level management meetings and give presentations is good hands-on training for the future. Work that involves strong emotions must be learned by doing and experiencing. Confidence and competence are the results of experience.

Reprogramming Somatic Markers: Give It Another Shot

A valuable tool for increasing and maintaining SREI is to reprogram selected somatic markers. This process has some overlap with over-learning, changing the dominant response hierarchy, and training, but at the same time, it is so specific that it needs to be discussed separately. The somatic marker hypothesis states that we attach, or mark, events with emotions, allowing faster processing the next time the need for a decision involving that event occurs. Once marked, the event has a positive or negative emotion attached to it. For example, if you ask me if I want to eat at a particular restaurant where I've had a bad experience before, I don't have to think or go through a rational decision-making strategy because the decision has been made previously. All I have to do is give you my decision: "No."

It is possible to change the marker from positive to negative, or vice versa, and to make it more or less negative or more or less positive than it was. If you talk me into trying the restaurant again and I have another bad experience, the negative marker is now stronger. Having a positive experience at the restaurant won't necessarily change the marker to positive, but I might be willing to try it again.

The Takeaway on Building SREI

Leaders who make a daily effort to continuously improve SREI will be surprised at their progress and the positive impact on decision making. The approach to building this ability is straightforward. A leader must use hands-on experiences to learn what the emotions feel like, experience the effect of emotions on decision making, and practice techniques for controlling them. This is not a "touchy-feely" process that causes many leaders to back away. Building SREI is not about doing group hugs. It's about learning the power of emotions and emotional intelligence; whether emotions have a positive or negative effect will become the choice of the leader. (*You* have the emotion; the emotion does not have you.)

SREI completes the third piece in the Stress Resilient System. When all three pieces are working in consonance, they generate a synergy that empowers the leader to engage high-stress situations and emerge successfully. The final chapter explains best practices for improving not only stress resilience but work performance, personal health, cognitive and emotional intelligences, and interpersonal relationships, all while maintaining lower stress. These best practices also increase your chances of living a longer, more active life. Let's begin to build an ARSENAL to combat the negative impact of stress on decision making. Some of these practices will produce results within hours.

9 The Seven Best Practices to Prevent Stress

Live in rooms full of light
Avoid heavy food
Be moderate in the drinking of wine
Take massage, baths, exercise, and gymnastics
Fight insomnia with gentle rocking or the sound of running water
Change surroundings and take long journeys
Strictly avoid frightening ideas
Indulge in cheerful conversation and amusements
Listen to music.
A. CORNELIUS CELSUS (25 B.C.–c. 50 A.D.)

A leader can get caught in an ever-accelerating downward spiral, and it starts with rising levels of stress. At first, the leader might think, "I can power through this. I am tough. That's how I got to where I am." But as his stress level begins to rise, he finds it more and more difficult to maintain the life style that helps keep stress manageable. The diet quickly turns unhealthy, there's no time or energy for exercise, no time for sleep or rest, no time for family or friends; his attitude turns negative, and learning halts. A reinforcing loop emerges that sends the leader into a downward spiral, like an airplane that has lost power and is out of the pilot's control, with little hope of recovery—unless the leader can break the cycle and begin to climb again.

The previous chapters have focused on understanding how leaders make decisions, the role of cognitive intelligence and emotional intelligence in the decision-making process, and, especially, how stress can significantly impair decision-making effectiveness. Stress has been shown to moderate all aspects of decision making—in some cases, changing the monetary value a person places on an object by as much as 50 percent.[1] When people experience the stress-related emotion of disgust, they tend to want to get rid of items they own and not purchase more. Consequently, they will sell their possessions at a lower price than they might ordinarily fetch. Sadness, another cousin of stress, may result in people placing a higher value on their items and wanting a higher price for them. They also tend to be willing to pay a higher price for things they want than do people experiencing disgust.

There are four steps in understanding the impact of stress on decision making and building a stress resilient system:

1. Develop knowledge of what the effects of stress are, particularly on the decision-making process.
2. Understand how and what these stress effects cause us to feel.
3. Be aware of the physiological and behavioral signs of being in the grip of stress.
4. Arm leaders with best practice strategies for managing specific stressors that take the biggest toll on decision making.

This chapter presents the seven most powerful best practices for building a holistic approach to managing stress and building stress management capacity, cognitive resilience, and stress resilient emotional intelligence, the triad of the Stress Resilient System. These practices work to halt the stress effect and break the downward spiral if a leader exerts the physical effort and mental discipline to make them a way of life.

ARSENAL: The Seven Best Practices

The seven best practices are Awareness, Rest, Support, Exercise, Nutrition, Attitude, and Learning. These best practices form the ARSENAL system and they quite literally become your arsenal against stress. Each of these best practices has been shown by a large body of research to be a key strategy for increasing stress management capacity, developing cognitive resilience, building stress resilient emotional intelligence, and making more effective decisions. This section presents a summary of each best practice to help you begin working on these areas immediately. *Keep in mind that success in each of these practices requires making it an emotional process.* The logic of rational thought can help you make the decision to begin an exercise program, but to follow through with the program requires an emotional commitment to keep you motivated.

Although the practices are presented separately, keep in mind that they are part of a system: each of the seven practices interacts with all the others (see Figure 9.1). Exercise, for example, helps the brain and body rest and sleep soundly. Rest helps recovery from exercise, which enables the leader to build strength and capacity. The reduction in stress and cortisol increases the desire to eat healthier food. Your brain functions more efficiently and you begin to look better, resulting in higher self-esteem, which contributes to a more positive attitude. Your support group will affirm these differences, improving your self-esteem further.

Exercise without rest, however, leads to high stress and eventually exhaustion. All rest and no exercise leads to a myriad of deteriorating effects that degrade decision making. The bottom line is that leaders need to work on increasing capacity and effectiveness in all seven practice areas.

FIGURE 9.1 The ARSENAL
System

Each practice area is presented in a format that tells what it is and why it is important, followed by a menu of techniques to use for putting together your customized ARSENAL developmental plan. Each practice area has its own self-assessment scale for identifying your current capacity in that area. As you read about each best practice, you will have an opportunity to complete a short self-evaluation of your current performance in that area. Think about each best practice as a continuum ranging from very little to high capacity. Your current capacity probably lies somewhere between the two extremes of the continuum.

After you read through the practices and complete your self-assessments, you can transfer this information to the ARSENAL Basic Assessment Graph (Figure 9.9) for a more complete picture of your current state of development and indications about how to prioritize your developmental plan. Some of the techniques around each best practice were presented in the preceding chapters. Rereading these chapters, highlighting key points, and making notes might be helpful in creating your customized ARSENAL developmental plan.

The dashboard concept, discussed in Chapters Seven and Eight, can be a valuable tool for monitoring these best practices. It provides a means for conducting quick self-evaluations of how stress might be having a negative impact on your decision making. Armed with this information, you can determine where you should apply more effort to reduce the danger of making ineffective decisions.

Awareness

It was a clear, crisp Tuesday morning in the fall of 1972 as the UH-1 helicopter slowly made its way toward the exit point seventy-five hundred feet above the small clearing in the valley below. Less than twenty minutes earlier, I had completed a parachute jump from this altitude and was looking forward to another thirty-second freefall before opening my ram-air parachute contained in my recently purchased state-of-the-art harness and container system; the reserve parachute was located on my back above the main parachute (to reduce the unbelievable shock delivered to the body if the reserve, normally worn on the front, is opened at terminal velocity of 120 miles per hour or more).[2]

After the pilot carefully positioned the helicopter over the exit point, I gave the signal to exit, and my fellow jumpers and I dived out of the helicopter and began the rapid descent toward the ground. We executed a few preplanned maneuvers, enjoyed the beautiful view of the north Georgia mountains around us, and separated. As a D-license holder, I was allowed to open my parachute at two thousand feet instead of twenty-five hundred feet. On this day, however, I fell just a little lower before pulling my ripcord and bracing for the opening shock. At this time, the deployment system on ram-air parachutes was still being perfected—meaning that they did not always open, and when they did, it was brain rattling.

At two thousand feet, a jumper is 11.36 seconds (or less, depending on individual speed) from impact with the ground. Pulling the ripcord and waiting for deployment takes about three seconds. In my case, three seconds went by, and I was still falling. I looked up and saw that my parachute was in a small wad incapable of opening. This gave me a shot of fear-driven noradrenaline, but at the same time I felt a burst of excitement because I would get to try out my brand new harness system. I began my emergency procedures (checklist) by cutting away my main parachute (to prevent the reserve from becoming entangled in the main parachute as it deploys), flared my body out, and waited for the reserve to open automatically (one of the features of my new harness and container system). Nothing happened. No opening shock! I went to the next step on the list, which was to reach behind my shoulders and try to manually pull out the reserve. It was not there! A lot of precious time had been used.

Moving my hands behind my shoulders caused me to assume a head down attitude, accelerating my freefall velocity toward 200 miles per hour. At this point, with the ground a few seconds away, the noradrenaline was really flowing. It was at that point that I saw my reserve on my abdomen. I was wearing my old harness! I pulled the reserve ripcord, watched it deploy up between my feet, and braced. It opened so hard that my heels literally hit the back of my helmet. The reserve oscillated a few times, and I hit the ground with the hard thud of a reserve landing. Another two seconds and it would have been too late to pull the ripcord. (It takes two seconds to read this sentence.)

I had practiced my emergency procedures so many times with my new harness that when my parachute malfunctioned, I automatically executed the new procedure. This would have been great if I had had on the new harness. My awareness level had dropped in my excitement about getting to make two quick, consecutive free falls, and I did not remind myself that I had on the old harness for the second jump. One of the lessons I learned was, "Don't keep switching emergency equipment for use in life-or-death situations." Your dominant response hierarchy will take over in a high stress situation and respond the way it was trained, regardless of which harness you are wearing.

Awareness is the foundation for developing all ARSENAL best practices, which leads to the development of stress management capacity, cognitive resilience, and stress resilient emotional intelligence. It can be thought of as the leader of the ARSENAL team. All ARSENAL best practices require some form of awareness to improve capacity. If Michael Phelps, a record-breaking Olympic swimmer, had practiced swimming every day without receiving any feedback, for example, on how fast he was swimming, he could not have become a world champion. Feedback is a component of all systems and provides information and understanding that the system can use to improve.

Awareness "watches" the other best practices. It should be used to monitor and collect feedback for the PFC. Awareness is part of the Perceiving component of the Perception-Appraisal-Motivation-Action model (PAMA). It provides oversight to the ARSENAL system and a reality check so critical to resilience. It also contributes information to the overall Appraisal process. Its position at the top of the ARSENAL graphic in Figure 9.1 indicates that it is the metaphorical system watchdog, keeping track of the other best practices.

Think about Awareness as a continuum ranging from the low end with a set of indicators such as these:

- Not being focused
- Not paying attention to details

- Spending time with your head in the clouds
- Experiencing gaps in time because of daydreaming or not paying attention

On the high end, indicators include:

- Being very focused on what's currently happening
- Feeling sensations (as opposed to "feeling nothing")
- Knowing how your brain and body are performing
- Knowing where you are at all times (checking the dashboards)

It is possible, with effort, to increase Awareness and thereby increase decision-making effectiveness.

Because each leader must create her own developmental program, I offer a menu of techniques for increasing awareness and the other ARSENAL components. Each person's brain and body differ in their response to these techniques and, especially, in overall capacity at the beginning of the developmental process. Each leader should create a specific developmental program based on needs and which of the techniques work for her. In many cases, the techniques that work are the ones a leader will commit to do. In the case of developmental plans, one size does not fit all.

Awareness should include assessments, feedback, metrics, and any other type of information that helps make and keep leaders aware of what is going on in the stress management capacity, cognitive resilience, and stress resilient emotional intelligence areas. A few techniques are listed in the menu that may be helpful in jump-starting a process for increasing and maintaining Awareness.

Awareness Menu
The Awareness Menu begins with four must do's followed by a menu of other proven techniques. You may find that you are already doing many of these to some degree. If so, then you should strive to increase your ability in the ones you are currently doing and add others from this list and from other sources. Create a customized plan that works.

1. Dedicate time daily to stepping outside yourself and observing your actions.
2. Get feedback from multiple sources on a daily basis.
3. Monitor and evaluate the information from your cognitive and emotional functioning dashboards so you know what's going on and why.
4. Take time to understand and identify what you feel and why.

Additional techniques for raising and maintaining Awareness include:

- Take a validated emotional intelligence assessment and receive professional feedback from a qualified feedback specialist.
- Take a brain development assessment to identify your strengths and weaknesses.
- Monitor and track the other six ARSENAL best practices.
- Create additional dashboards to monitor different areas.
- Closely monitor your stress level and its impact on decision making. How does your stress level vary during the day? Around different people? During different situations or events?
- Monitor your physiological conditions such as blood pressure, energy level, fatigue, anxiety, caffeine level, and others, and note their impact on your decision making.
- Use performance aids.

The Awareness Scale in Figure 9.2 can give you a quick indication of your current performance level on this best practice. The scale ranges from 1 to 10, with 1 meaning, *I have little or no capacity in this area,* to 10, meaning *I have very high capacity and require little or no improvement in this area.* Circle a number on the scale that best represents where you think you are this week on Awareness.

Awareness is a dynamic skill and varies from day to day. If you track it for a few months, you will discover a baseline around which it varies. To increase your awareness will require a dedicated developmental plan incorporating some or all of the techniques presented above. Remember that *an unaware brain is a surprised brain.*

FIGURE 9.2 Awareness Scale

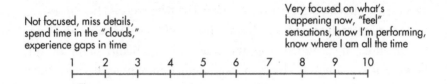

Not focused, miss details, spend time in the "clouds," experience gaps in time

Very focused on what's happening now, "feel" sensations, know I'm performing, know where I am all the time

1   2   3   4   5   6   7   8   9   10

Susan G. Komen for the Cure Breast Cancer Awareness Program

In 1980, after nine operations and three courses of chemotherapy and radiation, Susan G. Komen lost her three-year battle with breast cancer at the age of thirty-six. Two years later her younger sister, Nancy G. Brinker, inspired by her dying sister's desire to help other women with breast cancer, made good on the promise she made to Komen before she died—to do something about ending this disease forever. Brinker founded Susan G. Komen for the Cure, now a global leader in the fight to end breast cancer by raising awareness and funds, nearly $1.5 billion to date. Through the efforts of this foundation, today nearly 75 percent of women over forty receive mammograms routinely to detect breast cancer compared to just 30 percent in 1982. "We've made tremendous strides here in the United States in bringing breast cancer out of the shadows," Brinker says on the Komen for the Cure Web site. Through Brinker's efforts, breast cancer patients know more about the disease they are fighting and treatment options, knowledge that might have prolonged her sister's life.

Rest

In 2000, David Hempleman-Adams, the British adventurer, was the first man to fly over the North Pole in an open balloon. The flight was 132 hours, and he stayed awake for over 70 of those hours. After 24 hours, he struggled to write down radio messages containing vital information such as coordinates and speed, which he needed for navigation. The onboard video camera showed him struggling to remain awake and perform simple cognitive tasks.

More frightening than his inability to copy messages was when his brain finally forced him to sleep. While he slept, the balloon began losing altitude. When the emergency altitude alarm sounded inside the gondola, he awoke in a groggy and disoriented state. Not realizing where he was, just that he was hearing an alarm (which activated his dominant response hierarchy that told him to "flee") and needed to escape from the gondola, he climbed over the side and just before stepping off, became alert enough to realize he was almost nine thousand feet above the polar cap! It would have been a long first step.

When we fail to heed the brain's or body's signals that we need rest, we suffer consequences. It's not always a first step of nine thousand feet, but it could be an oncoming tractor trailer truck, running off onto the side of the road, making a critical calculation error, or forgetting what you wanted to buy at the grocery store. *All high performing systems require downtime.*

Rest allows the brain and body to repair, rebuild, regenerate, process activities, consolidate information into long-term memory, learn, and prepare for another round of activities. A broken bone, for example, requires rest and time to heal. If we forget and overdo, pain sensors from the injury send very strong taps—maybe even jerks—to remind us to take a break. The brain and other body systems also send taps to warn us of impending problems, but because the pain associated with them starts off at such a low level, we tend to ignore the warning.

Sleep is the most critical form of Rest.[3] You should avoid losing sleep if at all possible. Keep in mind that sleep loss is cumulative.[4] If you lose an hour tonight and an hour tomorrow night, you have lost two hours in terms of what your body needs. Cognitive and emotional abilities begin to degrade quickly as you enter into sleep deprivation, and you probably will not be aware of it until it is too late.[5]

Lack of sleep degrades the brain's and body's effective functioning. When the body and conscious mind, except for hearing, go to sleep, brain activity accelerates. This is the time when repairs are made, learning is consolidated, the day's activities are reviewed, and decisions are made about which, what, where, and how to store them. The brain is able to operate in an unstructured manner without the constraints imposed by consciousness.

Periodically during the night, the brain "paralyzes" the body for its own protection and goes into a dream state accompanied by rapid eye movement (REM). Not everything that happens during this state is known, but it does appear to be critical to the brain's recovery. Have you ever had a day in which you know you slept all night but feel as if you have not had any sleep? You feel groggy, not sharp mentally, and you might have a headache. Some people describe it as similar to a hangover. Actually the "hangover effect" comes from the alcohol interfering with REM sleep. The bottom line is that just getting sleep is not enough. It must be the right combinations of the different types of sleep.

Let me re-emphasize that sleep loss is cumulative. Tonight's lost hour and tomorrow night's lost hour equals two hours of sleep debt, and it has to be paid back. As your sleep debt increases, your cognitive and emotional effectiveness decrease. If you have sleep debt, when should you pay it back? Research suggests that in most cases, the best time to pay your sleep debt is on the front end. That is, go to bed earlier rather than sleep later. Sleeping later (or getting up earlier) throws off your normal wakeup time and sleep cycle more than staying up later or going to bed earlier. Napping, if done correctly, is also an effective way to repay sleep debt.

Rest is not only about sleep, although sleep is a critical piece of rest. Taking short breaks, creating mental distractions, or having a cup of green tea, for example, help to provide some rest during the day. Talking to friends, doing a Web search, walking, listening to music, scanning new tweets on Twitter, and other such mini-breaks not only add to maintaining peak performance, but make life less stressful and more enjoyable.

Rest can range from a set of indicators such as feeling very tired, not sleeping well, feeling overworked, and unable to relax on the low end of the continuum to waking up refreshed, feeling energized, taking frequent breaks or mini-vacations, and doing relaxing things on the high end. It is possible, with effort, to increase rest and thereby increase decision-making effectiveness.

Famous Power Nappers

Everyone must pay the sleep debt that results from not getting enough quality sleep. An effective way to stave off some of the negative effects of sleep loss is through napping: sleeping for fifteen to thirty minutes during the day (or night if you work at night and sleep during the day). Napping for longer than thirty minutes at a time may cause you to go into a sleep cycle, and you will have trouble waking up and may feel sleepy the rest of the day. The most effective time to nap is between 1:00 P.M. and 3:00 P.M. A study by the National Aeronautics and Space Administration found that a nap of just twenty-six minutes can boost performance by as much as 34 percent.[6] If you are sleeping only a few hours during a twenty-four hour cycle, you will require several naps to maintain minimal efficiency.

David Hempleman-Adams discovered that if the brain loses enough sleep, it will automatically declare nap time and you will fall asleep regardless of what you are doing. U.S. Army Ranger students regularly fall asleep on their feet (literally) and fall to the ground. I have seen them fall asleep midsentence while briefing me on a training mission. When this happens, the brain is sending a strong signal that it needs more sleep. An aware leader will recognize and respond to this idiot light.

Many historical figures have made their propensity for napping public—for example:

Bill Clinton	Albert Einstein
Eleanor Roosevelt	Thomas Edison
John D. Rockefeller	Leonardo da Vinci
Gene Autry	Ronald Reagan
Lance Armstrong	

A few basic rules for napping are:

- Plan your nap between 1:00 P.M. and 3:00 P.M. if possible. (Research has shown that you repay sleep debt faster during this time.)
- Find a quiet place where you will not be disturbed.
- Turn off your phone—no calls or e-mail alerts allowed!
- Set a timer to make sure you do not overnap.
- Enjoy your nap!

Rest Menu

The Rest Menu begins with five must do's for rest followed by a menu of other proven techniques. As with Awareness, you may find that you are already using many of these techniques. If so, then you should strive to increase your ability in the ones you are currently doing and add others from this list and from other sources. Create a customized rest plan that works—and follow it!

If you fail to do these five must do's for Rest, you risk not being able to develop this best practice beyond where you are today.

1. Force yourself to take breaks. The company, world, and cosmos can survive while you rest. Fatigue slips up on you and is cumulative. Get adequate rest every day. This includes getting eight hours or more sleep each night (some people require less, but most of us need at least eight).
2. Include some personal time in each day. This is very important.
3. Schedule vacations, trips, and other long rest breaks. Putting them on your calendar increases the chances of actually taking them.
4. Learn to say no and mean it. Don't overload yourself.
5. Identify multiple types of mental and physical breaks that work for you to ensure that you can always fit your schedule around Rest.

The following techniques can be used to augment the must do's:

- Determine whether you are a morning or evening person, and schedule your activities accordingly when possible.
- Play, have fun, and experience at least one belly laugh every day (watch a funny movie, for example).
- Learn to relax. Meditate, pray, or practice yoga.
- Listen to music; go to movies, plays, and concerts; play a musical instrument.
- Use biofeedback.
- Get a hobby.

- Take power naps in the early afternoon.
- Do a relaxation response session at least once daily (refer back to Chapter Six).

Resting, especially sleep, allows the brain to process the day's activities, transfer information into long-term memory, and repair itself.[7] Rest prepares you to function at your cognitive and emotional peak.[8] Matthew Walker, director of the Sleep and Neuroimaging Lab at the University of California, Berkeley, says, "Sleep essentially is resetting the magnetic north of your emotional compass."

The Rest Scale in Figure 9.3 can give you a quick indication of your current performance level on this best practice. The scale ranges from 1 to 10, with 1 meaning, *I have little or no capacity in this area,* and 10 meaning, *I have very high capacity and require little or no improvement in this area.* Circle a number on the scale that best represents where you think you are this week on Rest.

Resting is a dynamic skill that can be accomplished in a multitude of ways. Leaders must be prepared to rest whenever an opportunity presents itself. For example, during a taxi ride, listen to music on an MP3 player; waiting for a meeting to begin, practice tactical breathing (explained at end of this chapter); during your daily commute, look for teddy bears; when you get home, take a twenty-minute decompression break to transition from business leader to "super dad" or "super mom." Build a repertoire of short breaks you can always have available.

How much Rest you need varies from day to day. If you track your rest for a few months, you will discover a baseline for the amount of rest you typically need for different situations. To raise the baseline to

FIGURE 9.3 Rest Scale

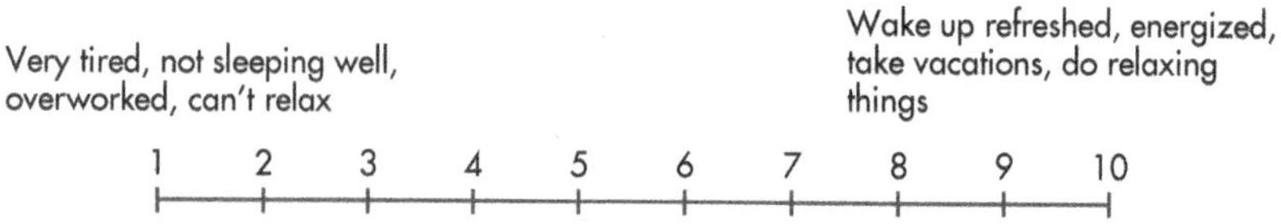

Very tired, not sleeping well, overworked, can't relax						Wake up refreshed, energized, take vacations, do relaxing things			
1	2	3	4	5	6	7	8	9	10

a higher level requires planning (using your PFC) and the motivation and focus to do it. Remember that *a tired brain is a grumpy brain.*

Support

When cancer touches your family, and especially your child, your world turns upside down. The ultimate goal becomes getting the cancer in remission—whatever it takes, knowing it will take a lot. You begin living the stress effect. This is what happened to Josh and Mollie when they received the news that their three-year-old son, Griffin, had leukemia. Josh runs the graphics department at High Performing Systems (HPS), and Mollie works part time out of their home while taking care of Griffin and eighteen-month-old Olive. In situations like this, support is critical to help the family survive the crisis and the series of very difficult decisions that must be made.

The HPS team rallied around Josh and Mollie to provide the time off Josh needed during the initial weeks while his family's future plans and needs unfolded. Both of their mothers took turns staying with Olive and helping to run the house. HPS did an initial fundraiser, which was followed by an outpouring of support from Josh and Mollie's church, family, friends, and even strangers who had heard about Griffin's situation through community groups and the Web. More than eighty people participated in a 5K "fun run" set up to raise awareness of Griffin's illness and provide financial support. When the decision to do a bone marrow transplant was made, over six hundred people showed up and volunteered to be tested, adding their names to a national list of bone marrow donors.

During the transplant and those critical weeks afterward, a virtual office was set up in the Ronald McDonald House so Josh could do some work remotely. (Doing your job can be a powerful form of stress management, particularly when circumstances away from the office are extremely stressful. In his case, Josh needed to get away from the excruciating stress of his personal situation, and the normalcy of work brought much needed relief.) Continuous support and adaptation have been necessary to get Josh, Mollie, and Olive through the high stress of working toward Griffin's recovery.

Support refers to the psychological, emotional, and physical help you get from others. This support typically comes from having a significant other, family, friends, colleagues, coaches, or mentors—people you can talk to, who will be there for you in difficult times and can help meet your needs in some way.

A substantial amount of research supports the health value of having a Support system. Research also suggests that the higher the quality of your relationships, the longer you may live. Family, friends, coworkers, and religious, civic, and professional groups can provide the needed Support to make you feel connected, included, secure, and self-worthy. Evidence suggests that married people who stay married to their original spouse tend to have longer life expectancies than those who don't stay married or remarry.[9]

Support ranges from a set of indicators such as *I am a loner, I have very few or no friends,* and *I don't have close family ties or a support group* on the low end of the continuum to *I have a strong support group, lots of friends,* and *close family ties* on the high end. It is possible, with effort, to increase Support and thereby increase decision-making effectiveness.

Support Menu
The following list contains the five must do's for Support. If you fail to do these, you risk not being able to develop this best practice beyond where you are today:

1. Identify the people in your support system and how they help you. Keep their contact information handy.
2. Offer Support to others, which often has a reinforcing effect.
3. Increase time around people who make you feel better.
4. Practice your faith, attend religious services, and volunteer or engage in charitable activities that involve the greater good.
5. Don't hesitate to use your safety net—the people in your support system.

These additional proven techniques will help you develop and maintain a high level of Support.

- Stay in touch with friends.
- Spend quality time with your family members and significant other.
- Nurture relationships at work. The people you work with are your second family.
- Use all available resources, including employee assistance programs.
- Belong to civic or religious organizations that help you feel a sense of community.
- Renew a relationship with a long-lost friend and reminisce about good times.
- Network. Find people with similar interests. Join professional groups, book clubs, alumni associations, or charitable organizations.
- Leave or replace groups that increase your stress or require too much personal time.

The Support Scale in Figure 9.4 can give you a quick indication of your current performance level on this best practice. The scale ranges from 1 to 10, with 1 meaning, *I have little or no capacity in this area,* and 10 meaning, *I have very high capacity and require little or no improvement in this area.* Circle a number on the scale that best represents where you think you are this week on Support.

Support is a more socially complex practice than the other six ARSENAL areas. There is a fine line between getting the Support you need and being overwhelmed by your supporters. Support is normally a two-way street. Getting Support also includes giving Support to a friend or dedicating time to a worthwhile cause. Tracking how you use your support system for a few months will help you discover how to improve

FIGURE 9.4 Support Scale

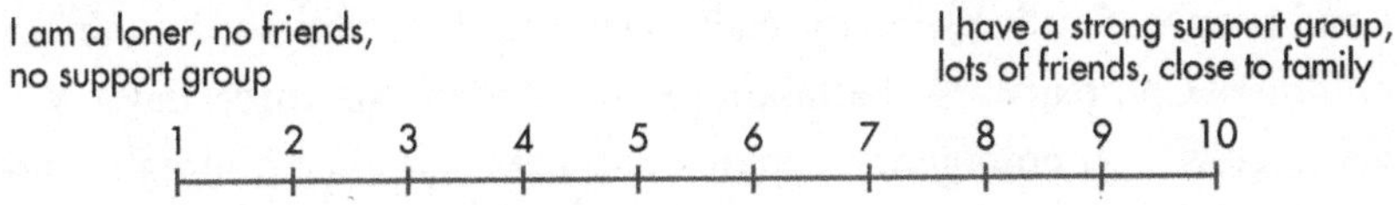

I am a loner, no friends,
no support group

I have a strong support group,
lots of friends, close to family

1   2   3   4   5   6   7   8   9   10

this practice area and allows you to adjust the techniques that work best in your life. Remember that *an unsupported brain is a sad brain.*

Support for Military Members and Their Families

The Fisher House program (www.fisherhouse.org) is a public-private partnership to provide support to America's military men and women and their families during their time of medical need. Members of the military are stationed worldwide and often find it necessary to travel great distances to specialized medical facilities—in most cases, leaving their families behind. The Fisher House Foundation constructs and donates "comfort homes" on the grounds of major military and Veterans Administration (VA) medical centers. These homes provide free living space for family members so they can be close to their loved ones during hospitalization and rehabilitation. These homes serve more than ten thousand families annually.

In addition, the Fisher House Foundation administers the "Hero Miles" program for the Department of Defense. Passengers from individual airlines donate frequent flyer miles to assist service members and their families. This program makes it possible for the Fisher House Foundation to provide free airline tickets to military members and their families who are undergoing treatment at military or VA medical centers.

A third form of support for military families is the Scholarship for Military Children and Spouses. In the first nine years of this program, $7.5 million in scholarships have been awarded.

The Wounded Warrior Project (www.woundedwarriorproject.org) provides support for severely injured members of the U.S. military by enlisting the public's aid, helping service members assist each other, and providing unique programs and services. Support provided includes advocacy for positive change in benefits and veterans' policies, benefits counseling, caregivers' retreats, coping and family services, peer mentoring, transition training, and the Warriors to Work program.

Exercise

I had been in South Korea for eight days and the commanding officer of Bravo Company, 1st Battalion, 23rd Infantry for three days. We had received an emergency deployment alert just after midnight and had moved out with the rest of our battalion to one of our specified battle positions to prepare for a potential North Korean attack. It had been a long walk and steep climb to get to our battle position. My soldiers had been digging in since our arrival and preparing for an attack.

It was just getting daylight when I heard the "Whop! Whop! Whop!" of a helicopter behind the ridge. Then there it was, positioned precariously on the ridge, and a tall, slim man with two stars (Major General) on his collar and helmet jumped out and shouted to a nearby soldier, "Where's your company commander?" Thirty seconds later, he was standing with me inside the fighting position (a hole in the ground), asking for an explanation of what I was doing. Five minutes later, he got back on the helicopter and disappeared behind the ridge. The platoon sergeant who was also in the hole with me said, "You done good, Sir!" and I asked what made him say that. He replied, "Because you're still the company commander."

Fifteen minutes later, the helicopter was back, and again the general came into the hole with the platoon sergeant and me, bringing a Lieutenant General (three stars) with him. (The fighting position is designed for two people, not four.) He said, "This is my boss. Tell him what you just told me." Five minutes later, they were back on the helicopter and gone. That was the beginning of my relationship with "the Gunfighter," who had visited us twice that day.

Major General Henry Emerson was a highly decorated Vietnam veteran who loved his soldiers and went to great lengths to take care of them. He often used the phrase, "Fatigue makes cowards of us all." Physical fitness was one of the principles of his "Pro-Life" (not to be confused with today's battle over abortion) program. In this program, every soldier's day started with a four-mile run. He set up competition in numerous sports such as basketball, tae kwon do, and "combat football" and gave division-wide recognition to winners at all levels. After creating a division of ten thousand extremely fit soldiers, he was promoted to Lieutenant General (three stars) and took his Pro-Life program to Fort Bragg, North Carolina, where he commanded the XVIII Airborne Corps. Soon Emerson had his more than fifty thousand soldiers running four miles each morning as well as participating in sports tournaments. The exercise program he implemented had a significant positive effect on the health and performance of his soldiers and their families.

Exercise as used here refers to physical activity that builds cardio-vascular and muscle strength. Cardiovascular health fights off diseases associated with high stress such as high cholesterol, high blood pressure, arteriosclerosis, blood clots, heart attacks, strokes, type II diabetes, obesity, back pain, and osteoporosis (particularly in women). Muscle tone and strength deteriorate quickly after the age of forty without adequate exercise. Exercise keeps the brain and body systems tuned and functioning well. Leaders will not only be able to resist stress better, but will recover from stressors more quickly than those who are not physically fit.

I have found that physical fitness is directly related to a leader's ability to resist cognitive and emotional degradation during prolonged periods of physical and mental stress. Research participants in a high physical fitness group demonstrated a much higher awareness of their fatigue level and cognitive and emotional performance levels than a low physical fitness group.[10] I have seen these findings validated many times during outdoor training exercises, ropes courses, and long planning sessions. A high level of physical fitness gives a leader an advantage when physical and mental performance is required to surge into the peak performance zone (see Chapter Six, especially Figure 6.2).

In my experience, leaders in the high fitness category tend to have a high level of awareness of how well they are functioning physically. This awareness can be expanded to include cognitive and emotional awareness through training and the use of cognitive and emotional dashboards.

Exercise done properly and responsibly not only builds cardiovascular and muscle strength, it increases blood flow to the brain, thereby increasing its working capacity and health. Exercise is directly related to the brain's ability to delay the onset of memory loss associated with aging, dementia, and even Alzheimer's disease.[11]

Exercise ranges from a set of indicators such as *not having an exercise program, sitting a lot during the day,* and *not being physically active* on the low end of the continuum to *exercising five or more times a week, being in excellent physical condition,* and *very active* on the high end. It is possible, with effort, to increase exercise and thereby increase decision-making effectiveness.

Exercise Menu

The Exercise Menu begins with six must do's, followed by a menu of other proven techniques. Exercise can be a particularly difficult practice area to increase for a number of reasons. For example, exercise is hard work (especially if you are starting at level 1), you get sore and tired, have to make time to exercise, find a place to exercise, get the right clothing, do it, then shower, and change clothes again. All of this takes time and scheduling.

These "difficulties" provide many overpowering "opportunities" (excuses) to quit. The mental difficulty surrounding physical Exercise can cause an exercise program to fail before it starts. Success requires getting through the first sixty days. You have to reach the point where Exercise transitions from cognitive to emotional. Once exercise becomes somatically marked (positively), you will feel guilty if you miss, or even think about missing, a workout. Now you are on your way!

If you fail to do these six must do's for Exercise, you risk not being able to develop this best practice beyond where you are today.

1. Get a complete physical prior to beginning your Exercise program.
2. Get off the couch or out of your chair, stop making excuses, and start moving. (Walking is a good place to start.)
3. Establish baseline measurements of factors such as heart rate, blood pressure, and cholesterol. Keep detailed daily records of your progress.
4. Get a partner, or Exercise alone. Find what works for you.
5. Do not miss an Exercise session during the first sixty days—not even one! While some say new habits are created in twenty-one

days, I find that for most people, sixty days tends to firmly transform any new behavior into a habit.

6. Set reasonable goals. Too much Exercise too fast or the wrong kind of exercise can make you sick.

Choose from these additional best practice techniques for exercise:

- Have your blood work checked annually.
- Do a blend of cardiovascular and anaerobic activities for twenty to thirty minutes, three to five times a week.
- Engage in activities that work on agility, such as balancing and jumping (these are also great brain exercises).
- Stretch, and practice yoga.
- Participate in a sport such as running, walking, endurance training, hiking, skiing, bicycling, swimming, or something else you enjoy. For added fun and motivation, try your hand at competitions (road races, local masters' teams) or group activities (cycling groups, ski trips).
- Keep records of your activities on how fast, how far, and how long to inspire your progress.

Exercise has the added effect of stimulating brain development. It pumps blood through the system and helps flush stress hormones out of your system faster than watching TV or other sedentary activities.

The Exercise Scale in Figure 9.5 can give you a quick indication of your current performance level on this best practice. The scale ranges from 1 to 10, with 1 meaning, *I have little or no capacity in this area,* and

FIGURE 9.5 Exercise Scale

10 meaning, *I have very high capacity and require little or no improvement in this area.* Circle a number on the scale that best represents where you think you are this week on Exercise.

Exercise is a mentally and physically demanding best practice that requires you to go into Selye's trough (alarm reaction stage) and work your way out the other side—which metaphorically is uphill. It is not easy, but if you continue to track your exercising for a few months, you will be pleasantly surprised at the progress you make—not just physically but in appearance, health, and reduction in medications and stress.

Exercise has been shown to have a significant positive effect on stress management and cognitive and emotional abilities by increasing blood flow, and thus oxygen, to the brain. Exercise regimes also increase attunement to physiological conditions and the ability to maintain a healthy prefrontal cortex (PFC).[12] The secret to exercise is that you have to do it. Remember that *an unfit brain is a slow brain.*

Blue Cross Blue Shield

Blue Cross Blue Shield's BluePrint for Health Fitness Center Discount program, available in many states, offers discounts and other incentives for joining health clubs. Their research has shown that increasing fitness reduces health costs, and Blue Cross Blue Shield is willing to make a financial contribution. The independent licensees of the Blue Cross Blue Shield Association offer numerous health and fitness programs to their employees and membership.

Nutrition

Grenae had started out early that morning with fifty-five thousand of her "closest friends," enduring the heat, humidity, and steep hills—especially "cardiac hill"—and conquering that little voice in her head saying, "What *were* you thinking? These people are *real* athletes. You're not going to make it!" Yet now, almost 6.2 miles later, she could hear the large crowd cheering and could see the entrance to the barriers that funneled all runners into a single lane to pass under the giant timer, counting off the minutes and seconds. It suddenly dawned on her that she was going to finish Atlanta's annual July 4 Peachtree 10K Road Race, a goal she had set for herself when she was almost seventy pounds heavier. A flood of emotions came over her as she crossed the finish line and began walking across the crowded field to get her very first Peachtree 10K T-shirt. There would be other Peachtree 10Ks and many 5Ks over the years, but never one that meant so much to her.

This was one of many highlights along the road to better health that had started nearly eighteen months earlier. She was committed to improving her overall health through nutrition and exercise. It was never about following a restrictive diet; it was about making better food choices, being aware of portion sizes, and establishing new habits. And it had paid off as she proudly wore her T-shirt and announced to the world, "Yes, I'm a *real* athlete."

Nutrition refers to what, when, and how you nourish your brain and body—eating, drinking, and digesting. The old saying that you are what you eat is certainly true with this best practice. A look at the growing girth of the U.S. population reveals that consuming food is not a problem for most people. The problem is what Americans consider good food and how much of it they consume. America has an obesity crisis. We eat too much of the wrong kinds of food. It usually starts in childhood, and for many people these bad eating habits continue right on through their teens into adulthood. Restaurants, from fast food chains to the fanciest establishments, serve gigantic portions, and we feel obligated to clean our plates. Food manufacturers supersize products like snacks and candy, and consumers flock to these perceived "bargains," only to pay the price by adding empty calories (and pounds).

Dick Yeomans, profiled in Chapter Three, set a goal of losing twenty-five pounds (and he was not obese) to set the example for his leaders in the area of fitness and nutrition. Leaders must be mentally and physically sharp all the time, and good nutrition goes a long way toward achieving this goal. Leaders struggling with obesity brought on by poor nutrition and lack of exercise rarely are able to operate at their full cognitive and emotional potential under stress.[13]

Nutrition ranges from a set of indicators such as *I am overweight, have poor eating habits, drink too much caffeine,* and *eat too much sugar and fat* on the low end of the continuum, to *I have very healthy eating habits and low body fat* and *drink plenty of water* on the high end. With effort, you can improve your Nutrition and experience improved decision-making effectiveness.

Nutrition Menu
The Nutrition Menu begins with nine must do's followed by additional proven techniques. Improving Nutrition can be as difficult a task as, or more so than, improving Exercise. Food, especially food that is not particularly healthy, tastes good and is readily available. It is easy to rationalize why eating fast food saves you time and therefore makes your life less "stressful." As with Exercise, good Nutrition requires some investment of time: planning, shopping for, and preparing healthy meals take time. You must also pay attention to what you eat. (It's easy to skip this step when you're constantly racing through the drive-through to pick up breakfast, lunch, or dinner.) In addition, you have to deal with the psychological effects of changing your diet, for example, feeling "hungry" or deprived, and feeling "guilty" if you eat the cookie. It doesn't take two months to transition to an emotional process. It already exists.

The "difficulties" outlined above provide many overpowering excuses to quit. The emotional difficulty surrounding a good Nutrition program can cause it to fail before it starts. Success, as with exercise, requires getting through the first sixty days. But once good Nutrition has become somatically marked (positively) over the course of that period, you'll find that you have lost your urge to eat the cookie and realize that it is all about choice: "I can eat the cookie if I want to, but I choose not to." Once you have reached the point where you have control over your eating behavior, you are well on your way to a lifetime of good Nutrition.

If you fail to do these nine must do's for Nutrition, you risk not being able to develop this best practice beyond where you are today.

1. Make healthy food choices using sound nutritional guidelines from a proven source. Consult with your physician if you are overweight to set a goal for how many pounds you should lose.
2. Write down what you eat and include *everything* (you might be shocked).
3. Weigh yourself every day, and keep a record.
4. Make small, gradual changes in your diet; allow your body and palate time to adjust.
5. Stay away from fad diets; research shows they don't keep the weight off permanently. Instead, strive to eat the way you want to eat for the rest of your life.
6. Minimize the amount of unhealthy or junk food in your environment.
7. Drink plenty of water.
8. Reduce your consumption of sodas and other drinks with empty calories.
9. Reduce the size of the portions of food you consume.

The food you put into your body influences your stress level and, consequently, cognitive and emotional performance. Consider these general guidelines:

- Minimize or avoid foods high in sugar, trans fats, saturated fats and harmful additives. Avoid processed foods, which are often high in sodium.
- Control what you eat for lunch at work by bringing meals from home when possible. If business lunches and dinners are part of your routine, pay attention to what you're ordering, including portion size.
- Monitor your caffeine intake. Caffeine has been shown to increase physical performance, but at the same time, it releases a cascade of stress hormones into your system. Recognize your "buzz" level, and don't go beyond it.

- Increase your intake of "brain" foods, such as omega–3s.
- If you drink alcohol, drink in moderation.
- Eat the right balance of protein, carbohydrates, and vegetables.
- Take a vitamin and mineral supplement. Women over the age of forty should also take a calcium supplement. (Check with your doctor to see if there are any other nutrients you should supplement with vitamins.)
- Don't skip breakfast. Your mother was right: it really is the most important meal of the day. Research shows that breakfast skippers start the day with less energy, have sluggish metabolisms, and tend to overeat at other meals.
- Try to make time for breakfast, lunch, and dinner, and avoid eating on the run, in the car, or in front of your computer. When you eat while you are multitasking, you are less aware of what you're eating and when you're full.

Everything entering your system—air, water, food, and chemicals (caffeine, vitamins and prescription drugs)—has an effect on your stress level, IQ, and emotional intelligence. What you put into your system determines your mental, emotional, and physical performance.

Although smoking doesn't fall under Nutrition, this habit is worth addressing here because it can inhibit your physical well-being, including your IQ and emotional intelligence, in the same way that poor Nutrition habits can. Nicotine significantly reduces the amount of oxygen carried to the brain, which needs a certain amount of oxygen to function effectively. One cigarette reduces the amount of oxygen to the brain as much as breathing air at an altitude of five thousand feet, thus reducing PFC performance.

The Nutrition Scale in Figure 9.6 can give you a quick indication of your current performance level on this best practice. The scale ranges from 1 to 10, with 1 meaning, *I have little or no capacity in this area,* and 10 meaning, *I have very high capacity and require little or no improvement*

FIGURE 9.6 Nutrition Scale

| I am obese, poor eating habits, too much caffeine, sugar, fats | Very healthy eating habits, low body fat, drink lots of water |

```
      1     2     3     4     5     6     7     8     9     10
      |-----|-----|-----|-----|-----|-----|-----|-----|-----|
```

in this area. Circle a number on the scale that best represents where you think you are this week on nutrition.

Nutrition is a mentally demanding best practice that, like Exercise, requires you to go into Selye's trough (alarm reaction stage) and work your way out the other side—which metaphorically is uphill. It is not easy, but if you continue to track Nutrition for at least sixty days, you will be pleasantly surprised at the progress you make in appearance, health, and reducing stress. Remember that *a hungry brain is a distracted brain.*

Corporate Good Practices in Nutrition

J. I. Rodale founded Rodale Inc. in 1930 with the belief that there was a relationship between America's soil health and the health of Americans. Rodale is a global leader in health, fitness, and wellness content, with a readership that exceeds 70 million. The company produces trade books on wellness topics and category-leading magazines such as *Men's Health, Prevention, Women's Health, Runner's World, Bicycling, Running Times, Organic Gardening,* and *Mountain Bike.*

Rodale encourages employees to lead "healthy, fulfilling and balanced lives." The company provides healthy meals and snacks at low or no cost. Fitness facilities, walking and running trails, regular health screenings, and more are provided for employees. Rodale has been repeatedly named as one of The 100 Best Companies to Work For by *Fortune* magazine.

The SAS Institute was founded in 1976 by Jim Goodnight and John Stall and is one of the largest software companies in the world. SAS originally stood for "statistical analysis system." It was affectionately known by most graduate students as "sass." The term "institute" was later dropped from the name and it is now known as SAS.

One of the founding principles was that satisfied employees create satisfied customers. The SAS campus at Cary, North Carolina, includes childcare and elder-care centers, recreation and fitness centers, a health care center, and many other work-life programs. SAS fitness centers offer everything from classes for kids and teens to aquatics, organized sports, and personal training. For twelve straight years SAS has been listed as one of The 100 Best Companies to Work For by *Fortune* magazine. SAS made a commitment from the beginning to take care of its employees by keeping them healthy.

Attitude

Marcia sat in the waiting room, flipping nervously through magazines while waiting on yet another doctor to attempt to diagnose what was wrong with her. This time she got the diagnosis, but it was not what she wanted to hear: she had lupus. She thought to herself, "How could I have lupus? I don't even know what it is." But she finally had an answer, and the prognosis was not good.

Upon returning from her next appointment with a lupus specialist, she realized that the people she had seen in the waiting room who were confined to wheelchairs had been walking just six months before. She determined then and there that she would not become like them, not without a fight. That was fifteen years ago, and she has been in a brutal fight, experiencing every "torture device" and procedure that medicine has to offer. She still works almost every day and has testified before Congress several times on behalf of the Lupus Foundation. She also raises money for a cure and provides Support to other lupus patients.

Marcia was born and raised in West Virginia, a coal miner's daughter and the youngest of eleven children. She attended West Virginia University, worked at the university for a while, got married, had children, and eventually became a management consultant and trainer for High Performing Systems. Marcia is very bright, has high emotional intelligence, and everyone loves her. Despite all of her setbacks with lupus and life in general, she takes care of her loving husband, wonderful daughter and son, and surviving brothers and sisters—and anyone else she can help.

People are drawn to Marcia to a large degree because of her exceptionally positive attitude. Just being around her makes people feel better. She has been a major source of inspiration for me and thousands of others over the years. Marcia is what happens when you have the right Attitude.

Your Attitude reflects your mindset, happiness, optimism, and contentment with your environment and those around you. It is a window into a leader's motivation, commitment, character, and self-esteem. Attitude drives energy level and focus for all ARSENAL best practices. It is pervasive and tends to spill over into everything else you do. If you have a strong, positive Attitude, you are likely to display optimism, commitment, and a "can do," "let's do it" approach to whatever tasks and projects you undertake or decisions you make.

The past thirty years have produced numerous studies that link positive attitude with good health, memory and cognitive and emotional performance. Glenn Ostir and his research team found that a positive attitude was related to people not becoming frail as they aged. In an interview with BBC News, Ostir affirmed, "I believe that there is a connection between mind and body—and that our thoughts and attitudes/emotions affect physical functioning, and overall health, whether through direct mechanisms, such as immune function, or indirect mechanisms, such as social support networks."[14]

Attitude also affects whom you associate with, promotability, job assignments, effort put into job tasks, completeness of tasks, and putting in the extra effort required without being asked. Attitude is contagious. Mirror neurons kick in and create a behavioral contagion that can be quickly replicated across the work group and in some cases the organization.

Attitude ranges from a set of indicators such as *constantly having a negative attitude, criticizing and blaming others,* and *saying it's "not my fault"* on the low end of the continuum to *being very positive, loving the challenge of life, accepting responsibility,* and *being adaptable* on the high end. It is possible, with effort, to improve Attitude and thereby increase decision-making effectiveness.

Attitude Menu

If you fail to do these six must do's on the Attitude Menu, you risk not being able to develop this best practice beyond where you are today.

1. Engage in activities that build your self-confidence and self-esteem.
2. Smile!
3. See the glass as being half full.
4. Get feedback from people you trust on how others perceive your Attitude. Listen and say, "Thank you."
5. Talk directly to the person you are unhappy with, not to your coworkers about that person.
6. Become a team player. Ask fellow team members what you can do to help them.

Attitude is critical in establishing motivation and commitment to manage stress and build resilience. How you think about life in general influences which hormones are released, the amount released, and the length of time they remain in your system. These hormones in turn influence all of the body's systems in a positive or negative manner. Consider these additional menu items for raising and sustaining attitude:

- Participate in activities, both at work and in your leisure time, that you enjoy.
- Always strive to do your best in whatever you undertake, even if no one else will know.
- Don't give up. Rely on other ARSENAL best practices for encouragement.
- Be socially responsible. Many everyday choices we make can have a deep impact—negative or positive—on others.
- Accept responsibility for your life and your actions.

- Discover (or rediscover) and use your talents.
- Find positive things to say about your coworkers and your job.
- Don't gossip, especially at work. It's a vicious cycle that drags everyone down.
- Be part of the solution, not the problem. For instance, don't simply complain about an inefficient process at work that you can influence; work alone or with others to craft a better solution.
- If you really don't like your job and the people you work with, it's time to find a new position.

The Attitude Scale in Figure 9.7 can give you a quick indication of your current performance level on this best practice. The scale ranges from 1 to 10, with 1 meaning, *I have little or no capacity in this area,* and 10 meaning, *I have very high capacity and require little or no improvement in this area.* Circle a number on the scale that best represents where you think you are this week on Attitude.

Attitude tends to be relatively robust across time, meaning that in most cases, your Attitude is not caused by your work associates or job. If you look across a leader's career, you will probably find her attitude has been about the same wherever she worked. This is not always true, but in a high percentage of cases, it is. Attitude comes from inside us. Track your overall Attitude for a few months, and you will discover how much it varies. Applying the techniques in this section will help to move your Attitude in a positive direction. Remember that *a negative brain is an angry brain.*

FIGURE 9.7 Attitude Scale

Southwest Airlines

Southwest Airlines has always been known as a low-cost, fun airline to fly. Safety briefings prior to takeoff are given in a humorous way that ensures even the hardcore road warriors listen. Passengers often participate in the briefing by clapping or repeating choruses. Southwest has a slogan—although they say it is not a slogan but a way of life: "Southwest Cares: Doing the Right Thing." This way of life covers the airline's dedication to using the warrior spirit to serve employees, customers, shareholders, and other stakeholders of Southwest as they "strive each and every day to do the right thing for our planet, our communities, our people and our suppliers."

The attitude of Southwest employees is not only obvious but contagious. They really seem to enjoy their work, and that attitude is passed on to their passengers. Longtime passengers from other major airlines may experience culture shock when they fly on Southwest, but most adjust quickly.

Learning

Although our brains do change with age, there is no reason to think we can't continue to teach ourselves new skills. For example, navigating the ins and outs of the dynamic social media world can be tricky, but not tricky enough to deter ninety-eight-year-old Marjorie Loyd of Carmichael, California, who recently joined Facebook. Loyd learned to use a computer just after she stopped driving at the age of ninety-five and told the *Sacramento Bee*, "I love people, and I love contact with people."[15] In preparation to celebrate her ninety-ninth birthday in 2010, she booked her airline ticket to Long Island online.

"It's kind of humbling because every time I learn something, I learn I have a lot more to learn," she said. The former owner of a used typewriter company (she ran it to support her family when her father died) faithfully reads the *Wall Street Journal* every day as well as *Forbes* magazine.

"Lifelong Learning"—the L in ARSENAL—means just that, no matter your age. Learning refers to actions taken to increase knowledge, skills, and abilities on a continuing basis—being a lifelong learner.

Leaders who continually engage in Learning tend to display learning agility, which enhances their ability to learn, adapt, flex, and function well during periods of high change. These leaders handle stress better than low-learning agility leaders, because they can learn and adapt faster to the changing environment.

One analogy is that the brain is like a muscle: maintaining good tone and strength requires regular exercise. Learning is exercise for the brain. The more you use it, challenge it, and give it different experiences—and adequate rest—the better and longer into old age it performs. The sharper and more agile the brain's functions are, the more it can help leaders make effective decisions under stress.

Learning ranges from a set of indicators such as *I don't like having to learn new things* and *I don't want more training or education* on the low end of the continuum, to *I'm a lifelong learner, I like puzzles, I read a lot, I take classes*, and *I'm always trying to learn something new* on the high end. It is possible, with effort, to increase Learning and, thereby, increase decision-making effectiveness.

Learning Menu

If you fail to do these five must do's on the Learning Menu, you risk not being able to develop this best practice beyond where you are today.

1. Set daily, monthly, quarterly, and annual Learning goals. For example, read two books monthly, or improve a foreign language skill over the course of a year.
2. Spend time with others who like to learn.
3. Spend time with people you consider intelligent.
4. Get out of your comfort zone. Learn something you have always wanted to learn but keep putting off.
5. Exercise all parts of your brain by choosing a variety of Learning goals.

Continuous Learning keeps the brain stimulated and growing. Solving problems and puzzles are great brain exercises. Novelty and whole-brain Learning are key factors in keeping the brain sharp. Doing just one kind of puzzle, such as Sudoku, does not give your brain a complete workout. The brain does more than just think. It controls all the functions of the body to include movement. You must also work your memory, eye-hand coordination, audio skills, and more.

Here are some other techniques for raising and sustaining Learning:

- Take online classes.
- Learn a new language.
- Listen to educational CDs, and watch educational programs and videos.
- Read nonfiction books in areas outside your professional field.
- Take notes during the day on topics you encounter but don't know very well. Look them up later to learn more about them.
- Search the Web.
- Use brain enhancement software.
- Solve puzzles, crosswords, Sudoku, and Mensa puzzles to stretch your brain.
- Work on expanding your memory.
- Practice doing mental math.
- Improve your balance: walk on uneven terrain or bounce on a trampoline, for example.
- Learn something new every day.
- Take trips, visit other countries, and learn about other cultures.
- Challenge yourself, for example, learn to play chess.
- Share what you learn with others. Discussions stimulate thinking.

The Learning Scale in Figure 9.8 can give you a quick indication of your current performance level on this best practice. The scale ranges from 1 to 10, with 1 meaning, *I have little or no capacity in this area,* and 10 meaning, *I have very high capacity and require little or no improvement in this area.* Circle a number on the scale that best represents where you think you are this week on Learning.

FIGURE 9.8 Learning Scale

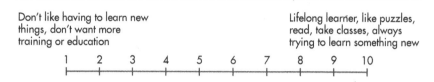

Remember that Learning is a dynamic skill that varies to some degree from day to day. If you track this area for a few months, you will discover what types of Learning activities you enjoy most, the range of your comfort zone for Learning, how well you are applying the techniques above, and, probably, that you have entered a brand new world filled with knowledge that you did not know existed. Remember that *an unused brain is a forgetful brain.*

Pixar Animation Studios

Pixar is a state-of-the-art animation company that uses its proprietary technology combined with some of the best creative talent in the world to produce Academy Award–winning animated films for audiences of all ages. A partial listing of Pixar films includes *Toy Story*, *Tokyo Mater*, *A Bug's Life*, and *Wall-E*, all of which pushed the envelope in the animated film world.

A portion of Pixar's success comes from Pixar University, run by Randy Nelson, which provides a complete curriculum in filmmaking and various creative courses. It is designed to provide a continuous Learning environment for all employees. In fact, each employee is encouraged to spend up to four hours a week—every week—working on his or her education. All levels and functions of the organization are mixed together in these classes, allowing for a better understanding of what everyone else does and bonding experiences.

Pixar is a company that exemplifies many things, one of which is the value of continuous Learning for everyone.

ARSENAL Basic Assessment

The ARSENAL Basic Assessment is a quick self-assessment of how well you are doing on the seven ARSENAL best practice areas.[16] Transfer your scores on each best practice to Figure 9.9 (graph a) by placing a dot

FIGURE 9.9 ARSENAL Assessment Graph

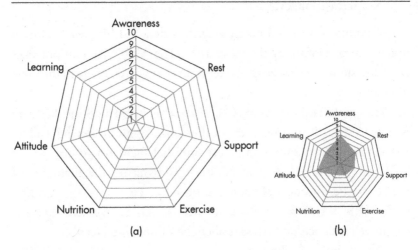

(a) (b)

Go to www.thestresseffect.com to download a blank graph or to take the expanded ARSENAL Individual Assessment.

at the appropriate point on each axis. (A score of 1 would be marked at the center of the graph, and a score of 10 would be marked on the bold outer line of the graph.) After plotting all seven areas, connect the dots with straight lines, moving around the figure from Awareness to Rest and so on, until you arrive back at Awareness. Now shade the inside area formed by the dots (see example in graph b).

This graph provides a quick visual of which best practice areas are your strongest and which areas need work. Ideally the entire graph would be shaded in, but that is not very realistic. Your goal should be to expand your ARSENAL ability levels to fill as much of the graph as possible. Become aware of how each best practice area is affecting your decision making in a positive or negative way. Keep a record of how decision-making effectiveness changes as these best practice areas change.

The seven ARSENAL best practices will help you in these areas:

- Increase brain functioning.
- Build stress resilience.
- Control emotions, and stay calm.
- Build new brain cells.

- Improve physical functioning.
- Increase longevity.

In addition, you will notice a synergistic effect, the result of each practice area reinforcing the other areas. The ARSENAL best practices act as a system—a change in one tends to change the others in the same direction.

The combination of ARSENAL best practices and the Stress Resilient System (SMC, CR, and SREI) create the Catastrophic Leadership Failure Prevention System shown in Figure 9.10 that increases your ability to resist catastrophic leadership failure by staying on the high side of the Leader Performance Response Surface (see Figure 5.4). Application of the ARSENAL best practices enhances stress management capacity, cognitive resilience, and stress resilient emotional intelligence.

The techniques, best practices, and self-awareness monitoring processes (dashboards, ARSENAL assessments, and graphs) discussed in this book provide enhanced opportunities for staying in your comfort zone and making effective decisions, even under high stress. There have been examples of leaders, such as Captain Sullenberger, who excelled under extreme stress. Through practice, determination,

FIGURE 9.10 Catastrophic Leadership Failure Prevention System Model

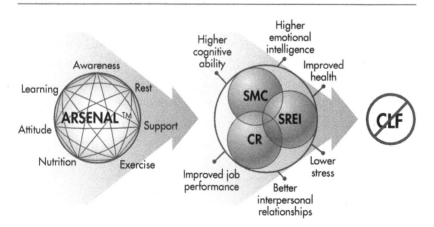

and using your cognitive and emotional intelligences, you too will make effective decisions under stress.

The Takeaway on ARSENAL

This chapter gives you the core best practices for immediately implementing a Stress Resilient System action plan. As a leader you should organize and begin your developmental plan today. Begin now by taking four tactical breaths. Slowly inhale through your nose for four seconds (count "one-one thousand, two-one thousand, three-one thousand, four-one thousand") while letting the air expand your belly; pause for the count of four, then exhale through your mouth, again counting to four, relaxing all your muscles as the air flows out. That's one tactical breath. Do three more, relaxing more deeply with each exhalation. When you sense your stress level rising, use tactical breathing. (Keep the counting to four seconds. Going longer might make you dizzy.)

The work presented in this chapter can be described by the following seven ARSENAL Axioms:

1. An unaware brain is a surprised brain.
2. A tired brain is a grumpy brain.
3. An unsupported brain is a sad brain.
4. An unfit brain is a slow brain.
5. A hungry brain is a distracted brain.
6. An negative brain is an angry brain.
7. An unused brain is a forgetful brain.

These axioms provide an easy way to remember the effects of not performing well in the ARSENAL areas.

You are now ready to move back into the real world. You will experience it differently than you have previously, see it differently, and maybe for the first time, "feel" it. You have the knowledge to make good decisions under very high stress, and life will provide you with opportunities to excel. Use these techniques and you will have the ability to make effective decisions in any situation.

Conclusion

No sensible decision can be made any longer without taking into account not only the world as it is, but the world as it will be.
Isaac Asimov

For decades, we have developed leaders to operate in a relatively stable and prosperous economy. When the market is great, almost anyone can appear to be a competent leader. The global economic crisis that began in 2008, however, rapidly exposed leaders who had risen to their level of incompetence and, consequently, were unable to make effective decisions under mounting economic and political stress. And the number of leaders exposed in this way is increasing. This epidemic of leaders who are making unsound decisions as a result of high stress levels has reached a critical threshold and can only guarantee a proliferation of the patterns seen in Bear Stearns, AIG, Fannie Mae and Freddie Mac, and others. Meanwhile, leadership development has lagged behind neuroscience and the *leadership body of knowledge*, resulting in a record number of leaders at all organizational levels losing their jobs in 2008 and 2009.

As we move farther into the twenty-first century, it is essential to optimize the human, organizational, and environmental factors that influence organizational performance to produce the most productive and resilient system possible. This will require a number of things, one of which is high performing leaders who can tolerate extreme levels of negative stress and also have the capability to create and manage positive stress. Leaders of the future will be required to be *masters of decision making under stress.*

Developing these masters will require a new focus for educating, training, and developing leaders. Corporate universities, business schools, and M.B.A. programs will have to adapt models that train leaders in a simulated high-stress, global environment—like the one in which they will lead—*before they actually get there.* Training leaders is similar to training parachutists: you have to train them to jump before pushing them out the door.

Teamwork and collaboration will become increasingly important as organizations emerge on the other side of the current global economic crisis.[1] Building stress resilient collaborative teams will become a necessity. People are the building blocks of teams. Consequently, teams take on the characteristics of their team members, and especially of their leader. When a team is placed in a stressful environment, its ability to make effective decisions changes in a fashion similar to that of a leader. Teams behave like people; they have their own personality or, as the influential psychologist Raymond Cattell called it, *syntality.*[2] Teams also demonstrate cognitive intelligence and emotional intelligence, which are affected by stress in the same manner as leaders' intelligences.[3] When stress goes up, cognitive and emotional intelligences go down—and so does effective team decision making.

More connectivity and teamwork mean more stress. We are seeing this today, and it will only increase in the future. More stress means lower team performance unless new, innovative preventive steps are taken. For example, team members may wear electronic stress monitors (similar to those being developed by the U.S. Army Natick Soldier Research Development and Engineering Center and discussed in Chapter Seven) that provide an overall stress level for the team as well as "stress alerts" for individual team members. At least one team member may be designated as the team stress monitor with the responsibility for monitoring the team's stress level and recommending actions to manage the stress. The team's stress level should also be displayed as a critical factor on the team's performance dashboard.

Teams are the building blocks of organizations. In their book *Companies Are People, Too,* Sandra Fekete and Lee Anna Keith make a convincing argument that companies have personalities and behave in ways similar to individuals.[4] Stressed people thus create stressed teams, which lead to stressed organizations. In my experience, you can sense the stress level of an organization as you begin to interact with its members—sometimes as soon as you walk into their building. There's good reason that some organizations are stressed. According to the PriceWaterhouseCoopers Twelfth Annual Global CEO Survey, 97 percent of CEOs believe that employees will have to do more work in the same amount of time they have today.[5] If that is true, we can expect the stress levels in organizations to continue to rise. Like leaders and teams, future organizations will need to make stress management a functional area similar to finance, operations, and human resources and will need to create a new C-level position: *Chief Stress Officer.* They will also need to add stress as one of the dimensions on the corporate dashboard.

Stress is a serious matter and must be addressed using all available resources. For example, organizations might create stress relief centers where employees can go to de-stress. Similar centers, which have already been established in some organizations, have relaxing music, aquariums, yoga, mindfulness training, massage chairs—or actual masseuses—and other forms of relaxation. Office environments will become much more calming in their layout and in noise and temperature management. Work spaces will conform to the work style of the individual, for example, more privacy for workers with introverted preferences and more openness for workers with extraverted preferences. Workers will monitor their own stress levels electronically, and leaders will automatically redistribute workload based on worker stress levels. The goal will be to work smarter, not harder—to work within the comfort zone, not the burnout zone.

The U.S. Army has taken the lead in developing not only resilient leaders but also resilient families and communities with their newly created Master Resiliency Training program.[6] This program is championed by the Army Chief of Staff, General George Casey, as a way to develop resilient soldiers, families, and civilians to meet the demands of today and the future. The years of continuous global conflict have brought to light the requirement for the military to have leaders who are masters of decision making under stress. Nonmilitary organizations will begin to adopt similar programs in the near future.

In preparing for the future, we should keep in mind the old Native American analogy that describes the past, present, and future as a log burning in a fire. The part of the log that has burned into ash is yesterday, the part that is burning is today, and the part that will burn soon is tomorrow. We are the fire. We can live only today, and what we do today determines whether our fire will still be burning tomorrow.

Notes

Introduction

1 The Flight 1549 Intra-cockpit communication and air-ground communication transcripts used in this book are excerpted versions from Brazy, D. P. (2009, April 22). *Group chairman's factual report of investigation: Cockpit voice recorder DCA09MA026* with names assigned to the various people communicating. Retrieved May 20, 2009, from http://www.tailstrike .com/150109.pdf. A twenty-four-hour clock time is used in this sequence beginning at 15:26:37. On a twelve-hour clock, the time is 37 seconds past 3:26 P.M.

2 A mistake by Captain Sullenberger in the actual flight number, one of several made during the ongoing conversations.

3 Another error in the flight's actual number, 1549. Sullenberger said "1539" earlier; now Harten says "1529." As the stress level continues to climb, remembering number sequences becomes increasingly difficult.

4 CEO turnover the highest since 2001. (2005, March 7). CNN/Money.com. This article reports data provided by Challenger, Gray & Christmas, 2005.

5 CEO turnover hits new high. (2009, January 16). Management-Issues.com. Based on a report by Challenger, Gray & Christmas, 2009.

6   Boyatzis, R. E. (2009). Competencies as a behavioral approach to emotional intelligence. *Journal of Management Development, 28*(9), 749–770.

7   Boyatzis, R. E., Smith, M. L., & Blaize, N. (2006). Developing sustainable leaders through coaching and compassion. *Academy of Management Learning & Education, 5*(1), 8–24.

Chapter One

1   CBS "60 Minutes." *Ken Lay: I was fooled.* (2005, March 13). Retrieved from http://www.cbsnews.com/stories/2005/03/11/60minutes/main679706.shtml.

2   Cohan, W. D. (2008, August 25). The rise and fall of Jimmy Cayne. *Fortune Magazine, 158*(3). Retrieved from http://money.cnn.com/2008/07/31/magazines/fortune/rise_and_fall_Cayne_cohan.fortune/index.htm.

3   For more information on the quotes by Fuld, Sullivan, and Killinger, see Megan Barnett, Regrettable comments by bank CEOs. Retrieved from http://finance.yahoo.com/career-work/article/105484/Regrettable-Comments-by-Bank-CEOs.

4   This is a reference to Senator Hillary Clinton's series of TV ads during the 2008 U.S. presidential campaign to encourage voters to select the candidate who was best prepared to respond and take action in a crisis.

5   Friedman, T. L. (2007). *The world is flat 3.0: A brief history of the twenty-first century.* New York: Picador.

6   Peter, L. J., & Hull, R. (1969). *The Peter principle: Why things always go wrong.* Cutchogue, NY: Buccaneer Books.

7   This average CEO IQ comes from the High Performing Systems database. The range of CEO IQs in the database is 110 to 145.

8   Peters, J. J., & Waterman, R. H. (1982). *In search of excellence.* New York: HarperCollins.

9   Collins, J. (2001). *Good to great: Why some companies make the leap and some don't.* New York: HarperCollins.

10 Kirkpatrick, S., & Locke, E. A. (1991). Leadership: Do traits matter? *Academy of Management Executive, 5*(2), 48–60.

11 Welch, J. (2005). *Winning.* New York: HarperBusiness.

12 Six Sigma, a statistical concept that originated with Motorola in the 1980s, refers to measuring a process in terms of defects. A process operating at the Six Sigma level produces only 3.4 defects per 1 million opportunities.

13 Owen Jacobs and I have remained in contact over the years.

14 The Leadership Potential Equation is a mathematical process for measuring the leadership potential of a leader in two major categories: learned abilities and innate abilities. The result of the equation shows not only the potential for success at various organizational role levels now, but also potential across the leader's career span.

15 The study of emotional intelligence began in earnest in the 1980s with the work of Reuven Bar-On, Peter Salovey, John Mayer, Howard Gardner, and others. It came to the attention of the general public when Daniel Goleman published his groundbreaking best-selling book, *Emotional intelligence: Why it can matter more than IQ* (New York: Bantam Books). Goleman's book created an explosion of research, publications, and public awareness of emotional intelligence.

16 Thompson, H. L. (2006). Exploring the interface of type and emotional intelligence landscapes. *Bulletin of Psychological Type, 29*(3), 14–19.

17 McClelland, D. C. (1988). *Human motivation.* Cambridge: Cambridge University Press. Also see Lawrence, P. R., & Nohria, N. (2002). *Driven: How human nature shapes our choices.* San Francisco: Jossey-Bass.

18 Cohan, W. D. (2008, August 25). The rise and fall of Jimmy Cayne. *Fortune.* Retrieved September 10, 2009, from http://money.cnn.com/2008/07/31/magazines/fortune/rise_and_fall_Cayne_cohan.fortune/index.htm.

19 Pearman, R. R. (1998). *Hardwired leadership: Unleashing the power of personality to become a new millennium leader.* Palo Alto, CA: Davies-Black Publishing.

20 Emotional Quotient Inventory is an assessment of emotional intelligence created by Reuven Bar-On and owned and published by Multi-Health Systems.

21 Stanovich, K. E., & West, R. F. (2000). Individual differences in reasoning: Implications for the rationality debate. *Behavioral and Brain Sciences, 23,* 645–665.

22 Gladwell, M. (2005). *Blink! The power of thinking without thinking.* New York: Little, Brown.

23 Boyd created the OODA loop and its tactics and laid the groundwork for many other U.S. Air Force innovations. Coram, R. (2002). *Boyd: The fighter pilot who changed the art of war.* New York: Back Bay Books.

24 Hillaker, H. (1997, July). John Boyd, USAF Retired, father of the F16. *Code One,* 12(3).

25 Klein, G. (1998). *Sources of power: How people make decisions.* Cambridge, MA: MIT Press; and Klein, G. (2009). *Streetlights and shadows: Searching for the keys to adaptive decision making.* Boston: MIT Press.

26 Simon, H. A. (1957). *Models of man: Social and rational.* Hoboken, NJ: Wiley.

27 Sun Tsu. (1994). *Sun Tsu: The art of war* (R. D. Sawyer, trans.). New York: Basic Books; and Krulak, C. C. (1999, January). The strategic corporal: Leadership in the Three Block War. *Marines Magazine.*

28 I created the Perception-Appraisal-Motivation-Action model (PAMA) in 2005 to help explain the processes involved in decision making, especially the cognitive and emotional components. Three sources for additional information about PAMA are Thompson, H. L. (2009). Emotional intelligence, stress, and catastrophic leadership failure, In M. Hughes, H. L. Thompson, & J. B. Terrell (Eds.), *Handbook for developing emotional and social intelligence: Best practices, case studies, and strategies* (pp. 111–138). San Francisco: Pfeiffer; Thompson, H. L. (2006). Exploring the interface of type and emotional intelligence landscapes. *Bulletin of Psychological Type,* 29(3), 14–19; and The Stress Effect Web site at www.thestresseffect.com.

29 "Schrödinger's cat" refers to a thought experiment created by the Austrian physicist Erwin Schrödinger in 1935. A cat is locked inside a steel box with a glass container of poison and a Geiger counter. If the Geiger counter detects radiation, it will cause the poison to be released. After a period of time, the cat can be assumed to be either alive or dead. According to the Copenhagen interpretation of quantum mechanics (the most widely accepted interpretation of quantum mechanics put forth by Niels Bohr and Werner Heisenberg in Copenhagen around 1927), until the lid is opened, the cat is both dead and alive (and all states in between). When the lid is opened and you can see the cat, all quantum states collapse into

one and you will see if the cat is alive or dead. Schrödinger coined the term *quantum entanglement* to refer to the connection of the cat's dead-or-alive state with the random event of the detection of radiation.

30 Hewitt, B., & Egan, N. (2009, February 23). Flight 1549: The right stuff. *People Magazine*, p. 64. Retrieved from http://www.people.com/people/archive/article/0,,20264356,00.html.

Chapter Two

1 Ackroyd, P. (2006). *Newton*. New York: Doubleday.

2 *The Wonderlic Personnel Test and Scholastic Level Exam user's manual.* (2002). Libertyville, IL: Wonderlic.

3 Schmidt, F. L., & Hunter, J. E. (1998). The validity and utility of selection methods in personnel psychology: Practical and theoretical implications of 85 years of research findings. *Psychological Bulletin, 124*(2), 262–274.

4 Gottfredson, L. S. (1997). Mainstream science on intelligence: An editorial with 52 signatories, history and bibliography. *Intelligence, 24,* 13–23.

5 Spearman, C. (1904). "General intelligence," objectively determined and measured. *American Journal of Psychology, 15,* 201–293.

6 Thurston, L. L. (1938). *Primary mental abilities.* Chicago: University of Chicago Press.

7 Cattell, R. B. (1963). Theory of fluid and crystallized intelligence: A critical experiment. *Journal of Educational Psychology, 54,* 1–22.

8 Carroll, J. B. (1993). *Human cognitive abilities: A survey of factor analytic studies.* Cambridge: Cambridge University Press.

9 Alfonso, V. C., Flanagan, D. P., & Radwell, S. (2005). The impact of the Catell-Horn-Carroll theory on test development and interpretation of cognitive and academic abilities. In D. P. Flanagan and P. L. Harrison (Eds.), *Contemporary intellectual assessment: Theories, tests, and issues* (2nd ed.). New York: The Guilford Press.

10 The Wonderlic Personnel Test has a correlation of .92 with the Wechsler Adult Intelligence Scale–III. This very high correlation indicates that the two tests make very similar predictions about a person's general mental ability.

11 For a more detailed presentation on this topic, see Bruer, J. T. (1999). *The myth of the first three years: A new understanding of early brain development and lifelong learning.* New York: Free Press.

12 Campbell, F. A., & Ramey, C. T. (1995). Cognitive and school outcomes for high-risk African-American students at middle adolescence: Positive effects of early intervention, *American Educational Research Journal, 32*(4), 742–772.

13 Some of the key researchers and their representative works in the field of cognitive intelligence development share this opinion: Steven Pinker (Pinker, S. [2009]. *How the mind works.* New York: W.W. Norton & Company); Howard Gardner (Gardner, H. [2007]. *Five minds for the future.* Boston: Harvard Business School Press); Judith Richard Harris (Harris, J. R. [1998]. *The nurture assumption: Why children turn out the way they do.* New York: Touchstone); Jerome Kagan (Kagan, J. [2009]. *The three cultures: Natural sciences, social sciences, and the humanities in the 21st century.* New York: Cambridge University Press); and Robert Sternberg (Sternberg, R. J. [2007]. *Wisdom, intelligence, and creativity synthesized.* New York: Cambridge University Press).

14 Piaget, J. (1950). *The psychology of intelligence.* Orlando, FL: Harcourt; Vygotsky, L. S. (1962). *Thought and language.* Cambridge, MA: MIT Press (Original work published 1934); Kagan, J., Herschkowitz, N., & Herschkowitz, E. (2005). *Young mind in a growing brain.* Mahwah, NJ: Erlbaum.

15 Deary, I. J. (2001). *Intelligence: A very short introduction.* New York: Oxford University Press.

16 An additional twenty-eight people were added a few weeks later, bringing the total number to 101.

17 Schaie, K. W. (1994). The course of adult intellectual development. *American Psychologist, 49,* 304–313.

18 Jones, D. (2008, August 12). Does age matter when you're CEO? *USA Today.*

19 Wearing, D. (2006). *Forever today: A true story of lost memory and never-ending love.* London: Corgi.

20 Summers, L. H. (2005, January 14). Remarks at NBER Conference on diversifying the science & engineering workforce, Cambridge,

Massachusetts. Retrieved from http://www.president.harvard.edu/speeches/summers_2005/nber.php.

21 Goldberg, E. (2009). *The new executive brain: Frontal lobes in a complex world*. Oxford: Oxford University Press.

22 Hyde, J. S. (2005). The gender similarities hypothesis. *American Psychologist, 60*(6), 581–592.

23 Spirduso, W. W., Poon, L. W., & Chodzko-Zajko, W. (Eds.). (2008). *Exercise and its mediating effects on cognition*. Champaign, IL: Human Kinetics.

24 Raichle, M. E., & Gusnard, D. A. (2002). Appraising the brain's energy budget. *Proceedings of the National Academy of Sciences, 99*(16), 10237–10239.

25 Fleming, M. K. (2003, October 1). The sleep factor. *Soldiers Magazine*, p. 40.

26 The average IQ score is 100. Ever wonder how IQ just happened to have an average score of exactly 100? It is 100 by the magic of mathematics. It could just as easily be 107.876 or 95.345. The publishers of IQ tests decided that it would be 100. This simple formula shows how it is done:

$$\text{Transformed Score} = (((\text{raw score-mean})/\text{Standard Deviation}) * 15) + 100$$

In transforming IQ test scores, or any test scores, to a standard deviation of 15 and an average of 100, 15 becomes the new standard deviation and 100 becomes the new average. If you want a different standard deviation, replace the 15 with what you want it to be. The same is true for the average. Just replace the 100 with what you want the new average to be.

27 I have found the following IQ variations by role level: Tactical role level, 85–140; Organizational role level, 105–140; Strategic role level, 115–145; and Visionary role level, 115–145.

28 Bass, B. M. (1990). *Bass & Stogdill's handbook of leadership: Theory, research, and managerial applications* (3rd ed.). New York: Free Press.

29 Gardner, H. (1999). *Intelligence reframed: Multiple intelligences for the 21st century*. New York: Basic Books. Gardner writes, "Leaders may need a modicum of intelligence; but, if anything, intelligence can get in their way if they want to connect to the public" (p. 125).

30   Research Australia. (2005, June 11). Shrinking brains but healthy
     memory—Does brain matter matter? *ScienceDaily*. Retrieved January 22,
     2010, from http://www.sciencedaily.com/releases/2005/06/
     050611153907.htm.

31   American Academy of Neurology. (2008, July 15). Exercise may prevent
     brain shrinkage in early Alzheimer's Disease. *ScienceDaily*. Retrieved
     January 18, 2010, from http://www.sciencedaily.com/releases/2008/07/
     080714162632.htm.

32   Cohen, G. D. (2006). *The mature mind: The positive power of the aging
     brain*. New York: Basic Books.

33   Goldberg, E. (2001). *The executive brain: Frontal lobes and the civilized
     mind*. Oxford: Oxford University Press; Goldberg, E. (2005). *The wisdom
     paradox: How your mind can grow as your brain grows older*. New York:
     Gotham Books; and Goldberg, E. (2009). *The new executive brain: Frontal
     lobes in a complex world*. Oxford: Oxford University Press.

34   Goldberg, E. (2009). *The new executive brain: Frontal lobes in a complex
     world*. Oxford: Oxford University Press, p. 21. For further reading see
     Neumayr, A. (1995). *Dictators in the mirror of medicine: Napoleon, Hitler*
     (D. J. Parent, Trans.). Bloomington, IL: Medi-Ed Press.

35   Investigation: United Airlines Flight 173. (2009, July 19). Retrieved from
     http://www.airdisaster.com/investigations/ua173.shtml.

36   Einstein's IQ is typically estimated to have been 160 to 165. There are many
     documented cases of people with IQs in the 200 range, many of whom
     have not made any significant contributions to science—except, perhaps,
     that they have not made any significant contribution to science.

Chapter Three

1   Honoré, R. L., with Martz, R. (2009). *Survival: How a culture of
     preparedness can save you and your family from disasters* (p. 100). New
     York: Atria Books.

2   Honoré, R. L., with Martz, R. (2009). *Survival: How a culture of
     preparedness can save you and your family from disasters* (p. 164). New
     York: Atria Books.

3   Caruso, D. R., & Salovey, P. (2004). *The emotionally intelligent manager*.
     San Francisco: Jossey-Bass.

4 Plutchik, R. (2002). *Emotions and life: Perspectives from psychology, biology and evolution*. Washington, DC: American Psychological Association. Plutchik chose this set of eight emotions based on his analysis of the most agreed-on common emotions identified by researchers. For more information about Newton's color wheel, see Varley, H. (1980). *Colour*. London: Marshall Editions.

5 Marsh, B. (2009, February 14). The voice was lying, the face may have told the truth. The NYTimes.com. Retrieved May 15, 2009, from http://www.nytimes.com/2009/02/15/weekinreview/15marsh.html.

6 Azar, B. (2000). What's in a face? *Monitor on Psychology, 31*, 1. Also see Fridlund, A. (1994). *Human facial expression: An evolutionary view*. San Diego, CA: Academic Press.

7 Frijda, N. H. (1994). Emotions are functional, most of the time. In P. Ekman & R. J. Davidson (Eds.), *The nature of emotion—Fundamental questions*. New York: Oxford University Press.

8 Darwin, C. (1872). *The expression of the emotions in man and animals*. New York: Oxford University Press. Darwin also made use of the latest technology of the time period and included photographs in his book.

9 Leuner published the first article using the term "emotional intelligence" (Leuner, B. [1966]. Emotional intelligence and emancipation. *Praxis der Kinderpsychologie und Kinderpsychiatrie, 15*, 193–203). Reuven Bar-On coined the term "emotional quotient" in 1985 (Bar-On, R. [1985]. The development of an operational concept of psychological well-being [p. 419]. Unpublished doctoral dissertation. Rhodes University, South Africa.) He also provided a definition of emotional intelligence (a noncognitive type of intelligence): Bar-On, R. (1997). *The Bar-On Emotional Quotient Inventory (EQ-i): Technical manual* (p. 14). Toronto, Canada: Multi-Health Systems. Others have provided similar definitions, for example: Salovey, P., & Mayer, J. D. (1990). Emotional intelligence. *Imagination, Cognition, and Personality, 9*, 185–211; and Thompson, H. L. (2006). Exploring the interface of type and emotional intelligence landscapes. *Bulletin of Psychological Type, 29*(3), 14–19.

10 Goleman, D. (1995). *Emotional intelligence: Why it can matter more than IQ*. New York: Bantam Books.

11 Thompson, H. L. (2006). Exploring the interface of type and emotional intelligence landscapes. *Bulletin of Psychological Type, 29*(3), 14–19.

12 MacLean, P. D. (1970). The triune brain, emotion and scientific bias. In F. O. Schmitt (Ed.), *The neurosciences: Second study program* (pp. 336–349). New York: Rockefeller University Press. MacLean, P. D. (1990). *The triune brain in evolution: Role in paleocerebral functions.* New York: Plenum.

13 Paul MacLean introduced the term *limbic system* as a new name for what had been called the *visceral brain.* This part of the brain is also called the old mammalian brain, intermediate brain, rational brain, or paleopallium. MacLean, P. D. (1952). Some psychiatric implications of physiological studies on frontotemporal portion of limbic system (visceral brain). *Electroencephalography and Clinical Neuropsychology, 4,* 407–418.

14 Goldberg, E. (2009). *The new executive brain: Frontal lobes in a complex world* (p. 117). New York: Oxford University Press.

15 The MSCEIT scales have a mean of 100 and a standard deviation of 15. See Mayer, J., Salovey, P., & Caruso, D. (2002). *Mayer-Salovey-Caruso Emotional Intelligence Test manual.* Toronto: Multi-Health Systems.

16 The EQ-i scales have a mean of 100 and a standard deviation of 15. See Bar-On, R. (1997). *Bar-On Emotional Quotient Inventory: A measure of emotional intelligence (technical manual).* Toronto: Multi-Health Systems.

17 Abess, L. (2009, April 29). Sharing the wealth: Leonard Abess and the $60 million gift to his employees. Interview with Knowledge@ Wharton. Retrieved June 13, 2009, from http://knowledge.wharton.upenn.edu/ article.cfm?articleid=2228.

18 Stone, H., Parker, J.D.A., & Wood, L. M. (2005, February). OPC leadership study: Exploring the relationship between school leadership and emotional intelligence. Presented at the Ontario Principals' Council executive meeting, Toronto, Ontario.

19 This finding stems from my ongoing study of the leadership styles, abilities, and effectiveness of public school system assistant principals, principals, directors, and superintendents. Emotional intelligence is being measured using the EQ-i and MSCEIT.

20 Stein, S. J., & Book, H. E. (2006). *The EQ edge: Emotional intelligence and your success* (rev. ed.; pp. 260–264). Mississauga, Canada: Jossey-Bass. In addition, Dries and Pepermans (Dries, N., & Pepermans, R. [2007]. Using emotional intelligence to identify high potential: A metacompetency perspective. *Leadership and Organizational Development Journal, 28*[8], 749–770) conducted a study of 102 managers and found that high-potential managers had higher EQ-i scores than "regular" managers. This was especially true for the EQ-i subscales of Assertiveness, Independence, Optimism, Flexibility, and Social Responsibility. The authors suggest that these five subscales might be "covert" high-potential criteria.

21 Bar-On, R. (2006). The Bar-On model of emotional intelligence (ESI), *Psicothema, 18*, supplement, 13–25.

22 Bechara, A., Damasio, H., Tranel, D., & Damasio, A. R. (1997). The Iowa gambling task and the somatic marker hypothesis: Some questions and answers. *TRENDS in Cognitive Sciences, 9*(4), 159–162.

23 Goleman, D. (1995). *Emotional intelligence: Why it can matter more than IQ*. New York: Bantam Books.

24 LeDoux, J. E. (2002). *Synaptic self: How our brains become who we are* (p. 226). New York: Penguin Books.

25 Loewenstein, G., & Lerner, J. S. (2002). The role of affect in decision making. In R. J. Davidson, K. R. Scherer, & H. H. Goldsmith (Eds.), *Handbook of affective sciences* (pp. 619–642). New York: Oxford University Press.

26 Damasio, A. (2000). *The feeling of what happens: Body and emotion in the making of consciousness*. New York: Harcourt.

27 Damasio, A. (1997). *Descartes' error*. New York: Avon Books.

28 Drexler, M. (2009, Winter). Science of decisions; At the Kennedy School, the art of decision making is brought into the lab. *John F. Kennedy School of Government Bulletin*. Retrieved January 15, 2010, from http://www.hks.harvard.edu/ocpa/pdf/HKSBulletin_winter2009.pdf.

29 Damasio, A. (2000). *The feeling of what happens: Body and emotion in the making of consciousness*. New York: Harcourt.

30 *The EQ-i Technical Manual* (p. 81) shows total EQ-i scores with groups of people aged sixteen to nineteen, 95.3; twenty to twenty-nine, 96.8; thirty to thirty-nine, 101.8; forty to forty-nine, 102.7; and fifty and over, 101.5.

31 These data come from research using the EQ-i. See Bar-On (1997).

Chapter Four

1 Ekman, P. (2003). *Emotions revealed: Recognizing faces and feelings to improve communication and emotional life.* New York: Owl Books.

2 Lumsden, D. P. (1981). Is the concept of "stress" of any use, anymore? In D. Randall (Ed.), *Contribution to primary prevention in mental health: Working papers.* Toronto: Toronto National Office of the Canadian Mental Health Association, as reported in Lazarus, R. S. (1999). *Stress and emotion: A new synthesis.* New York: Springer Publishing Company. Robert Hooke, a prominent physicist-biologist in the seventeenth century, developed the later definition as reported by Hinkle, L. E. (1973). The concept of "stress" in biological and social sciences. In Z. J. Lipowski, D. R. Lipsitt, & P. C. Whybrow (Eds.), *Psychosomatic medicine: Current trends and clinical implication.* New York: Oxford University Press; and Lazarus, R. S. (1999). *Stress and emotion: A new synthesis.* New York: Springer Publishing Company, p. 31.

3 Selye, H. (1978). *The stress of life.* New York: McGraw-Hill.

4 Cofer, C. N., & Appley, M. H. (1964). *Motivation: Theory and research.* Hoboken, NJ: Wiley, p. 449.

5 Selye, H. (1936). A syndrome produced by diverse nocuous agents. *Nature, 138,* 32.

6 Tangri, R. (2003). *Stress costs, stress cures.* Victoria, Canada: Trafford Publishing. At the time of this writing, the United States is caught up in a global economic catastrophe. Thus, the data presented here are probably out of date: stress is much higher and is causing much more damage than reflected in these statistics.

7 Sapolsky, R., Romero, M., & Munck, A. (2000). How do glucocorticoids influence the stress response? Integrating permissive, suppressive, stimulatory, and preparative actions. *Endocrine Reviews, 21,* 55.

8   Mujica-Parodi, L. R., Renelique, R., & Taylor, M. K. (2009). Higher body
    fat is associated with increased cortisol reactivity and impaired cognitive
    resilience to acute emotional stress. *International Journal of Obesity, 33,*
    157–165. Also see About.com, Stress Management, February 5, 2008.
    Scot, E. Cortisol and stress: How to stay healthy. Increased abdominal fat
    has been linked to heart attacks, stroke, "bad" cholesterol (LDL) and
    lower "good" cholesterol (HDL).

9   McGaugh, J. L. (2000). Memory—A century of consolidation. *Science,*
    287, 248–251.

10 Roberts, R. O., Geda, Y. E., Knopman, D. S., Cha, R. H., Pankratz, V. S.,
    Boeve, B. F., Ivnik, R. J., Tangalos, E. G., Petersen, R. C., & Rocc, W. A.
    (2008). The Mayo Clinic study of aging: Design and sampling,
    participation, baseline measures and sample characteristics.
    Neuroepidemiology, 30(1), 58–69.

11 Sapolsky, R. M., Romero, L. M., & Munck, A. U. (2000). How do
    glucocorticoids influence stress responses? Integrating permissive,
    suppressive, stimulatory, and preparative actions. *Endocrine Reviews, 21,*
    55–89.

12 Khalsa, D. S. (1997). *Brain longevity.* New York: Warner Books.

13 University of California at Los Angeles. (2000, May 22). UCLA researchers
    identify key biobehavioral pattern used by women to manage stress.
    ScienceDaily. Retrieved January 22, 2010, from http://www.sciencedaily
    .com/releases/2000/05/000522082151.htm.

14 Taylor, S. E. (2000). Biobehavioral responses to stress in females: Tend-
    and-befriend, not fight-or-flight. *Psychological Review, 107,* 411–429.
    Taylor, S. E. (2002). *The tending instincts of women: Women, men and the*
    biology of our relationships. New York: Holt.

15 Thompson, H. L., & Walsh, P. (2000). Is there really a difference between
    "job type" and "home type"? *Bulletin of Psychological Type, 23*(1), 14, 16, 18.

16 Zillman, D. (1978). Attribution and misattributions of excitatory
    reactions. In J. H. Harvey, W. J. Ickes, & R. F. Kidd (Eds.), *New directions*
    in attribution research (Vol. 2, pp. 335–368). Mahwah, NJ: Erlbaum.

17 Treasurer, W. (2003). *Right risk: 10 powerful principles for taking giant leaps*
    with your life (p. 25). San Francisco: Berrett-Koehler Publishers.

18   Sapolsky, R. M. (2004). *Why zebras don't get ulcers* (3rd ed.). New York: Owl Books. Sapolsky, R. M. (2002). *A primate's memoir: A neuroscientist's unconventional life among the baboons.* New York: Touchstone.

19   Seligman, M. E., & Maier, S. F. (1967). Failure to escape traumatic shock. *Journal of Experimental Psychology, 74*(1), 1–9.

20   Sanderson, W. C., Rapee, R. M., & Barlow, D. H. (1988). Panic induction via inhalation of 5.5% CO_2 enriched air: A single subject analysis of psychological and physiological effects. *Behavior Research and Therapy, 26*(4), 333–335.

21   Marmot, M., Bosma, H., Hemmingway, H., & Stansfeld, S. (1997, July 26). Contribution of job control and other risk factors to social variation in coronary heart disease incidence. *Lancet, 350*(9073), 235–239. Retrieved from http://www.ncbi.nlm.nih.gov/pubmed/9242799.

22   Noise-induced hearing loss. (2009). National Institute on Deafness and Other Communication Disorders Web site. Retrieved October 15, 2009, from http://www.nidcd.nih.gov/health/hearing/noise.asp#sounds.

23   Rhudy, J. L., & Meagher, M. W. (2001). Noise-induced changes in radiant heat pain thresholds: Divergent effects in men and women. *Journal of Pain, 2,* 57–64.

24   Thompson, H. L. (1981). Baby crying as an antecedent of child abuse. Unpublished doctoral dissertation, University of Georgia.

25   Yerkes, R. M., & Dodson, J. D. (1908). The relation of strength of stimulus to rapidity of habit-formation. *Journal of Comparative Neurology and Psychology, 18,* 459–482. For a more advanced and current view of performance curves, see the Hancock Optimal Performance Curve in Hancock, P. A., & Szalma, J. L. (2008). *Performance under stress.* Burlington, VT: Ashgate Publishing Company.

26   The "Optimal Performance Curve" shown in Figure 4.7 is a generic curve for discussing this concept. The shape and location of the curve on the graph will vary with the type of performance measured. For example, if the task being performed is primarily cognitive (a calculus test), the optimal level tends to be reached with a somewhat lower level of stress than if the task is primarily physical (say, football or wrestling).

27   Holmes, T., & Rahe, R. (1967). Holmes-Rahe life changes scale. *Journal of Psychosomatic Research, 11,* 213–218.

Chapter Five

1   Cooper, M. (1999, February 5). Unarmed man dies after police fire 41 shots at him. *The New York Times.* Retrieved from http://partners.nytimes .com/library/national/regional/020599ny-diallo.html.

2   Peter, L. J., & Hull, R. (1969). *The Peter principle.* Cutchogue, NY: Buccaneer Books.

3   Andreassen, P. B. (1987). On the social psychology of the stock market: Aggregate attributional effects and the regressiveness of prediction. *Journal of Personality and Social Psychology, 53*(3), 490–496.

4   Schwartz, B. (2004). *The paradox of choice: Why more is less.* New York: HarperCollins. The quotation is from Schwartz, B. (2009, May 24). The impact of too many options in modern life. Retrieved from http:// psychology.suite101.com/article.cfm/do_we_have_too_many_choices _part_1_of_2.

5   Simon, H. A. (1971). Designing organizations for an information-rich world. In M. Greenberger (Ed.), *Computers, communication, and the public interest* (p. 40). Baltimore: The Johns Hopkins Press.

6   Craik, K.J.W. (1967). *The nature of explanation* (rev. ed.). Cambridge: Cambridge University Press. This book laid the foundation for mental models.

7   Bazerman, M. H., & Moore, D. A. (2009). *Judgment in managerial decision making.* Hoboken, NJ: Wiley. The "confirmation trap" is from Zuckerman, M., Knee, C. R., Hodgins, H. S., & Miyake, K. (1995). Hypothesis confirmation: The joint effect of positive test strategy and acquiescence response set. *Journal of Personality and Social Psychology, 68,* 52–60.

8   Jung, C. G. (1976). *Psychological types* (para. 847). (A revision by R.F.C. Hull of the translation by H. G. Baynes.) Princeton, NJ: Princeton University Press.

9   For a different but excellent version of the cave, see Hutchens, D. (1999). *Shadows of the Neanderthal: Illuminating the beliefs that limit our organizations.* Waltham, MA: Pegasus Communication.

10 Morgan, G. (2006). *Images of organization* (p. 339). Thousand Oaks, CA: Sage Publications.

11 Coined by Arien Mack and Irvin Rock in 1992. Rock, I., Linnett, C., Grant, P., & Mack, A. (1992). Perception without attention: Results of a new method. *Cognitive Psychology, 24,* 502–534.

12 Simons, D. J., & Chabris, C. F. (1999). Gorillas in our midst: Sustained inattentional blindness for dynamic events. *Perception, 28,* 1059–1074. Also see Chun, M. M., & Marois, R. (2002). The dark side of visual attention. *Current Opinion in Neurobiology, 12*(1), 184–189. Neisser, U. (1967). *Cognitive psychology.* New York: Appleton-Century-Crofts.

13 Study by Bernard Brown and Lilian Rosenbaum of Georgetown University. Study ties IQ scores to stress. (2009, August 13). *The New York Times.*

14 Malik, P. R., & Balda, S. (2006). High IQ adolescents under stress: Do they perform poorly in academics? *Anthropologist, 8*(2), 61–62. The Bisht Battery of Stress Scale was devised by Swati Bisht in 1987.

15 Saltzman, K. M., Weems, C. F., & Carrion, V. G. (2006). IQ and post-traumatic stress symptoms in children exposed to interpersonal violence. *Child Psychiatry and Human Development, 36,* 261–272.

16 Shiv, B., & Fedorikhin, A. (1999). Heart and mind in conflict: The interplay of affect and cognition in consumer decision making. *Journal of Consumer Research, 26*(2), 278–292. For additional, less technical information, see Krakovsky, M. (2008, February). How do we decide? *Stanford Business Magazine.* Retrieved from http://www.gsb.stanford.edu/news/bmag/sbsm0802/feature-babashiv.html.

17 Thompson, H. L., & Richardson, D. R. (1983). The rooster effect: Same-sex rivalry and inequity as factors in retaliative aggression. *Journal of Personality and Social Psychology Bulletin, 9*(3), 415–425.

18 Some mathematical models can be used to examine nonlinear, multivariable scenarios such as Catastrophic Leadership Failure (CLF). One such model is Thom's catastrophe model (Thom, R. [1975]. *Structural stability and morphogenesis.* New York: Benjamin-Addison-Wesley). See Thompson, H. L. (2007). *Catastrophic leadership failure: An overview.* Retrieved from http://www.hpsys.com/PDFs/CatastrophicLeadership FailureOverviewv2_18SEP2007.pdf, for an explanation of how catastrophe theory explains catastrophic leadership failure. Catastrophe theory has been widely used to explore phenomena in the biological sciences (Scherer, K. [2000]. Emotions as episodes of subsystem synchronization.

In M. Lewis & I. Granic [Eds.], *Emotion, development and self-organization: Dynamic systems approaches to emotional development.* New York: Cambridge University Press), psychology (Guastello, S. J. [2001]. Nonlinear dynamics in psychology. *Discrete Dynamics in Nature and Society, 6,* 11–19; Guastello, S. J. [2002]. *Managing emergent phenomena: Nonlinear dynamics in work organizations.* Mahwah, NJ: Lawrence Erlbaum Associates; Nowak, A., & Vallacher, R. (1998). *Dynamical social psychology.* New York: The Guilford Press), and education (Stamoviasis, D. [2006]. The nonlinear dynamical hypothesis in science education problem solving: A catastrophe theory approach. *Nonlinear Dynamics, Psychology, and Life Sciences, 10*[1], 37–70). CLF (dependent variable y) is driven by two state parameters, or states of stable equilibrium. The change in the states is a function of stress and EI (a, b) and can be represented by the following equation.

$$V_{(y,a,b)} = \frac{y^4}{4} - \frac{by^2}{2} - ay$$

Dynamical systems, such as the one represented by CLF, try to maintain a stable state. Thus, when "an instability" occurs, the system will change to reach a stable state. The following graphic represents the 3-D visualization described by the previous mathematical equation.

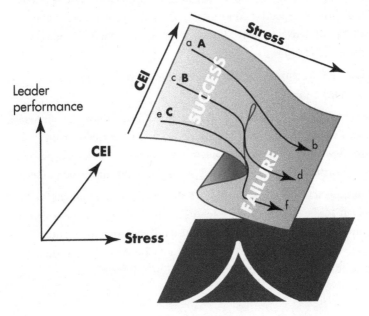

19 Pickens, T. B. (2009, July). Now is the time: Pass the NAT GAS Act. *The Huffington Post*. Retrieved from http://www.huffingtonpost.com/t-boone-pickens/now-is-the-time_b_229099.html.

20 Freud's quotation comes from a conversation between Freud and Theodor Reik as they walked along the Ringstrasse in Vienna. Reik published Freud's comment in his book, Reik, T. (1948). *Listening with the third ear: The inner experience of a psychoanalyst* (p. vii). New York: Grove.

21 Gonzales, L. (2003). *Deep survival: Who lives, who dies, and why*. New York: Norton, p. 196.

22 Schutz, W. (1958). *FIRO: A three-dimensional theory of interpersonal behavior*. New York: Rinehart.

23 Tamm, J., & Luyet, R. (2005). *Radical collaboration*. New York: HarperCollins.

24 Adapted from The Human Element workshop participant materials "Signs of Defensiveness," developed by Will Schutz in 1997.

Chapter Six

1 Tsai, S. P., Wendt, J. K., Donnelly, R. P., de Jong, G., & Ahmed, F. S. (2005, October 21). Age at retirement and long-term survival of an industrial population: Prospective cohort study. BMJ, doi:10.1136/bmj.38586 .448704.Eo. Retrieved May 21, 2009, from http://www.bmj.com/cgi/reprint/331/7523/995.

2 Nixon, P.G.F. (1976). The human function curve. *Practitioner, 217*, 765–769, 935–944.

3 Schapiro, R., & Melago, C. (2008, September 13). California train wreck caused when engineer failed to stop say officials. Retrieved from http://www.nydailynews.com/news/national/2008/09/13/2008-09-13_california_train_wreck_caused_when_engin.html#ixzzodSJH8y63.

4 Counting allows the jumper to track the passage of time since leaving the aircraft so she knows if the parachute has had enough time to open. The jumper counts loudly, "One-one thousand! Two-one thousand! Three-one thousand! Four-one thousand! Check canopy!" If the parachute is not open, emergency procedures are initiated.

5 Damasio, A. (1997). *Descartes' error.* New York: Avon Books.

6 Thompson, H. L. (1985). StressTrain: Training for high performance. *Military Review, 65*(2), 54–62.

7 FoxNews.com (2009, July 9). Amtrak train crashes into car, kills 5 near Detroit. Retrieved from http://www.foxnews.com/story/0,2933, 531120,00.html.

8 Benson, H., & Klipper, M. Z. (1976). *The relaxation response.* New York: HarperTorch.

9 For a more detailed explanation of how to elicit the relaxation response see Benson's book or visit the Benson-Henry Institute at http://www .massgeneral.org/bhi/basics/eliciting_rr.aspx.

10 Benson, H., & Stark, M. (1997). *Timeless healing.* New York: Fireside.

Chapter Seven

1 Logotherapy is a type of existentialist analysis focused on a will to find meaning. It is sometimes known as the Third Viennese School of Psychotherapy (Freud's was the First and Adler's was the Second).

2 Frankl, V. E. (1959). *Man's search for meaning* (p. 7). Boston: Beacon Press. Published originally in 1946, this book is still in print and has sold over 10 million copies worldwide in many languages.

3 Frankl, 1959, p. 109.

4 Frankl, 1959, pp. 113–114.

5 Thompson, H. L. (2009, June 29–30). *Stress resilient emotional intelligence.* Paper presented at the 2009 International Conference on Emotional Intelligence, Toronto.

6 Coutu, D. (2002). How resilience works. *Harvard Business Review, 80*(5), 46–55.

7 Frankl, 1959.

8 Crawford, K. (2004, July 20). Martha: I cheated no one. Retrieved January 23, 2010, from http://money.cnn.com/2004/07/16/news/newsmakers/ martha_sentencing/.

9   Collins, J. (2001). *Good to great: Why some companies make the leap and others don't.* New York: HarperBusiness.

10 Collins, 2001.

11 Edwards, E. (2009). *Resilience: Reflections on the burdens and gifts of facing life's adversities.* New York: Broadway.

12 Kobasa, S. C. (1979). Stressful life events, personality, and health: An inquiry into hardiness. *Journal of Personality and Social Psychology, 37,* 1–11.

13 Bartone, P. T. (1995, July). *A short hardiness scale.* Paper presented at the annual convention of the American Psychological Society, New York.

14 Csikszentmihalyi, M. (1990). *Flow: The psychology of optimal experience.* New York: HarperPerennial.

15 Isaacson, W. (2007). *Einstein: His life and universe.* New York: Simon & Schuster.

16 Kaplan, R. S., & Norton, D. P. (1996). *The balanced scorecard: Translating strategy into action.* Boston: Harvard Business School Press.

17 Mariotti, J. (2009, August 16). The yin and the yang: Woods choked. Retrieved from http://jay-mariotti.fanhouse.com/2009/08/16/the-yin-and-the-yang-woods-choked.

18 Arnsten, A. (1998). The biology of being frazzled. *Science, 280,* 1711–1713.

19 Hewitt, B., & Egan, N.W. (2009, February 23). Flight 1549: The right stuff. *People.com,* p. 64. Retrieved from http://www.people.com/people/archive/article/0,,20264356,00.html.

20 Thompson, H. L. (1983). *Physical fitness as a moderator of cognitive degradation during sleep deprivation.* Unpublished master's thesis, U.S. Army Command and General Staff College, Fort Leavenworth, KS.

21 Arora, V. M., Georgitis, E., Woodruff, J. N., Humphrey, H. J., & Meltzer, D. (2007). Improving sleep hygiene of medical interns: Can the sleep, alertness, and fatigue education in residency program help? *Archives of Internal Medicine, 167*(16), 1738–1744.

22 TruckSeries.com. Retrieved from http://truckseries.com/cgi-script/csArticles/articles/000004/000470.htm.

23 Drowsiness study with Ford VIRTTEX simulator a success: New Volvo safety technology on its way. (2004, April 7). *Accident Reconstruction*

Newsletter, 6(4). Retrieved from http://www.accidentreconstruction.com/newsletter/apr04/drowsy_study.asp. A related article can be found at http://truckseries.com/cgi-script/csArticles/articles/000004/000470.htm Newstream (2004, April). New study on drowsy driving has eye-opening results. Retrieved July 15, 2009, from http://www.theautochannel.com/news/2004/04/08/188584.html.

24 Military parachute jumps tend to be very different from civilian skydiving, where the only equipment is a parachute, a helmet, and an altimeter. The military parachutist can easily have, including the parachute, 150 pounds of equipment when exiting the aircraft.

25 Buckingham, M., & Coffman, C. (1999). *First break all the rules: What the world's greatest managers do differently* (p. 81). New York: Simon & Schuster.

26 Kauffman, S. (1995). *At home in the universe: The search for the laws of self-organization and complexity.* New York: Oxford University Press.

Chapter Eight

1 Personal interview with Chris Carter on June 20, 2009. As this book is being written, he is on his third tour of duty in Iraq.

2 I have repeated this research using different administration sequences and emotional intelligence instruments and found the same results. I have also found the same stress effect using various other psychological instruments. A more detailed description of the research can be found in the *Handbook for Developing Emotional and Social Intelligence.* Thompson, H. L. (2009). Emotional intelligence, stress, and catastrophic leadership failure. In M. Hughes, H. L. Thompson, & J. P. Terrell (Eds.), *Handbook for developing emotional and social intelligence: Best practices, case studies, and strategies* (pp. 111–138). San Francisco: Pfeiffer.

3 Mozumder, S. G. (2009, April 16). Nooyi on her toughest decision & her Pepsi family. *Rediff News.* Retrieved June 14, 2009, from http://specials.rediff.com/money/2009/apr/16sld1-nooyi-on-her-toughest-decision.htm.

4 Gallagher, R. A. (2001). T-Groups. Retrieved from http://www.orgdct.com/more_on_t-groups.htm.

5 Boyatzis, R. E., & McKee, A. *Resonant leadership: Renewing yourself and connecting with others through mindfulness, hope, and compassion.* Boston: Harvard Business School Press.

Chapter Nine

1 Cryder, C. E., Lerner, J. S., Gross, J. J., & Dahl, R. (2008). Misery is not miserly: Sad and self-focused individuals spend more. *Psychological Science, 19,* 525–530.

2 This jump was made when the ram-air parachutes (rectangular parachutes that fly like the wing of an airplane) had just come out. Today they are the standard parachute and have deployment systems that provide a relatively soft and reliable opening. The harness described here was also new and is today's standard, except ripcords are used only in special situations. Modern parachutes are deployed by manually pulling out the "pilot chute" and tossing it out. It catches the air and pulls out the main parachute.

3 Mass, J. B. (1998). *Power sleep: The revolutionary program that prepares your mind for peak performance.* New York: Quill.

4 Dement, W. C., & Vaughan, C. (1999). *The promise of sleep: A pioneer in sleep medicine explores the vital connection between health, happiness, and a good night's sleep.* New York: Dell.

5 Thompson, H. L. (1983). *Physical fitness as a moderator of cognitive degradation during sleep deprivation.* Unpublished master's thesis, U.S. Army Command and General Staff College, Fort Leavenworth, KS.

6 Bishnar, J. (2009, January 14). Napping in the new year—The Da Vinci sleep cycle. *American Chronicle.* Retrieved March 12, 2009, from http://www.americanchronicle.com/articles/view/87892.

7 Thompson, H. L. (1983). Sleep loss and its effect in combat. *Military Review, 63*(9), 14–23.

8 Pleban, R., Thomas, D., & Thompson, H. L. (1985). Physical fitness as a moderator of cognitive work capacity and fatigue onset under sustained combat-like operations. *Behavior Research Methods, Instruments and Computers, 17*(1), 86–89.

9 DePaulo, B. (2009, February 10). No, getting married does not make you live longer. *Psychology Today.* Retrieved May 26, 2009, from http://www

.psychologytoday.com/blog/living-single/200902/no-getting-married-does-not-make-you-live-longer.

10 Thompson, H. L. (1983). Physical fitness as a moderator of cognitive degradation during sleep deprivation. Unpublished master's thesis, U.S. Army Command and General Staff College, Fort Leavenworth, KS.

11 Larson, E. B., Wang, L., Bowen, J. D., McCormick, W. C., Teri, L., Crane, P., Kukull, W. (2006). Exercise is associated with reduced risk for incident dementia among persons 65 years of age and older. *Annals of Internal Medicine, 144,* 73–81.

12 Thompson, H. L. (1983). Physical fitness as a moderator of cognitive degradation during sleep deprivation. Unpublished master's thesis, U.S. Army Command and General Staff College, Fort Leavenworth, KS.

13 Templeton, D. (2009, August 27). Obesity can inflict big toll on brain. Retrieved September 20, 2009, from http://www.post-gazette.com/pg/09239/993543–114.stm.

14 Ostir, G. (2004, September 12). Positive attitude delays aging. BBC News.

15 Kim, G. (2009, September 12). Carmichael woman, 98, conquers Facebook. *Sacramento Bee.* Retrieved September 20, 2009, from http://www.sacbee.com/seniors/story/2177179.html.

16 The ARSENAL Basic Assessment is a quick high-level assessment. The ARSENAL Individual Assessment is a comprehensive assessment of each practice area that produces an individual report and action plan. The ARSENAL Team Assessment is a comprehensive team assessment that produces a team report and action plan. More information can be found at www.hpsys.com/ARSENAL.htm and www.thestresseffect.com.

Conclusion

1 Team collaboration (and overall collaboration in an organization) can be measured using the Collaborative Skills Climate Survey created by Henry L. Thompson, James Tamm, and Ron Luyet (www.radicalcollaboration .com) and published by High Performing Systems (http://www.hpsys.com/Assessments_CSCS.htm).

2 Cattell, R. B., Saunders, D. R., & Stice, G. F. (1953). The dimensions of syntality in small groups. *Human Relations, 6,* 331–356.

3 Team emotional intelligence can be measured using the Team Emotional and Social Intelligence survey created by Marcia Hughes and James Terrell of Collaborative Growth (www.theemotionallyintelligentteam.com) and published by High Performing Systems (http://www.hpsys.com/Assessments_TESI.htm), or on a less complex level by using the Emotional Quotient-Inventory Group Report published by Multi-Health Systems (www.mhs.com).

4 Fekete, S., & Keith, L. A. (2003). *Companies are people too: Discover, develop, and grow your organization's true personality.* Hoboken, NJ: Wiley.

5 PriceWaterhouseCoopers Twelfth Annual Global CEO Survey (2009) is an extensive report based on 1,124 CEOs from more than fifty countries.

6 Reed, J., & Love, S. (2009, August 5). Army developing master resiliency training. Retrieved from http://www.army.com/news/item/5768.

Acknowledgments

This book represents the culmination of over thirty years of experiencing, observing, and studying decision making under high stress. I have learned from many people over the years, but focus these acknowledgments on those directly involved in the publication of this book.

I thank Jossey-Bass for providing an outstanding team, led by my editor, Genoveva Llosa. Genoveva could "see" the book and path for completion from our first meeting. She used her excellent cognitive and emotional intelligences, decision-making skills, inspiration, and structure to guide me through the maze of decisions, sometimes stressful, required for creating a meaningful and compelling story. She did an excellent job in bringing out the best in all of us.

The rest of the Jossey-Bass team was also critical to the process. Becky Cabaza spent many hours working closely with me to help me tell my story in language that was not too technical. She suggested stories and transitions and pushed for examples while providing encouragement. Gayle Mak made sure work by others that I mention was properly referenced. Mary Garrett kept the production process moving once my thoughts became a completed manuscript. Beverly Miller did outstanding copyediting work on the final manuscript. Erin Moy helped the team position the book in the marketplace so you could find it—and want to read it.

Bernadette Blanco checked references and managed marketing meetings. Cynthia Shannon helped the book and me become visible. Adrian Morgan provided creativity, adaptability, and patience through the many possible designs of and colors for the dust jacket.

My colleagues at High Performing Systems deserve special mention for their ideas, feedback, and many hours of listening to me, and for reading and editing the manuscript while doing extra work to allow me time to focus on the content. Debra Cannarella provided many ideas, such as the acronym ARSENAL, examples, feedback, editing, proofing, and encouragement. Julie Gentry found many examples, provided feedback and proofing, and assisted with collecting data over the Web. Farrell Bowdoin provided administrative support, data collection, proofing, and a reality check. Karen Schwind spent many hours reading, editing, and proofing versions of the manuscript—and asking questions. Curt Cisrow always had ideas, suggestions, and ways to make the material real. Josh Billings made my rough drawings and concepts come to life as professional illustrations and graphics while demonstrating great patience with my numerous requests for changes. Josh did all of this while experiencing tremendous personal traumatic stress—which has had a very positive outcome. Josh's family experienced firsthand what strong positive support from ARSENAL can do. Merry Maxey contributed her creativity, support, and graphic skills. Dana Smith led our marketing team through the process of making the book visible and available to our clients. Marcia Swoger was always there with her wit, stories, creativity, and encouragement, keeping me in touch with people and the real world.

Grenae Thompson, my wife, constant inspiration, and the most creative person I have ever known, was always there providing encouragement, ideas, editing, and more editing, proofing, understanding, constant Web searches, stories, feedback on the status of my various dashboards, and constantly reminding me that "there's a book for that." She asked difficult questions and challenged my language, ideas, and concepts until I could make them understandable. She helped me look at this work from new perspectives and gain better understanding and insights. The book could not have become a reality without her effort and determination.

My daughter Michele Bruce was a constant source of ideas and real life experiences. My son, Stephen Thompson, offered depth of complexity and prescience. His ability to traverse the landscape of unconsciousness with me and add noetic meaning to what we discovered provided a new level of consciousness and source of excitement to the journey and future possibilities. Jennifer Brown, my down-to-earth, practical daughter, provided structure and inspiration to keep moving toward the objective. Butch Thompson, my brother in family and in "arms," who has experienced decision making under the stress of combat, provided a perspective and understanding of this book that most people, fortunately, will never grasp. And thanks to my sons-in-law, Jerry Bruce and Eric Brown, for their support and encouragement.

I want to thank my mother, Christine Thompson, who continues to inspire me to create a work that will help people at all stages of life manage those difficult and stressful decisions that must be made and to have the resilience to keep moving forward. I also want to thank my parents-in-law, Roy and Johnnie Gowder, who have always inspired me and provided me with real-life examples of resilience.

To colleagues Reuven Bar-On, who provided numerous insights and research papers on topics covered in the book; Martin Delahoussaye, who saw the book in my idea; and Marcia Hughes, who along with Martin encouraged me to submit the manuscript to Jossey-Bass; and to the many friends, colleagues, and clients who provided ideas and encouragement before and during the writing of this book, I extend heartfelt thanks.

About the Author

Henry L. (Dick) Thompson, Ph.D., is president and CEO of High Performing Systems (HPS), an international management consulting and training firm he founded in 1984. Throughout his career, he has gained experience, insights, and expertise building and leading high-performing teams—from the battlefield to the boardroom—using a systems approach. Thompson conducts research in areas that include leadership, emotional intelligence, cognitive ability, psychological type (personality), and group dynamics and is recognized as a leading authority on assessing and integrating these concepts. He is a certifying/qualifying instructor for the Bar-On EQ-i (Emotional Quotient Inventory), the MBTI instrument, and Element B. His work on selecting leaders, incorporating concepts such as emotional intelligence, has resulted in the Leadership Potential Assessment System, a scientific process for identifying best-fit leaders and determining their potential for growth across time. Thompson works with organizations, executives, and managers in all areas of leadership, including consulting, leader selection and transitions, succession planning, mentoring, coaching, stress management, decision making, and organizational development.

Index

A

Abecedarian Project, 58, 59

Abess, L., 98, 99

Ability model classification, 95, 97

Academic achievement, effect of stress on, 154

Accountability, lack of, 15

Accreditation Council for Graduate Medical Education, 209

Action, awareness followed by, as key, 142

Action patterns, changing, issue of, 88

Action phase, 42, 47, 85, 92, 100, 117–118, 139, 164

Acute stressors: in the bubble model of stress management, 188; defined, 140

Adaptability, 201

Adaptation response, 117, 118, 164, 165

Adolescents: academic achievement of, 154; risky behavior of, 186–187

Adrenaline, 45, 222, 247

Age: and cognitive intelligence, 59–62; and emotional intelligence, 104–105; as a factor in decision making, 16

Aging, 71–72, 262, 272, 275

AIG, 6, 12, 13, 283

Air India, 206

Air traffic controllers, and stress management capacity, 179. *See also* US Airways Flight 1549

Alarm reaction stage, 120–121, 153, 265, 270

Allegory, involving mental models, 147–148

Allport, G. W., 194

Alpha Company scenario, 221–224

Alzheimer's, 65, 116, 262

American Express Financial Advisers, 221

American Psychological Association, 54

Amygdala: and emotional intelligence, 93, 94, 95, 96, 100–101; and stress, 113, 121, 125, 138, 139, 156–157, 226, 233; time focus and the, 235

Analysis paralysis, 32, 77, 143. *See also* Indecision

Andreassen, P., 143

Anterior cingulate cortex, 95, 96

Appley, M. H., 111

Appraisal phase, 42, 43–46, 117, 139; awareness and, 92, 248; and emotional intelligence, 84, 92, 100; under stress, 152–162

Aristotle, 49, 81

Armstrong, L., 254

Arnsten, A., 204

Arora, V., 208

ARSENAL Basic Assessment Graph, 246, 279

ARSENAL system: assessment of the, 246, 278–279; axioms of the, 281; benefits of the, 279–280; combining the stress resilient system and the, 280;

described, 246–278; importance of the, 9; interaction among practices within the, 245; overview of the, 244–246; as a performance aid, 239; reviewed, 281. *See also* Attitude; Awareness; Exercise; Learning; Nutrition; Rest; Support

Asimov, I., 283

Assessment, self-evaluation and. *See* Self-assessment

Assessments/tests. *See specific assessment/test*

Assimilation, and cognitive ability, 26

Attitude: in the ARSENAL system, 9, 245, 272; as a best practice, described, 271–275; development of, menu of techniques for, 273–274; indicators of, range of, 272–273; negative, 243; self-assessment of, 274

Attitude Scale, 274

Augustyn, J., 210, 211

Automatic response, 203–204

Automobile drivers, sleep loss and, 209

Autry, G., 254

Available working memory, 153, 200, 202, 210

Awareness: in the ARSENAL system, 9, 245, 248; as a best practice, described, 246–251; and cognitive resilience, 200, 201, 207–208, 211; development of, menu of techniques for, 249–250; and emotional intelligence, 91–92; indicators of, range of, 248–249; as key, to staying in control, 142; of performance levels, exercise and, 262; self-assessment of, 250, 251; and stress resilient emotional intelligence, 231–232, 236

Awareness program, example of, 251

Awareness, Rest, Support, Exercise, Nutrition, Attitude, and Learning (ARSENAL). *See* ARSENAL system

Awareness Scale, 250, 251

B

Baby boomers, 132

Balda, S., 154

Bandura, A., 167

Bar-On, R., 91, 95, 97, 100

Bartone, P., 198

Bass, B., 68

Bass fishing analogy, 235–236

Bazerman, M., 146

Bear Stearns, 12, 13, 28, 161, 187, 231, 283

Bechara, A., 95, 100

Behavioral contagion, 227, 228, 272

Behavioral responses, to stress, 115

Belenky, G., 66

Benson, H., 189, 190

Benson-Henry Institute for Mind Body Medicine, 189

Bias, 147, 151

Bibb County school system, 149

Bipolarity, emotional, 85

Bisht Battery of Stress Scale, 154

Blaize, N., 8

Blind spots, 149

Blink! (Gladwell), 34

Blue Cross Blue Shield, 265

BluePrint for Health Fitness Center Discount program, 265

Boring tasks, dealing with, 218

Bounded reality, 38

Boyatzis, R., 8, 239–240

Boyd, J. R., 34, 35, 40

Brain, the: aging of, 71–72, 262, 275; cognitive intelligence and, 69–73; emotional intelligence and, 93–97; exercise for, 276; knowledge of, and awareness of, 231; most common senses of, and their functions, 144, 145; stimulating, 218. *See also specific areas of the brain*

Breast cancer awareness program, 251

Bredehoft, J., 149–150

Brigade commander, decisions of, 30, 32

Brinker, N. G., 251

Brown, B., 154

Bryant, P. "Bear," 174

Bubble model of stress management, 187–189

Buffett, W., 62

Bureaucracies, 17

Burnout zone, 127, 173, 174, 175, 176

Bush pilot, 109–110

Byrd, R., 59

C

Campbell, F., 58

Cancer, 257

Carrion, V., 155

Carroll, J., 56, 57

Carter, C., 221–224, 230

Caruso, D., 84, 95

Casey, G., 286
Castaway (movie), 196
Catastrophe theory, 159–161
Catastrophic leadership failure, 161, 162
Catastrophic Leadership Failure Prevention
    System, 280
Cattell, R., 55, 284
Cattell-Horn theory, 55–56
Cattell-Horn-Carroll theory, 56
Cayne, J., 12, 28, 161, 187, 231
Celsus, A. C., 243
Cerebral cortex, 93–94
Chabris, C., 150
Chairman, role level complexity of, 23
Challenge, 198, 199
Challenger, Gray & Christmans, 6
Challenger, J., 6
Change, and the comfort zone, 176
Changes, types of, in response to stress, 114,
    115, 138, 237
Changing mental models, 148
Checklists, using, 214–215, 247
Chemical changes, in response to stress, 114,
    115, 138
Chief executive officers (CEOs): age of, 62;
    average IQ of, 15; awards given to, 231;
    decisions of, 30, 32; role level
    complexity of, 23; survey of, on
    workload, 285; turnover of, increase
    in, 6. *See also names of specific CEOs*
"Choking," 203, 204
Christensen, H., 71
Chronic stress, 122, 172
Chronic stressors: in the bubble model of
    stress management, 188; defined, 140
Chrysler, 15
Chugani, H., 212
Chunking, 39, 212–213, 216, 217
City National Bank, 98
Clark, H., 82
Clinton, B., 254
Cofer, C. N., 111
Cognitive ability: and the aging brain, 72;
    decline in, 65, 66, 225; described,
    25–27; differentiating, from cognitive
    intelligence, 49; and flying a
    commercial airliner, 206; variation
    in, 54
Cognitive ability assessment, 20–22
Cognitive attributes of resilience, 199

Cognitive Bias Test, 64
Cognitive changes, in response to stress,
    115
Cognitive component, role of, during
    appraisal, 44–45
Cognitive decline, 65
Cognitive functioning dashboard, 200–202,
    209, 211, 219
Cognitive intelligence: accessing, increase in,
    benefits of, 9; age and, 59–62; and the
    brain, 69–73; center of, 72–73; and
    cognitive demands on quarterbacks,
    50–51; and deciding how to decide,
    73–78; and decision making, aspects
    of, 49–79; defining, 53–54;
    environment and, 58–59; exercise
    and, 65; gender and, 64–65;
    hierarchical model of, 56, 57; impact
    of stress on, 7, 8, 125, 153–156, 225;
    importance of, for leaders, 52–53;
    influence of, 73–78; intuitive decision
    making and, 76–78; measuring, 56–58;
    memory and, 63–64; and moderating
    factors, 58–67; nutrition and, 65–66;
    and overload, 155, 156; and processing
    speed, 201; and role level, 52, 67–68,
    76, 78; stress that shuts down
    emotional intelligence and, 159–162;
    teams demonstrating, 284; using a
    blend of emotional intelligence and,
    157. *See also* Cognitive resilience
    (CR); IQ score/level; IQ tests
Cognitive resilience (CR): aspects of,
    193–219; developing, enhancing, and
    maintaining, 211–218, 219; examples
    of, 193–194, 196–197; importance of
    developing, 8–9; monitoring,
    200–202; sleep loss and, 205–210;
    stress and, 203–205; in the stress
    resilient system, 171. *See also* Stress
    resilient system
Cognitive science, 55–56
Cognitive tools, 214–215, 216, 217
Cognitive workload: easing, using
    performance aids for, 214–215;
    measuring, 210–211
Cognitive-emotional index (CEI), 159–160
Collaboration, 284
Collins, J., 17, 196, 197
Combat situations, leading in, 221–224, 230

Comfort zone: in the bubble model of stress management, 187, 188; described, 126–128, 172; extending the, 175–176; life in the, 172–175; and peak performance, 173, 175; regularly being pushed out of the, situations involving, 177–181; and stress intensity, 140

Commercial pilots: decisions of, *30, 32*; and sleep loss, 206–208. *See also* United Flight 173; US Airways Flight 1549

Commitment, 175, 198, 199, 245, 272

Communication, by the brain, 70–71

Companies Are People Too (Fekete and Keith), 285

Complexity levels, issue of, 19–33, 68, 75–76, 78. *See also* Role level

Confirmation traps, 146–147, 150, 152

Conscious emotion, 84

Conscious perception, 42, 43, 44

Consciousness, 100, 143, 203, 204, 213

Continental Flight 3407, 207

Contingency plans, 216

Control: as a factor in emotional functioning, *234, 235*; as a factor in psychological hardiness, 198, 199; over emotions, stress and, 155, 156; over situations, 128–129, 175; staying in, 142. *See also* Emotional intelligence

Control aids, emotional, 238, 239

Corporate nutritional good practices, 270

Cortisol, 114, 116, 117, 245

Coutu, D., 193, 195, 197, 199

Craik, K., 145

Crystallized intelligence, defined, 55

Csikszentmihalyi, M., 199

Cubic, 62

D

Damasio, A., 95, 100, 102, 103

Damasio, H., 100

Darwin, C., 89–90

Dashboards: cognitive functioning, 200–202, 209, 211, *219*; emotional functioning, 234–235; for monitoring best practices, 246

Data inconsistency, 25–26

Death: following retirement, issue of, 174; leading causes of, stress linked to, 112

Decision complexity, 29–33

Decision making: cognitive intelligence and, aspects of, 49–79; as the core essence of leadership, 6, 17, 29; critical component of, 23; emotional intelligence and, aspects of, 81–107; ethical, 9; future, influence on, 140; how leaders engage in, 11–48; impact of stress on, 7, 8, 109–136, 244; influence of emotions on, 103, *104,* 155, 156, 157–158; and the prefrontal cortex (PFC), 72–73; process of, inherent pitfalls along the, 142, 204; stress capacity and, 176–181; stress management capacity and, 176–181. *See also* Good decision making; Poor decision making

Decision-making strategies: described, 7, 33–40; development of, 16; emotionally intelligent, 224, 230; using a combination of, 7–8

Decisions: executing, failing at, 217; overthinking, 77; types of, 29–30, *32*

Defensive behaviors, 165

Delta Airlines, 7

Dementia, 65, 116, 262

Descartes' Error (Damasio), 102

Descartes, R., 149

Desensitization, 240

Dialing 911, 217

Diallo, A., 137–139, 141, 146, 157, 226, 227

Diet and nutrition. *See* Nutrition

Disraeli, B., 1

Dodson, J., 134

Dominant response hierarchy, 182, 183, 233, 236

Dopamine, 114

E

Earthquake in Haiti, 217–218

Edison, T., 254

Edwards, E., 197

Edwards, J., 197

Edwards, W., 197

Effective decision making. *See* Good decision making

Einstein, A., 49, 75, 76, 175, 200, 214, 254

Ekman, P., 88–89, 109–110, 131

Electronic stress monitors, 210–211, 284–285

Emerson, H., 261–262

Emotional attributes of resilience, *199*

Emotional awareness and management, 92
Emotional changes, in response to stress, *115*
Emotional component, role of, during
     appraisal, 45–46
Emotional control aids, 238, 239
Emotional dyads, 85–86, *87*
Emotional functioning dashboard, 234–235
Emotional hijacking: avoiding, 100–103;
     example of, 139; and the influence of
     time focus, 235
Emotional intelligence: accessing, increase
     in, benefits of, 9; age and, 104–105;
     and avoiding emotional hijacking,
     100–103; as awareness and
     management, 90–92; and the brain,
     93–97; core level of, 92; and decision
     making, aspects of, 81–107; defined,
     91; gender and, 105; impact of stress
     on, 7, 8, 156–157, 225–227, 229; as an
     innate ability, 28; and intuitive
     decision making, 102–103; and
     leadership, 98–100; loss of access to,
     safeguarding against, way of, 228–231;
     measuring, 32–33, 95–97; and
     moderating factors, 104–105;
     nutrition and, 105; and rational
     decision making, 102; sleep and, 105;
     starting, prediction involving, 162;
     stress that shuts down cognitive
     intelligence and, 159–162; teams
     demonstrating, 284; using a blend of
     cognitive intelligence and, 157; using,
     to respond to bias, 151; at work, 106.
     See also Stress resilient emotional
     intelligence (SREI)
Emotional intelligence aids, 238, 239–240
*Emotional Intelligence: Why It Can Matter
     More Than IQ* (Goleman), 91
Emotional process, stress prevention best
     practices as an, 245
Emotional Quotient Inventory (EQ-i), 32–33,
     97, 99, 105, 197, 229, 230
Emotional system, 93–95, *96*, 141, 157, 232
Emotional tagging, 103
Emotional tools, 238–241
Emotions: blending of, 85–87; development
     of, 87–88; expressions of, 88–90;
     identifying and thinking about, 237;
     influence of, on decision making, 103,
     104, 155, 156, 157–158; monitoring

sensations and physiological
     responses to, 237; and the motivation
     phase, 162, 163; negative,
     predisposition to, 225;
     understanding, 84–90
Energy, 234, 235, 272
Enron, 6, 11, 13, 15, 162
Environment, and cognitive intelligence,
     58–59
Environmental stressors, *130*, 132–133
Epinephrine, 114, 184
Estrogen, 119
Ethical decision making, 9
Excitation Transfer Model, 123–125
Executing decisions, failing at, 217
Exercise: in the ARSENAL system, 9, 245; as a
     best practice, described, 260–265; and
     the brain, 71, 276; cognitive
     intelligence and, 65; and corporate
     good practices, 270, 271; development
     of, techniques for, 263–264;
     emotional commitment to, 245;
     indicators of, range of, 263; lack of,
     243; self-assessment of, 264–265
Exercise Scale, 264–265
Exhaustion stage, 123, 153, 175, 185
Experts: becoming, training required for,
     184–185; thinking and execution by,
     204
*Expression of the Emotions in Man and
     Animals, The* (Darwin), 89–90

F

Facial expressions, 88, 89
Family and friends, having no time for, 243.
     See also Support
Fannie Mae, 6, 13, 283
Fastow, A., 11
Fedorikhin, A., 155
Feedback: and awareness, 231; and cognitive
     ability, 26, 27
Feelings: vs. emotions, 84; identifying and
     thinking about, 237
Fekete, S., 285
Fight-or-flight response, *117*, 118, 119, 164. *See
     also* Emotions
FIRO (fundamental interpersonal relations
     orientation) theory, 165
Fisher House Foundation, 260
Fisher House program, 260

Flight response. *See* Fight-or-flight response
Fluid intelligence, defined, 55
Flynn effect, 67
Flynn, J. R., 67
Forbes (magazine), 196, 230, 275
Ford Motor Company, 209
Fortune (magazine), 270, 271
Frankl, V., 193–194, 195, 199
Frazzled behavior, 204
Freddie Mac, 6, 13, 283
Freeze response, *117*, 118, 164, 165
Freud, S., 164
Fridlund, A., 89
Friedman, T., 13
Frijida, N., 89
Frontline supervisors, role level complexity
        of, 23
Fry, B., 51
Fuld, R., 12
Funeral arrangements, preplanning, 216–217
Future decision making, influence on, 140
Future leaders, requirement for, 284
Future planning, 216–218
Fuzzy logic reaction, 146

G

Galilei, G., 49
Game wardens vs. police officers, 149–150
"Garbage in, garbage out" result, 144
Gardner, H., 68, 91
Gender: cognitive intelligence and, 64–65;
        emotional intelligence and, 105; as a
        factor in decision making, 16; and
        noise levels, 133; and the stress effect,
        119
Gender equality, 65
Gender Gap Index, 65
General Adaptation Syndrome Model,
        120–123, 185
General Electric, 23
General Motors, 13
Generational differences, IQ scores and, 67
Georgia Pacific, 7
Georgia school system, 149
Georgitis, E., 208
G-factor, 55, 56, *57*, 60
GiantLeap Consulting, 127
Gladwell, M., 34
Glaucon, 147
Global CEO survey, 285

Global economy, 13, 15, 283
Global Supply Chain Leaders Group, 231
Go! Airlines Flight 1002, 206–207
Goal setting, 162, 163
Goldberg, E., 64, 72–73, 94
Goleman, D., 91, 100, 137
Golf tournament, 203–204
Gonzales, L., 165
Good decision making: abilities required for,
        7; as a crucial for leadership, 8;
        drivers of, 16; masters of, requiring,
        284, 286; scenario exhibiting, 1–5, 7–8.
        See also Cognitive intelligence;
        Emotional intelligence
Good to Great (Collins), 17, 196
Goodnight, J., 270
Gottfredson, L., 53
Greed, culture of, creating a, 15
Gregory, J., 180
Gregory, R. L., *146*
Grip Meter, the, 140, 141–142
Grosser, T., 193

H

Haiti earthquake, 217–218
Hangover effect, 253
Hank, T., 196
Hardwired Leadership (Pearman), 29
Hardwoods Group, 106
Harten, P., 1, 2, 3, 4–5
Harvard Business Review, 195
Health stressors, *130*, 132
Hempleman-Adams, D., 251–252, 254
Hepler, F., 82
"Hero Miles" program, 260
High Performing Systems, 6–7, 15, 68, 106,
        126, 205, 228, 257
Hillaker, H., 34–35
Hippocampus, 93, *94*, 116
Holmes, T., 135
Holocaust survivors, resilience of, 193–194
Holyfield, E., 101
Home stressors, 130–131
Homeostasis, 176
Honoré, R., 81–83, 99, 218
Horn, J., 55
Human Cognitive Abilities (Carroll), 56
Humphrey, H., 208
Hunter, J., 52
Hurricane Katrina, 6, 81–82, 83

Hyde, J., 64–65
Hypothalamus, 93, *94*

I

Icahn, C., 62
Idiot lights, 214–215, 232, 254
Imagination and reality, telling the difference
    between, issue of, 141, 148
In Search of Excellence (Peters and
    Waterman), 17
Indecision, 6, 12, 32, 161. *See also* Analysis
    paralysis
Individual leader complexity, 24–29
Information processing, 144
Information retrieval, 75, 200, 201–202, *219*
Innate ability, 24, 24–29, 91
Insular and somatosensory cortex, 95, *96*
Intelligence. *See* Cognitive intelligence;
    Emotional intelligence
Intelligence quotient (IQ) rating. *See* IQ
    score/level; IQ tests
Intensity: emotional, 85; of stress, as a factor,
    140–142
Intentional blindness, 150–151
Interpersonal interactions, and cognitive
    ability, 26–27
Interpersonal skills, 24
Intuitive decision making: cognitive
    intelligence and, 76–78; described, 7,
    33, 34–40; emotional intelligence and,
    102–103; emotions and, 102; by
    experts, 184–185; using, combined
    with rational decision making, 8, 41,
    76, 78
IQ score/level: age and, 60, 61; of CEOs, 15,
    54; environment and, 58, 59; of the
    general population, 15, 59;
    generational differences and, 67;
    gifted, 54; high, 15, 75, 154, 155; and
    processing power, 75; and role level,
    68, 76; when under stress, 159
IQ tests: age and, 60, 61, 62; environment
    and, 58; used in football, 51, 52;
    variance in, 55
Iranian Air Bus Flight 655, 35–36
Iraq war, scenario involving, 221–224

J

J. P. Morgan Chase, 12
Jacobs, O., 20

Jaques, E., 20
Joint Task Force Katrina, 82
Jordan, M., 185, 212, 213
"Jump school," 182–184
Jung, C. G., 147

K

Kagan, J., 60
Kaplan, R., 200
Kauffman, S., 213
Kay, K., 11
Keith, L. A., 285
Kerkorian, K., 62
Kideopolis, 228
Killinger, K., 12
Kirkpatrick, S., 18
Klein, G., 35, 36, *37*, 38, 102, 157
Kobasa, S., 198, 199
Komen, S. G., 251
Krulak, C. C., 40

L

Law enforcement officers: in the Diallo
    incident, 137–139, 141, 143, 146, 154,
    157, 226–227; game warden vs. police,
    149–150; and stress management
    capacity, 180; training of, 180–181
Leader skills, 24
Leaders: choosing, art of, 14–17; differences
    in stress management capacity
    among, testing, 229; future,
    requirement for, 284; hiring, primary
    selection measure for, 52–53;
    individual, complexity of, 24–29;
    matching, to the job, 22–24; research
    on, 18, 20; resonant, 240; young,
    desensitizing, 240
Leadership: antiquated notion about, 14;
    core essence of, 6, 17, 29; critical
    component of, 23, 159; emotional
    intelligence and, 98–100; essential
    qualities of, 8; redefining what it
    takes for, 17–19; research on, 7, 8, 52;
    skills component of, 24; stratified
    systems theory of, 20; as stressful,
    110–111; traditional descriptions of,
    8. *See also specific aspects of
    leadership*
Leadership development, lag in, 283
Leadership reaction courses, 181, 182

Leadership training: adapting, importance of, 284; benefits of, 144; using a standard problem-solving model for, 30, *31*, 36
Leading by example, 106
Learned ability, 23, 24
Learning: in the ARSENAL system, 9, *245*; as a best practice, described, 275–278; development of, menu of techniques for, 276–277; indicators of, range of, 276; lack of, 243; lifelong, 9, 275; self-assessment of, 277–278
Learning Scale, 277, *278*
LeDoux, J., 100
Leeper, R. W., 90
Lehman Brothers, 12
Lennick, D., 221
Leonardo da Vinci, 254
Lerner, J., 101, 103
Leuner, B., 90
Lifelong learning, 9, 275. *See also* Learning
Limbaugh, R., 147
Limbic system, 93, *94*, 156, 199
Lloyd, M., 275
Locke, E., 18
Loewenstein, G., 101
Loewi, O., 70–73
Log burning analogy, 286
Logotherapy, 193, 199
Lupus Foundation, 271
Luyet, R., 165

M

Mack, A., 150
Maddi, S., 198, 199
Maier, S., 129
Malik, P., 154
Management, emotional awareness and, 91–92
Mandela, N., 196
Man's Search for Meaning (Frankl), 193–194
Manufacturing supervisor, decisions of, *30*, *32*
Mariotti, J., 203
Marmot, M., 129
Marriage, 258
Marriott, B., 62
Marriott International, 62
Master Resiliency Training program, 286
Math gender gap, issue of, 64–65

Math problems, 205
Mayer, J., 91, 95
Mayer-Salovey-Caruso Emotional Intelligence Test (MSCEIT), 95–97, 99, 229, 230
McCain, J., 13, 62
McKee, A., 239–240
McKinsey Company, 182
McLean, P., 93–94
Meagher, M., 132–133
Meaning, search for, 193–194, 195
Medical interns, sleep loss and, 208–209
Meltzer, D., 208
Memory, 63–64, 75. *See also* Working memory
Memory loss, age-related, 65, 116, 262
Mental dashboard, 201, 202
Mental models, 145–152
Mental stimulation, 38–39
Military agencies, U.S. *See specific military branch*
Military members, support for, 260
Military pilots, 34, 143–144
Military training, 167, 169, 170, 177–179, 182–184, 214, 221
Miller, G., 39
Mind-body connection, 272
Mindfulness training, 285
Mirror neurons, 227, 228, 272
Misinformation and overload, avoiding, 142–152
Mixed model classification, 95, 97
Mob behavior, 228
Mohawk Industries, 7
Monetary value, impact of stress-related emotions on, 244
Mood, 234–235
Moore, D., 146
Morgan, G., 149
Morgenthau, R., 59
Motivation, 28–29, 175
Motivation phase, 42, 43, 44, 46, 47, 117, 139, 162–163; and emotional intelligence, 84, 92, 100
Multiple intelligences, 68
Multidimensional approach, 26
Murdoch, R., 59, 62
Muscle analogy, 276
Myers-Briggs Type Indicator, 120
Myhrvold, N., 11

N

Nagin, R., 81
Napoleon, 40, 73, 238
Napping, 207, 212, 238, 253, 254
National Aeronautics and Space
    Administration (NASA), 254
National Football League (NFL) Scouting
    Combine, 50, 51
National Highway Traffic Safety
    Administration, 209
National Institute on Deafness and Other
    Communication Disorders, 132
National Training Laboratories Institute
    T-group sessions, 237–238
National Transportation Safety Board, 74,
    207
Native American analogy, 286
Nature of Explanation, The (Craik), 145
Negative reinforcing loop, 207, 225, 243
Nelson, R., 278
Neocortex, 93–94
New York Police Department's Street Crimes
    Unit, 137–139. *See also* Law
    enforcement officers
News Corp., 62
Newton, I., 49, 85
Nicomachean Ethics (Aristotle), 81
9/11, 30, 118
Nixon, P., 175
Noise levels, 132–133
Nonroutine decisions: described, 29–30, 31;
    examples of, 32
Nooyi, I., 230–231
Norepinephrine, 114, 138
Normal conditions, stress changing, 139–140
North Vietnam POW camp, 196–197
Northwest Flight 188, 207, 208
Norton, D., 200
Novelty, importance of, 218
Novices, thinking and execution by, 204
Nurturing responses, 119
Nutrition: in the ARSENAL system, 9, 245; as
    a best practice, described, 265–271;
    cognitive intelligence and, 65–66;
    corporate good practices in, 270–271;
    development of, menu of techniques
    for, 267–269; emotional intelligence
    and, 105; indicators of, range of, 267;
    lack of, 243; self-assessment of,
    269–270
Nutrition Scale, 269–270

O

Obama, B., 13
Obesity crisis, 266
Observe-orient-decide-act loop (OODA),
    34–35, 40, *48*
Olbermann, K., 147
100 Best Companies to Work For, 270, 271
100 Most Powerful Women, 230
Ontario Principals Council Leadership
    study, 99
Optimal performance zone, 134–135
Optimism, 197, 272
Orbitofrontal/ventromedial prefrontal
    cortex, 95, *96*
Organizational complexity, issue of, 19–22
Organizational level, 21, 68, 76
Organizational size, 19, 23
Organizational type, 19
Organizations, stressed, 285
Ostir, G., 272
Other awareness, 91–92
Overall cognitive functioning, rating, 200,
    201
Overall emotional functioning, rating, 234
Overlearning, 212, 213–214, 217, 240
Overload: and cognitive intelligence, 156; and
    misinformation, avoiding, 142–152; of
    the prefrontal cortex, 143, 155, 156,
    205; and working memory, 153
Overthinking, 77, 204
Overtraining, 224
Oxytocin, 119

P

Parachutists, 182–184, 209–210, 213, 240,
    246–248, 284
Paradox of Choice, The (Schwartz), 143
Parker, J., 207–208
Pattern recognition, 145–146. *See also* Search
    pattern
Patterson, S., 149
Peak performance, 173, 175
Pearman, R., 29
PepsiCo, 230
Perceived control, and stress, 129
Perception (conscious/unconscious) phase,
    42, 43, 44, 139; awareness and, 92, 248;
    and emotional intelligence, 84, 92,
    100; and mental models, 145–146, 149;
    and reality, 149; under stress, 117, 141,
    142–152

Perception-Appraisal-Motivation-Action model (PAMA): awareness and, 92, 248; described, 41–48; and emotional intelligence, 84–85, 88, 92; and reflexes, 233; under stress, 142–164, 225; stress and the, 117–120

Performance aids: cognitive, 214–215, *216*, 217; emotional, 238–241. *See also specific type of aid*

Performance indicators, list of: for cognitive functioning, 200; for emotional functioning, 234. *See also specific indicators*

Performance level: awareness of, exercise and, 262; and stress level, relationship between, 134–135, 159–161, 173, 175, 186

Performance Response Surface, 159–160, 280

Perseverance, 171. *See also* Resilience

Personal paradigm lens, 145, 148, 149, 150. *See also* Mental models

Personality, 29, 120

Peter, L., 15

Peter principle, 15

Peters, T., 17

Phelps, M., 248

Phillips, R., 179

Physical activity/conditioning. *See* Exercise

Physical changes, in response to stress, 115, 141

Physiological changes, in response to stress, 115, 237

Piaget, J., 60

Pickens, T. B., 62, 162–163

Pilots: bush, 109–110; commercial, *30, 32,* 206–208; military, 34, 143–144; and sleep loss, 206–208, 210. *See also* United Flight 173; US Airways Flight 1549

Pirates of the Caribbean 3 (movie), 161

Pixar Animation Studios, 278

Pixar University, 278

Planning, 200, *201,* 202, 216–218, *219*

Plato, 49, 147

Plutchik, R., 85–87

Police officers. *See* Law enforcement officers

Poor decision making: culture of, creating a, 15; decreasing, 9; epidemic of, 283; how stress leads to, aspects of, 137–166; other causes of, 142; and the prefrontal cortex (PFC), 73; smart leaders engaging in, reasons for, 6, 7;

statements indicating, 12. *See also* Stress

Post-traumatic stress disorder, 155

Power naps, 254

POWs (prisoners of war), resilience of, 196–197, 214

Prefrontal cortex (PFC): ability of, to plan ahead, 216; and building stress management capacity, 185, 186; capacity of the, 179; and chunking, 212; and cognitive intelligence, 63, *70,* 72–73, 74, 75, 76, 104; and emotional hijacking, 100; and emotional intelligence, 94–95, *96,* 102, 105; functions associated cognitively with the, 199; healthy, maintaining a, 265; maturation of the, and risky behavior, 186–187; measuring current workload of the, 210–211; monitoring and collecting feedback for the, 248; overload of the, 143, 155, 156, 205; reengaging the, process for, 237; and sleep loss, 207; smoking and the, 269; and stress, 113, 118, 121, 125, 139, 152, 153, 154, 156–157, 161, 226; time focus and the, 235

Preplanning, 216–218

PriceWaterhouseCoopers survey, 285

Primary emotions: development of, 87; learning to recognize, 238; model of, 85–86

Primate's Memoir, A (Sapolsky), 128

Prisoners of war (POWs), resilience of, 196–197, 214

Problem Solving scale, 32–33

Problems, complexity of, 75–76, 78

Problem-solving model, seven-step, 30, *31*

Process improvement classes, 30

Processing capacity, measuring, in real time, 210–211

Processing power, 75–76

Processing speed, 75, 200, 201, *219*

Production level, 21, 68

Psychological hardiness, 198–199

Purpose, sense of, 174

Q

Quarterbacks, cognitive demands on, 50–51

Quick decisions, making. *See* Rapid-fire decision-making style

Quitting urge, overcoming, 121

R

Rahe, R., 135

Ramey, C., 58

Rapid eye movement (REM) sleep, 105, 253

Rapid-fire decision-making style, 31–32, 35,
48. *See also* Intuitive decision making

Rational decision making: cognitive
intelligence and, 75; decision making
seemingly in conflict with, 36;
described, 7, 33–34; and emotional
intelligence, 102; emotions
overriding, issue of, 101; getting so
caught up in, 74–75; by novices, 185;
and the prefrontal cortex (PFC), 73,
74, 75, 185; and the stress prevention
best practices, 245; using, combined
with intuitive decision making, 8, 41,
76, 78

Reagan, R., 254

Reality: confronting, 171, 175, 195, 197; effect
of stress on, 149; and imagination,
telling the difference between, issue
of, 141, 148

Reality check, 248

Recognition-primed decision model (RPD),
35–40, *48*, 102–103, 157

Recovery, rest and, 175, 212, 237, 245

Reinforcing loop, negative, 207, 225, 243

Relationship management, 92

Relaxation response, 189–190

Reprogramming, 240–241

Reptilian brain, 93

Republic, The (Plato), 147

Reputation, choosing leaders based on, issue
with, 23

Research findings, 7, 8

Resilience: attributes of, and core set of
common factors, 199; as the core of
stress management, 195–197; defined,
170; described, 195; example of,
170–171; scientific foundation of,
197–199. *See also* Stress resilient
system

*Resilience: Reflections on the Burdens and
Gifts of Facing Life's Adversities*
(Edwards), 197

Resiliency training program, 286

Resistance stage, 121, 123, 153, 185, 186

Resonate Leadership (Boyatzis and McKee),
239–240

Response hierarchy, 232–234

Rest: in the ARSENAL system, 9, 245;
baseline for, 256–257; as a best
practice, described, 251–257;
development of, menu of techniques
for, 255–256; having no time for, 243;
indicators of, range of, 253; and
maintaining cognitive resilience, 212;
and maintaining stress resilient
emotional intelligence, 237–238;
self-assessment of, 256; and stress
management capacity, 175, 186, 189;
supplementing, with other actions,
239–240. *See also* Sleep

Rest periods, 206, 238

Rest Scale, 256

Retirement: leading past the age of, 62; stress
of, issue of, 174–175

Rhudy, J., 132–133

Richardson, D., 157

Risk, 162, 163, 186–187

Ritualized ingenuity, 195, 196

Rock, I., 150

Rockefeller, J. D., 254

Rodale, Inc., 270

Rodale, J. I., 270

Rodriguez, A., 88

Rogers, W., 35

Role level: and cognitive intelligence, 52,
67–68, 76, 78; decisions by, *30, 32*;
described, 22–24; and emotional
intelligence, 99; and U.S. Navy SEAL
training, 178

Roosevelt, E., 254

Rooster effect, 157–158

Ropes courses, 77, 181, 262

Rosenbaum, L., 154

Routine decisions, 29, *30*

Rush hour traffic, 227–228

Rustout zone, 127, 173, 174, 176

S

Salovey, P., 84, 91, 95

Saltzman, K., 155

Sanderson, W. C., 129

Sapolsky, R., 114, 116, 128

SAS Institute, 270–271

Satisficing solution, 38

Schaie, K. W., 61, 62

Schmidt, F., 52

Scholarship for Military Children and
Spouses, 260

School administrator, decisions of, *30, 32*
Schutz, W., 165
Schwartz, B., 143
Scottish Mental Survey, 60, 61
SCUBA divers, 227
Search pattern, 149–150, 152. *See also* Pattern recognition
Seattle Longitudinal Study, 62
Self-assessment: of the ARSENAL system, 246, 278–279; of attitude, 274; of awareness, 250, *251*; of exercise, 264–265; of learning, 277–278; of nutrition, 269–270; of rest, 256; of support, 259–260
Self-awareness: development of, 87–88; as a process, 91
Self-conscious emotions, 87–88
Self-conscious evaluative emotions, 88
Self-management, 91
Seligman, M., 129
Selye, H., 111–112, 120, 153, 185, 265, 270
Senior-level executives, role level complexity of, 23
Senses, most common, and their functions, 144, *145*
September 11, 2001, 30, 118
Seven ARSENAL Axioms, 281
Seven-step problem-solving model, 30, *31*
Shell Oil, 174
Shiv, B., 155
Short-term goals, role of, in maintaining cognitive functioning, 214
Similarity, emotional, 85
Simon, H., 38, 143
Simons, D., 150
Situational awareness, 207–208
Six Sigma, 19, 30
60 Minutes, 11
Skiles, J., 1, 2, 3, 4, 5, 42, 47, 214
Sleep: cognitive intelligence and, 66; and cognitive resilience, 205–210, 212; emotional intelligence and, 105; as a factor in decision making, 16; having no time for, 243; need for, 205, 252, 253; and a negative reinforcing loop, 207; stress and, 209–210; and stress management capacity, 175, 177, 178, 179; and stress resilient emotional intelligence, 237–238. *See also* Rest

Sleep, Alertness, and Fatigue in Residency (SAFER) program, 208, 209
Sleep and Neuroimaging Lab, 256
Sleep debt, 253, 254
Smith, N., 8
Smoking, 269
Socially responsible business practices, supporting, 230, 231
Socrates, 49, 147
Somatic markers, 103, 185, 224, 232, 233, 240–241, 263, 267
Sources of Power (Klein), 35
Southwest Airlines, 275
Spearman, C., 55
Spirduso, W., 65
Stall, J., 270
Stamp, G., 20
Stanford-Binet, 57
Stewart, M., 196
Stimulus: constantly changing, 47; detection of, 41–42, 44
Stockdale, J. B., 196–197, 212, 213, 214
Stockdale paradox, 196, 197
Stored memory, 63
Strategic level, 22, 68
Strategic planning, 33
Stratified systems theory, 20
Stratum III model, 57
Stress: as additive, 125; chronic, 122, 172; and cognitive intelligence, 7, 8, 225; and cognitive resilience, 203–205; cost of, 111–112; and decision making, 7, 8, 109–136, 244; defined, 111; and emotional intelligence, 7, 8, 156–157, 225–227, 229; and how it leads to poor decision making, aspects of, 137–166; intensity of, as a factor, 140–142; of leadership, 110–111; and a negative reinforcing loop, 207; releasing, on demand, 189–190; responses to, 114, 115, 237; and sleep, 209–210; sources of, 129–133; teamwork and, 284–285; that shuts down both cognitive and emotional intelligence, 159–162; ubiquitousness of, 205; understanding the impact of, steps in, 244
Stress Aftereffects Model, *122*
Stress Comfort Zone Model, 126–128

Stress effect: described, 113–117; and gender, 119; living the, cancer and, 257; research on the, 7, 8
Stress effect models, 117–129
Stress hormone. *See* Cortisol
Stress management capacity (SMC): aspects of, 172–191; building, 172–176; and decision making, 176–181; differences in, among leaders, testing, 229; importance of increasing, 8–9; scenario involving, 167–170; in the stress resilient system, 171; techniques for building, 182–190. *See also* Stress resilient system
Stress monitors, electronic, 210–211, 284–285
Stress prevention, best practices for. *See* ARSENAL system
Stress relief centers, creating, 285
Stress resilient emotional intelligence (SREI): aspects of, 221–241; defined, 225; developing and maintaining, 238–241; importance of building, 8–9; key components of, 231–235; need for building, examples reflecting a, 225–227; as a safeguard against loss of access to emotional intelligence, 228–231; in the stress resilient system, 171; techniques for building, 235–238; using, 227–228. *See also* Stress resilient system
Stress resilient system: combining ARSENAL best practices and the, 280; model of the, *171*; most productive, producing the, importance of, 284; steps in building the, 244; triad of the, 171–172, 239, 244, 245, 248, 280. *See also* Cognitive resilience (CR); Stress management capacity (SMC); Stress resilient emotional intelligence (SREI)
Stress responses, basic, *117*, 118, 119, 164, 165
Stress Transfer Model, *124*, 227
Stress waves, 114, 116
Stressors: in the bubble model of stress management, 188; defining, 140; different types of, scores for, examples of, 135; environmental, *130*, 132–133; major, identifying, 189
StressTrain, 185–186

Sullenberger, C., 1, 2, 3, 4, 5, 7–8, 37–38, 39, 42, 44, 45–46, 47, 143, 204, 214, 215, 231, 280
Sullivan, M., 12
Summers, L., 64
Sun Tsu, 40
Support: in the ARSENAL system, 9, 245; as a best practice, described, 257–260; development of, menu of techniques for, 258–259; indicators of, range of, 258; lack of, 243; for military members and their families, 260; self-assessment of, 259–260
Support Scale, 259
Survival instincts, 118, 164–165, 233
Susan G. Komen for the Cure, 251
Sustained high performance, 173
Swiss cheese approach, 188–189
Syntality, 284
Systems thinking training, 149

T

Tactical level, 21, 22, 68
Tamm, J., 165
Taylor, S., 119, 120
Teams, 284–285
Teamwork, 284
Technical skills, 24
Tend-and-befriend pattern, *117*, 119, 164
Thalamus, 113
"Thinking" preference, 120
Thompson, H., *41*, *141*
Thompson, L., 144
Thorndike, E., 90
Three block war, 40
Thurstone, L., 55
Time focus, *234*, 235
Time period, extended, outside the comfort zone, 173
Timing, as critical, 30
Toastmasters, 240
Tracinda, 62
Train crash, 179
Training: to develop master resiliency, 286; and exercise, 262; experts and, 184–185; law enforcement, 137, 180–181; mindfulness, 285; pilot, 144; ropes, 77, 181; and stress resilient emotional intelligence, 240; systems

thinking, 149. *See also* Leadership training; Military training
Tranel, D., 100
Treasurer, B., 126, 214–215
Tsai, S., 174
Tyco, 6, 13, 162
Tyson, M., 101

U

Unconscious, the, 40, 42, 43, 44, 84, 164, 203, 204, 213, 232; working with the, 235–236, 240
United Flight 173, 73–74, 76, 77
US Airways Flight 1549, 1–5, 7–8, 37–38, 41–47, 214, 215
U.S. Army, 6–7, 40, 66, 181, 221, 260–261, 286
U.S. Army Center for Army Leadership, 19–20, 197–198
U.S. Army Natick Soldier Research Development and Engineering Center, 210–211, 284
U.S. Army Ranger and Special Forces, 7, 167–170, 177–179, 254
U.S. Army Research Institute, 20
U.S. Army's Airborne School, 182–184
U.S. Department of Defense, 260
U.S. Federal Aviation Administration (FAA), 206, 207
U.S. financial crisis, 13
U.S. government, 15, 35
U.S. Marine Corps, 40
U.S. Military Code of Conduct, 213–214
U.S. Navy SEAL training, 178–179, 182, 214
U.S. presidential campaign, 13
Use of Force Decision-Making Lab, 180–181
USS Vincennes, 35–36

V

Value systems, decision making based on, 224, 230
Veterans Administration (VA), 260
Visionary level, 22, 68
Vygotsky, L., 60

W

Walker, M., 256
Wall Street Journal, 275

Walsh, P., 120
Walters, B., 196
War: casualties of, 224; involving Iraq, scenario depicting, 221–224; prisoners of, resilience of, 196–197, 214
War for talent, 8
Warning signs, awareness of, 231–232
Washington Mutual, 12, 15
Waterman, R., 17
Wearing, C., 63, 212
Wechsler Adult Intelligence Scale—III, 57
Wechsler, D., 90–91
Weems, C., 155
Welch, J., 18
Welsh, Tricia Evert, 228
Why Zebras Don't Get Ulcers (Sapolsky), 128
Wipro, 7
Wonderlic Personnel Test, 51, 52, 57
Woodruff, J., 208
Woods, T., 203–204, 212
Work stressors, *130*, 131
Working memory: available, 153, 200, 202, 210; and cognitive intelligence, 63–64, 75, 156; and cognitive resilience, 200, *201*, 202, 213, *219*; and emotional intelligence, 101, 157; measuring, 210; under stress, 153; and stress management capacity, 186
Workload distribution, 285. *See also* Cognitive workload
World Economic Forum, 65
World Trade Center attack, 118
WorldCom, 6, 13, 162
Wounded Warrior Project, 260

Y

Yang, Y.-E., 203
Yeomans, D., 106, 266
Yerkes, R., 134
Yerkes-Dodson law, 134, 162
Young leaders, desensitizing, 240

Z

Zable, W., 62
Zillman, D., 123

Handbook for Developing
EMOTIONAL AND SOCIAL INTELLIGENCE
Best Practices, Case Studies,
and Strategies

**Marcia Hughes | Henry L. Thompson
James Bradford Terrell
Foreword by James M. Kouzes**

ISBN: 978-0-470-19088-3 | US $75.00 | CAN $90.00

"This handbook will be of great use for any practitioner involved in the development of emotional intelligence abilities and competencies, and is a must-read for those who want a state-of-the-art overview of the many applications of emotional intelligence theory."—**Daniel Goleman, author, *Emotional Intelligence***

The ***Handbook for Developing Emotional and Social Intelligence*** features a wealth of case studies, best practices, and proven tools that show how emotional and social intelligence can be harnessed to deliver improved individual, team, and organization effectiveness. Written for executive coaches, consultants, workplace learning, and human resource professionals, this book is designed for anyone who works with executives, managers, and teams to improve their effectiveness in relationships and productivity.

The book also includes proven strategies that can be used to help leaders and teams develop their emotional and social effectiveness.

In addition, the Handbook contains best practices and case studies of applications throughout the world of how emotional intelligence training and coaching programs have been used to rebuild effectiveness and team performance in every type of organization. The authors also demonstrate how the benefits of emotional and social intelligence reverberate in education from elementary school through MBA programs. The book includes testimonies from executives who have increased meaning, connection, and effectiveness in both the workplace and their personal lives.

For more information, visit www.pfeiffer.com

An Imprint of WILEY
Now you know.